The Present State of Scholarship in Historical and Contemporary Rhetoric

The Present State of Scholarship in Historical and Contemporary Rhetoric

Edited by Winifred Bryan Horner

University of Missouri Press
Columbia & London, 1983

© 1983 by The Curators of the University of Missouri
University of Missouri Press, Columbia, Missouri 65211
Library of Congress Catalog Card Number 82–20002
Printed and bound in the United States of America
First paperback printing 1984

Library of Congress Cataloging in Publication Data
Main entry under title:

The Present state of scholarship
in historical and contemporary rhetoric.

Includes bibliographies.
1. Rhetoric—Historiography. I. Horner, Winifred Bryan.
PN183.P71983   808'.0072   82–20002
ISBN 0–8262–0467–8

PREFACE

This book is built on the work of scholars in rhetoric, and it is their research that makes this compilation possible. It stands as a tribute to them, and its purpose is to make their work available to scholars in a number of different fields.

This work is an attempt to put together under one cover the wide variety of scholarship in the diverse field of rhetoric. The classical period is included since much that follows is either a reinforcement of or a reaction against the first canon. Rhetoric dominates the life of the middle ages, as is evident in Professor Murphy's chapter, and Professor Abbott's study suggests that the reassertion of rhetorical scholarship is making possible and necessary a rewriting of Renaissance literature. In my chapter I describe the shift in rhetoric's focus in the eighteenth century and trace the decline of the old rhetoric and the emergence of the new in the epistemology of the period. Donald Stewart traces this new rhetoric through the nineteenth century, bringing the present book's historical record to a close.

Finally, James L. Kinneavy concludes with an account of the contemporary concepts that have their roots in this history. In this section he traces the blossoming of the traditional rhetorical concerns as they invade a number of disciplines and theoretical constructs in the modern academy. Kinneavy does not attempt to follow the historical thread set up by the earlier chapters, since narrating a history that is still in the making is an impossible undertaking. Rather he gives an account of the contemporary scene.

Given the nature and scope of this project, it has been necessary to place some limitations on the reviews of the scholarship for each period. Obviously, it would not be possible thoroughly to cover the rhetoric of any of these periods in the space of just one chapter. Each of the above contributors has attempted to provide information and recommendations about primary and secondary works that should be most beneficial to readers who wish to pursue the study of the rhetoric of one of the periods. It is hoped that readers will use this work as a point of departure for further study; thus, evaluative comments that are offered are with the intent of helping the reader choose those works that most deserve more careful attention.

This book is a gathering of the works of many scholars from a number of fields, but it is finally a collection for those students and scholars who see in rhetoric the core of humanistic studies.

W. B. H.
Columbia, Mo.
December 1982

Contents

Abbreviations

ABR	*American Benedictine Review*
AFM	*Archivum Franciscanum Historicum*
AJP	*American Journal of Philology*
Archiv	*Archiv für das Stadium der Neueren Sprachen und Literaturen*
BCRE	*British and Continental Rhetoric and Elocution Microfilms.* Ann Arbor, Mich.: 1953
Cahiers	*Université de Copenhague Cahiers de l'Institut du Moyen-Âge Grec et Latin*
C&M	*Classica et Mediaevalia*
CCC	*College Composition and Communication*
CE	*College English*
CF	*Classical Folia: Studies in the Christian Perpetration of the Classics*
CJ	*Classical Journal*
CM	*Communication Monographs* (formerly *Speech Monographs*)
CP	*Classical Philology*
CS	*Critical Sociology*
CSSJ	*Central States Speech Journal*
EAI	*Early American Imprints, 1639–1800.* Edited by Clifford K. Shipton. Published for the American Antiquarian Society. Worcester, Mass.: Readex Corporation, 1969
ECS	*Eighteenth-Century Sources for the Study of English Literature and Culture.* Micrographics, 11, Keswick, Va., 1979
Ed	*Education*
EJ	*English Journal*
ELH	*Journal of English Literary History*
HLQ	*Huntington Library Quarterly*
HSCP	*Harvard Studies in Classical Philology*
JEGP	*Journal of English and Germanic Philology*
JHI	*Journal of the History of Ideas*
JMRS	*Journal of Medieval and Renaissance Studies*
MAE	*Medium AEvum*
M&H	*Medievalia et Humanistica: Studies in Medieval and Renaissance Culture*
MARS	*Medieval and Renaissance Studies*
MKNAL	*Mededelingen der Koninklijke Nederlandse Akademie, Afdeling Letterkunde*
MLN	*Modern Language Notes*

MLR	*Modern Language Review*
MP	*Modern Philology*
MS	*Mediaeval Studies*
NEQ	*New England Quarterly*
NUC	*National Union Catalog*
PAPS	*Proceedings of the American Philosophical Society*
PBA	*Proceedings of the British Academy*
PMLA	*Publications of the Modern Language Association of America*
PQ	*Philological Quarterly*
PR	*Philosophy and Rhetoric*
QJS	*Quarterly Journal of Speech Communication*
RES	*Review of English Studies*
RQ	*Renaissance Quarterly*
RSQ	*Rhetoric Society Quarterly*
RUO	*Revue de l'Université d'Ottawa*
SM	*Speech Monographs* (see *CM, Communication Monographs*)
SMC	*Studies in Medieval Culture*
SMed	*Studi Medievali*
SP	*Studies in Philology*
Spec	*Speculum*
SQ	*Shakespeare Quarterly*
SRen	*Studies in the Renaissance*
SSJ	*Southern Speech Communication Journal* (formerly *SSB, Southern Speech Bulletin*)
ST	*Speech Teacher*
TAPA	*Transactions and Proceedings of the American Philological Association*
TCBS	*Transactions of the Cambridge Bibliographical Association*
TS	*Today's Speech* (now *Communication Quarterly*)
TSLL	*Texas Studies in Literature and Language*
UTQ	*University of Toronto Quarterly*
WMQ	*William and Mary Quarterly*
WS	*Western Speech* (now *Western Journal of Speech Communication*)

FOREWORD
Walter J. Ong, S.J.

The emergence and continued presence of rhetoric as a subject of academic study and as a focal point for academic and para-academic life is one of the central features of Western civilization. Although verbal performance in all cultures across the globe can be highly sophisticated and effective, nothing quite like the rhetoric worked up by the ancient Greeks and their successors developed anyplace else in the world.

Apart from its present specialized reference in the United States to courses in effective writing, the term *rhetoric* commonly suggests to the modern mind, in the United States as elsewhere, verbal profusion calculated to manipulate an audience, an operation whose aims are suspect and whose typical procedures are mostly trivializing. Yet in centuries past *rhetoric* was commonly used in the West to refer to one of the most consequential and serious of all academic subjects and of all human activities. As the art of persuasion, the art of producing genuine conviction in an audience, rhetoric affected the entire range of human action as nothing else in theory or in practice quite did. The study and use of rhetoric enabled one to move others, to get things done.

To many Renaissance humanists, as Jerrold E. Seigel has shown in *Rhetoric and Philosophy in Renaissance Humanism*, by contrast with rhetoric most if not all other academic subjects were trivializing: philosophical and scientific theorizing was utterly inconsequential because it had no effect on events, on the way people actually behaved. The study of rhetoric required engagement in the totality of human affairs, in politics and other decisionmaking fields, in real life, as the ancient Greeks and Romans had already appreciated. Rhetoric conferred power, and admirably humane power, for its power depended on producing conviction in others, on giving others grounds to act on out of free human decision resulting from deliberation. Such power befitted human beings. It was radically different from the brute power exerted by war and other uses of

1

physical force. Compared to knowledge of rhetoric, with its power to determine the course of history, the rest of knowledge in itself was ineffectual twaddle, unless it could be put to rhetorical use—as any or all of it might be, for, as Cicero insisted, it is the business of the orator or practicing rhetorician, who is the leader in public affairs, to know everything. The demands of rhetoric defined for Cicero what liberal education was.

Yet the ancient and Renaissance worlds also had some misgivings about rhetoric. Socrates and Plato and Aristotle professed to believe that the Sophists of their day generally were dishonest rhetoricians, using their intellectual and verbal skill to trick their audiences and teaching their disciples to do the same. This charge illustrates in another way the power of rhetoric. There are dangers of deception at many levels inherent in its use: if the charge is true, the Sophists were rhetorical deceivers; if it is not, their accusers were guilty of the rhetorical deception of which they accused the Sophists. It seems that honors here were in fact somewhat even. Much modern scholarship has shown that the Sophists were in fact often brilliant and learned men, though more concerned with training for practical life than with theories of "philosophy," and that they did not all profess or teach intellectual or verbal irresponsibility or chicanery.

Aristotle defined the art of rhetoric as the faculty of finding in any given case the available means of persuasion. As this definition astutely indicates, one who wants to persuade needs skills that are essentially heuristic, an art of finding. Rhetoric starts with the conclusion, the position it wants to convince others to take, for which it must find supporting reasons. In this it contrasts with logic. Logic lets premises lead to whatever conclusions they lead to. Rhetoric knows its conclusions in advance, and clings to them. This heuristic nature of rhetoric is what makes it open to charges of opportunism. With its end in view, it will use any means, moral or immoral, that work to achieve that end.

Aristotle notes that the practice of rhetoric grows at first from a natural ability. Most people attempt to support or assess or attack one or another opinion verbally or to defend or attack other persons verbally, and through hit-and-miss experience many eventually develop a certain knack for highly effective procedures. Presumably such was the case from the beginning of humankind in all cultures. Rhetoric remained pretty much in this relatively unreflective state in the West until the effective interiorization of alphabetic writing among the ancient Greeks by the fifth century B.C. Such writing made possible the lengthy, analytic linear organization of thought that we call scientific and that, once it had become more or less a habit of mind, could transform orally composed thought itself into a new literate orality, using thought processes unavailable before writing. Like Plato, Aristotle felt the new drive to the more abstract, logically sequential thought and undertook to investigate and state in abstract scientific form, among other things, how successful speakers in his milieu gained their ends and why. The result was the book we know as his *Art of Rhetoric*. In Pope's words, Aristotle "methodized" what had previously been a "natural" rhetoric into a consciously reflective, analytic "art." Of course, as Pope had perhaps not been entirely aware, developing "nature" into an "art" changes nature a bit. Reflection always entails creation.

Like all developments deeply embedded in human existence, the new "art" of rhetoric faced into the past as well as into the future. On the one hand its development into a scientized "art" depended on the mind's having interiorized writing, which was the wave of the future leading quickly not only to abstractly organized science but also to the foundation of empires. But on the other hand, the subject matter of rhetoric among the ancient Greeks belonged to the past: in Aristotle and elsewhere rhetoric was in fact concerned not with written discourse primarily but with oral discourse, the earlier mode of verbal expression, of course still very much alive. *Rhētōr* in Greek means orator, public speaker, and *technē rhētorikē*, or, more simply, *rhētorikē*, means public speaking. To Aristotle's world, teaching students rhetoric meant teaching them to become orators. Deflection of rhetoric from oral performance to written argumentation as such, vaguely incipient at best in Aristotle, would occur only very slowly and imperceptibly over the centuries. Yet it must be remembered that the oral speeches Aristotle was concerned with were in fact no longer purely oral but were already being shaped by the chirographic milieu to post-oral thought forms. The mental processes of academically educated Greeks in Plato's day and later, as Eric Havelock has shown in *The Greek Concept of Justice*, differed considerably from those of Homer's age, and these processes, though grounded in literacy, showed clearly not only in written treatises such as the *Art of Rhetoric* but also in the oral performance of literates.

Its longstanding commitment to orality over the centuries, a commitment not consciously designed or even adverted to, suggests that the deepest roots of rhetoric are archaic, though now covered by a centuries-old tangle of academic and other cultural growth. Rhetoric plays an important part in the growth of consciousness that marks human psychic and cultural history and that is accelerated vastly as verbal discourse is technologized through writing, then print, and now electronics and as thought processes are transformed while greater and greater stores of knowledge are accumulated. In its overall effect, rhetoric raises consciousness, as Gilbert Durand has shown in *Les Structures anthropologiques de l'imaginaire*, moving thought from the older, more purely imaging stages toward the greater abstractions of logic. Rhetorical antitheses are negotiable: *yes, more or less; no, more or less*. The antitheses of formal logic are typically nonnegotiable, absolute—setting up irreducible binarism that ultimately makes its way into the computer. *It is, or it isn't*.

The patterns whereby consciousness grows out of the unconscious of course differ from culture to culture—indeed, such patterns in the last analysis may constitute the most basic differences between cultures. And rhetoric is of course not the only factor that determines and registers the patterns of growth. But certainly in the West rhetoric is a central determinant and indicator. In other parts of the world, rhetoric was managed differently. In *Polarity and Analogy*, G. E. R. Lloyd has shown how ancient Greek thought generally specialized in differences (polarities) as against likenesses (analogies) more than any of the many other cultures that he examines from across the globe. Greek rhetoric, specifically, certainly specialized in antitheses, and out of this specialization, as I. M. Bochenski has shown in *A History of Formal Logic*, grew the logic that underlay Greek analytic thinking and that underlies modern science and the changes in human life that science has wrought. In *Communication and Culture in Ancient India and China*, where of course rhetoric was practiced, as it has been everywhere, Robert T. Oliver reports no interest in formalized rhetoric comparable to that of ancient Greece. (Formal logic came into being also in India, as Bochenski points out—perhaps independently of the Greek invention—but some five hundred years later than in Greece.)

The centrality of rhetoric in the West is tied in largely with its conspicuous academic and para-academic presence. But academic rhetoric has led no eremetical existence. From the ancient Greeks to the present, the teaching of rhetoric has affected and been affected by political and other social institutions, philosophical theories (themselves often partly rhetorical in origin), educational practices and aims, the growth of science, and much else.

From patristic times and earlier, rhetoric has also much affected and been much affected by the Judeo-Christian ethos—a fact more taken for granted then discussed by historians of rhetoric. Judeo-Christian teaching sets up a kind of rhetorical situation between human beings and God. Job argued with God. He argued with utter reverence—observed decorum, as a later rhetoric would put it—but unabashedly, for the relationship of each human being to God in faith is personal and personally interactive. Christian teaching regarding the Incarnation intensified the interaction. The Word himself became flesh, the Word who is also the Son, the Second Person of the Trinity of Father, Son, and Holy Spirit. The Word or Son is the communication of the Father—Son inasmuch as he is Word, and Word inasmuch as he is Son (*eo verbum quo filius*, as the succinct Latin logion puts it), and he came as a human being to announce the Good News, the Gospel, the *kerygma*. Human speaking and persuasion are of the essence of Christianity, though Christian faith as such transcends the human action with which it meshes. *Pistis*, the Greek term for faith among the early Christians, which Paul says "comes from hearing" (Romans 10:17), is the same word that occurs in rhetoric texts for the conviction that the public speaker undertakes to establish in his hearers. Moreover, the Word, the Son, brings human beings to the Father, and Christians plead rhetorically with the Father "through him, with him, and in him." The Holy Spirit, who enables the faithful to pray, is identified by Jesus as the *Paraklētos*, the "advocate," one who pleads another's case as in court. In this protreptic milieu, it is little wonder that the liturgy of the Christian Church, Eastern and Western, is shot through with highly self-conscious rhetoric: the hundreds of opening prayers at Mass in the Latin Liturgy, for example, and comparable prayers in other liturgies, Protestant as well as Catholic, are rhetorical showpieces, as are also countless homilies.

As the studies in this book make abundantly clear, rhetoric as an academic subject persisted, with varied fortunes and intensities, from classical antiquity through the Middle Ages, the Renaissance, and intervening centuries down to the present. Drilled into students in the earlier years of the curriculum, rhetoric inevitably extended itself with greater or lesser force far beyond the classroom, for rhetorical skills were supposed to be applied everywhere: in law and politics, in public celebrations marked by the florid oratory that into the present century bears the mark of academic rhetorical (oratorical) training, in preaching, in medicine (before the present century, physician-patient relationships often depended more upon vocal exchange promoting trust than on precisely targeted pharmaceuticals), in letter-writing and in poetry and fiction (novelists such as Hawthorne and Melville clearly show speechifying tendencies in their prose), and in general through all affective human relations.

The persistent presence of rhetoric as a recognized force in Western culture can be seen in the number of major intellectual figures known today chiefly for their work in a variety of other subjects who at one time or another taught rhetoric or wrote about it. In the recent English-speaking world alone one finds, for example, the scientist Joseph Priestley, the economist Adam Smith, the political scientist and diplomat and sixth president of the United States of America John Quincy Adams, who became professor of rhetoric and belles-lettres at Harvard after being in the United States Senate, the physician James Rush, the litterateur Thomas De Quincey, and the engineer cum physical scientist cum philosopher Herbert Spencer—all noted, along with others, in the present book.

Perhaps partly because of the very pervasiveness of rhetoric, the history of rhetoric has only begun to shape up effectively in recent times. Early histories of the subject, even as late as John Quincy Adams's brief account, could not achieve the distance required for historical effectiveness. As Donald C. Stewart indicates in his chapter here, Adams did not at all understand the complex relationship of rhetoric to cultural history and assimilated rhetoric in his own day uncritically to that of ancient Greece. The period between ancient Greece and Adams's own time he felt as nonexistent.

In recent times rhetoric has become more vigorous and more protean than ever before. The modern world has found new ways of exercising the persuasion that used to be practiced chiefly through verbal performance. Rhetoric has spread from its original habitat in the world of direct vocal exchange into newly created arenas, first to the written page, then to the printed page, with its charts and diagrams and illustrations— presenting the reader with what William M. Ivins, Jr., in *Prints and Visual Communication*, has called "exactly repeatable visual statements"—then to display advertising, a quite new development that utilizes dramatic arrangements of variously printed words as well as illustrations, on to skywriting, television, and all the rest. The present human lifeworld is saturated with rhetoric. Concern with various kinds of human interaction has alerted the present age, perhaps more in the United States than elsewhere, to the precise rhetorical elements in business transactions, in storytelling, in professedly objective reporting, in documentary films, and in philosophy and science, to name only a few of rhetoric's domains. Suddenly, rhetoric, the art of persuasion originally connected chiefly with oratory, has become totally amoeban, surrounding and consuming our entire lifeworld. The reason for this is essentially simple, although it is unfashionable to note it: paradoxically, in our technological world interpersonal relations have become more frequent and more complex in many ways than before. In his chapter here on Contemporary Rhetoric, James L. Kinneavy lists some of the specialized kinds of rhetoric he might have treated but, if only for want of space, could not: the rhetoric governing marketing, managerial science, interviewing, oral interpretation, film and radio and television production (he does treat rhetoric in the mass media), rhetoric as viewed in general semantics, literary criticism, theory of description (the old rhetoric had ample room for persuasive description, no room at all for exact visual description of a clinical sort), axiology, learning theory, cognitive sciences, and much else.

The recent foundation of the International Society for the History of Rhetoric registers the growing scholarly interest in the provenience and significance of this massive and pervasive subject that has meant so much in the history of Western culture, as well as other cultures in our now one world. The need is obvious for a book such as the present one, which undertakes to sum up the state of scholarship today and to suggest lines of study for the future, providing both discussion and invaluable bibliographic guides for each period it treats. The book concerns itself chiefly with verbal rhetoric, basically as represented in the academic teaching of rhetoric in the West. It starts with the ancient tradition, in Greek originally and then more and more in Latin, that underlies all Western academic rhetoric; then, in its later chapters, dealing with the vernacularized academic world that took shape gradually after the Renaissance, it narrows its focus to the history of rhetoric in the English-speaking world of the British Isles and the United States of America.

Richard Leo Enos begins the book where one must begin the study of all academic and para-academic life in the West, with the ancient Greeks and then the Romans. James J. Murphy provides an exhaustive account of scholarship concerned with medieval rhetoric, a subject to which he has given his super-abundant energies for many years. Don Paul Abbott treats the complexities of the Renaissance, where a turnaround took place, largely under the influence of Peter Ramus, that signaled the beginning of a new rhetorical era marked by the subtle and pervasive effects of print. Winifred Bryan Horner, to whom credit and gratitude go for the conception of this book, shows that what we already know of rhetorical history in the eighteenth century makes this century one of the most fascinating of all. Donald C. Stewart shows how much has been done to provide modern editions of the rhetorical writings of the nineteenth century that have so much influenced the teaching of written composition in our own day, and James L. Kinneavy discusses work on the manifold shapes that rhetoric has taken in our own time and reviews the vast literature on the relationship of various kinds of rhetoric and rhetorical theories to the teaching of writing.

In the historiography of rhetoric in the West, it appears that a disproportionate amount of work has been done by United States scholars. The reasons for this are various, but the fact itself suggests that rhetoric relates to social structures and to psychic life in the United States somewhat differently than it does in the other parts of the Western World. It is sometimes said the Europeans and Latin Americans learn how to practice rhetoric and United States scholars study it. The rhetorical heritage is a part of the ethos of Europe. It is less familiar, more distanced, and more intellectually interesting to scholars in the United States. Whatever the case, this book should be of great practical value to scholars around the world and of special value to those teaching writing as well as to those interested in many areas of literary study not often associated with rhetoric, such as reader-oriented criticism and speech-act theory, structuralism, textualism, deconstructionism, and much else. It is a book for all seasons.

1

THE CLASSICAL PERIOD

Richard Leo Enos

Primary Works

Pre-Socratic Philosophers and Sophists: Homeric to ca. the Peloponnesian War

There are several primary works that provide evidence for rhetoric's early evolution to a discipline. Often, such notions about the suasory power of discourse, and techniques of articulating thoughts and sentiments, are revealed indirectly in such literary works as Homer's *Iliad* and *Odyssey* and Hesiod's *Works and Days*. Yet, explicit attention to concepts that would become subsumed under rhetoric are evident in the fragments of pre-Socratic thinkers. The most comprehensive collections of this material are the *Die Fragmente der Vorsokratiker* (ed. Hermann Diels and Walther Kranz, 1972) and *Artium scriptores: Reste der voraristotelischen Rhetorik* (ed. Ludwig Radermacher, 1951). These two collections are acknowledged as invaluable sources for philological research, but all references are left in the original Greek. Fortunately, excellent translations of many such fragments are available. Kathleen Freeman's *Ancilla to the Pre-Socratic Philosophers* (1971) provides a fine, but laconic, summary of fragments that bear directly on the earliest notions of rhetoric. A more literal and thorough treatment of relevant fragments is presented in her other work, *The Pre-Socratic Philosophers: A Companion to Diels*, Fragmente der Vorsokratiker (1966). Rosamond Kent Sprague's *The Older Sophists* (1972) is a valuable translation of fragments in *Die Fragmente der Vor-*

Richard Leo Enos is an Associate Professor of Rhetoric in the Department of English at Carnegie-Mellon University. In addition to his doctoral work in rhetoric, classical studies, and history at Indiana University, Professor Enos has studied at the American School of Classical Studies at Athens. He has been involved in research and study programs in Italy and Greece since 1972.

sokratiker. Readers will find George Kennedy's "Gorgias" and Sprague's "Dissoi Logoi or Dialexis" important sources for early notions on rhetoric. Unfortunately, *The Older Sophists* is currently out of print and, therefore, difficult to obtain. Lastly, a neglected but important collection of early fragments is G. S. Kirk and J. E. Raven's *The Presocratic Philosophers* (1973). The advantage of the Kirk and Raven collection is their integration of extended analysis and explication of fragments, which are presented both in the original Greek and in English. Other collections of such primary material exist, but readers of English will find those mentioned above the most beneficial, primarily because of the accessibility of translations and the thoroughness of the commentary.

Plato

One of the most important issues in classical rhetoric is the debate over the legitimacy of rhetoric as a serious discipline. Several primary sources reveal the controversy; in fact, the epistemological issues articulated by sophists such as Gorgias are evident in the fragments cited above. Essentially, the Platonic view on the acceptability of rhetoric as a system for acquiring knowledge is a counterstatement to the relativism that characterized sophistic thought. Students who are introduced to classical rhetoric will benefit from an exposure to both sides of this debate. While Plato's views on the credibility of rhetoric are evident in many dialogues, two are often seen as representative of his position, the *Gorgias* (ca. 387–385 B.C.) and the *Phaedrus* (ca. 370 B.C.). The *Gorgias* calls to question the sophistic claim that rhetoric has any systematic *techne,* or "art," and the *Phaedrus* examines the possibility of a rhetoric that could be acceptable as a *techne.*

Several translations of the *Gorgias* and the *Phaedrus* are available, and the choice of the most appropriate one depends on the needs of the reader. W. R. M. Lamb's translation of the *Gorgias* (1925) and N. H. Fowler's translation of the *Phaedrus* (1914), both of which appear in the Loeb Classical Library series, are excellent with the original Greek and the English appearing on facing pages. A minimum knowledge of the Greek alphabet makes these works uniquely valuable, since critical terms in Greek can be isolated easily and discussed in class. Two other editions of the *Gorgias* and the *Phaedrus* also warrant citation. The Greek edition of the *Gorgias* by E. R. Dodds (1959) provides excellent background information about the transmission of the text and the place of the *Gorgias* in Plato's dialogues. Similarly, the translation of the *Phaedrus* (1972) by R. Hackforth is an excellent edition for providing a brief, but synoptic, introduction with commentary throughout and headnotes paraphrasing each section. As indicated above, several other dialogues also capture the issues over rhetoric's province, but discussion of these would extend the essay beyond its limits. All of the extant dialogues of Plato are available through the Loeb Classical Library series, with several dialogues often appearing in each edition. Although outside the province of this essay, the writings of Isocrates (436–338 B.C.) provide a valuable source of comparison with Plato on the practice of rhetoric in classical Athens. An excellent three-volume English translation of Isocrates' writing is provided by George Norlin and Larue Van Hook (1966, 1968) in the Loeb Classical Library series.

Aristotle

For many years the *Rhetorica ad Alexandrum* (ca. 340 B.C.) was believed to have been authored by Aristotle, and the work was even transmitted through the ages in the Aristotelian canon. Most scholars now agree that the work was probably authored by Anaximenes, but it is possible that this *techne*—considered the oldest extant manual of rhetoric—would have perished had it not been included among the writings of Aristotle. Two important works are available for readers of English. The Loeb Classical Library series offers a translation of the *Rhetorica ad Alexandrum* by H. Rackham (1937) that includes a helpful (and necessary) outline of this intricate, highly detailed treatise. E. M. Cope (1877) presents an analysis and commentary of the *Rhetorica ad Alexandrum* that makes an excellent companion volume to the Rackham edition cited above.

The primary work for Aristotle and, as some scholars believe, of classical rhetoric itself is his *Rhetorica* (ca. 335–330 B.C.), essentially because the *Rhetorica* established rhetoric as a serious discipline. Reading the *Rhetorica* in isolation from Aristotle's other treatises is a disservice to his objective of harmonizing knowledge, but only the English editions of the *Rhetorica* will be discussed here. Two of the most popular English editions of the *Rhetorica* are W. Rhys Roberts and Ingram Bywater's *Rhetoric and Poetics of Aristotle* (1954) and Lane Cooper's *The Rhetoric of Aristotle* (1960). Both of these works provide lucid translations, explanations, and—particularly in reference to the Cooper edition—a synoptic overview. Serious work on interpretation of philological issues within the *Rhetorica*, which is currently involving several researchers, is unavailable in these editions because of the exclusion of the Greek text. The translation by J. H. Freese, *The "Art" of Rhetoric* (1926), is an established version of the English edition and has the advantage of providing the Greek and English on facing pages along with a glossary of key terms.

Although analyses and commentaries are technically not considered "primary works," there are studies that so greatly facilitate the English editions of the *Rhetorica* that they are included in this section. Edward M. Cope's *An Introduction to Aristotle's Rhetoric* (1867) is one of the distinguished contributions to scholarship in classical rhetoric and is essential for explicating Aristotle's views. Similarly, Edward M. Cope and John Edwin Sandys's *The Rhetoric of Aristotle* (1877), while providing only the Greek text, offers three volumes of commentary that have served as the standard reference to the primary source for over one hundred years. Only recently has an updated, and excellent, commentary been published that bridges the one-hundred-year gap since the Cope and Sandys edition, William M. A. Grimaldi's *Aristotle, Rhetoric I: A Commentary* (1980). As the title indicates, Grimaldi's edition is a commentary of only the first book of the *Rhetorica*, but that in no way limits its contribution as an excellent scholarly study, and it is highly recommended. Readers will find Grimaldi's discussion on *pistis* in the "Appendix" a brilliant statement on the role of proof in Aristotle's methodology of rhetoric. On an introductory level, Larry Arnhart's *Aristotle on Political Reasoning: A Commentary on the "Rhetoric"* (1981) provides a good general overview and explication of the text.

Cicero

For centuries the *Rhetorica ad Herennium* (ca. 86–82 B.C.) was believed to have been authored by Marcus Tullius Cicero and was included in the corpus of his *Rhetorica*. The work is now believed almost certainly not to have been written by Cicero but remains in his canon of treatises because exact authorship has yet to be determined. Similar to its Greek counterpart, the *Rhetorica ad Alexandrum*, the *Rhetorica ad Herennium* is the earliest complete Latin version of a technical manual. Reading of the text could be tedious, except that the storehouse of rhetorical figures and patterns of organization provide invaluable evidence for historians of rhetoric. Fortunately, readers of English will benefit from the excellent translation of the *Rhetorica ad Herennium* by Harry Caplan (1954). Titled *Ad C. Herennium de Ratione Dicendi (Rhetorica ad Herennium)*, Caplan's is one of the best editions of primary sources on rhetoric in the Loeb Classical Library series. The inclusion of the Latin text is an advantage to the reader, and Caplan's introduction and bibliography, while dated, are still regarded as a contribution in their own right.

Cicero's own works on rhetoric are extensive; in fact, much of the study of classical rhetoric in the Roman period is devoted to the analysis of his treatises. Earliest of these is the *De Inventione* (86 B.C.), a work that, although discounted by Cicero in his *De Oratore* as the product of a youthful mind, was one of the dominant rhetorical artifacts in the Latin-speaking West throughout the Middle Ages. Only one edition is readily available to readers of English, the H. M. Hubbell translation in the Loeb Classical Library series (1949). As is characteristic of the Loeb series, the original language of the text is also provided along with a bibliography. Many readers find that the *De Inventione* appears to be more on the arrangement of discourse than on invention and that important concepts of Cicero's developing views on the structure of rhetorical discourse are buried in wordy commentary. While such reactions to this important document are common, the Hubbell edition is helpful in providing a synoptic introduction and a bibliography.

Cicero's most famous treatise on rhetoric, and one of the primary texts for historians of rhetoric, is his *De Oratore* (55 B.C.). Written after his consulship, and after years of deliberative and forensic experience, the *De Oratore* is a comprehensive statement on rhetoric that is grounded in both theory and practice. While the dialogue form of *De Oratore* makes the interpretation of rhetorical principles difficult, the richness and utility of rhetoric for the welfare of the individual and of the state, revealed in the extended discussion, make it a valuable statement. Two major English translations are available. Although the J. S. Watson translation served for years as the standard edition, his *Cicero on Oratory and Orators* (reprinted 1970) is dated. Readers will find the introduction and foreword by Ralph A. Micken and David Potter helpful. The Loeb Classical Library edition of *De Oratore* (1942, revised 1948) offers excellent translations by H. Rackham and E. W. Sutton. The difficulty of interpreting Cicero's own position on issues throughout the dialogue is aided greatly by a thorough summary at the beginning of the two-volume edition, which includes section-markings throughout and allows a quick and reliable reference to key passages. The Latin edition of Augustus S. Wilkins (1965), while not providing an English text, does give valuable commentary along with an insightful summary and analysis. Readers of *De Oratore* are strongly encouraged to examine Wilkins's Latin edition for serious study.

From 55 to 46 B.C., Cicero wrote a number of treatises on rhetoric, many of which are believed to be responses to comments he received about his *De Oratore*. The *Partitiones Oratoriae* (ca. 50 B.C.)—also referred to as *De Partitione Oratoria*—while not normally the subject of study by historians of rhetoric, does provide extended evidence on his later views of the compositional structure and arrangement of rhetorical discourse. Perhaps, with increased attention of historians to the heuristic procedures that guide the structuring of composition, this work will gain renewed attention, but it is now considered only a minor statement in the Ciceronian canon. To date, the only readily available English text of *Partitiones Oratoriae* is found in the Loeb Classical Library series (1942). H. Rackham is best known for his translation of *De Oratore*, which is included in the same volume, but readers will find his rendering of the *Partitiones Oratoriae* lucid if brief.

Similar to the *Partitiones Oratoriae*, Cicero's *De Optimo Genera Oratorum* (46 B.C.) is also a brief, and overlooked, statement on rhetoric. The major importance of this treatise is that it illustrates Cicero's relationship with, and indebtedness to, Hellenic rhetoric. The *De Optimo Genera Oratorum* was intended to serve as an introduction to Cicero's Latin edition of Demosthenes' *On the Crown*. His comments on the qualifications of the best sort of rhetor give insight to the values upon which his theory for the welfare of the state was based and complement his praise of Demosthenes in his *Orator*. A more detailed commentary on this relationship would enhance the merits of the translation by H. M. Hubbell in the Loeb Classical Library series (1949), but the standard of excellent translations that characterizes the series is maintained in this edition.

Cicero's *Brutus* (46 B.C.) is an invaluable work for historians of rhetoric. Through his accounting of scores of Roman orators, many of whom would be unknown without this treatise, Cicero indirectly reveals his admiration for the rhetors who preceded his generation. The major difficulty of the work is that the thorough chronicling of Roman orators makes mastery of the treatise, and synthesis of the precepts, difficult. The Loeb Classical Library translation by G. L. Hendrickson (1952) aids in providing a summary and introduction, but for a thorough accounting of this history of Roman rhetoric readers will need to consult G. V. Sumner's *The Orators in Cicero's* Brutus: *Prosopography and Chronology* (1973).

It could be argued that Cicero's *Topica* (44 B.C.) is a treatise that can strictly be considered outside of the province of rhetoric, since the author's initial comments and reference to Aristotle's *Topica* imply that it ought to be taken only as a statement on dialectic. A reading of the treatise, however, reveals an extensive discussion of *loci communes* and their relationship to Greek *topoi*. The implications of Cicero's analysis reveal not only his indebtedness to Greek thought, and Aristotle in particular, but also his ability to integrate the methods and substance of other disciplines into his rhetorical theory. Similar to many other works in the Ciceronian *Rhetorica,* the English edition of his *Topica* is readily available only through the Loeb Classical Library series (1949). The translation by H. M. Hubbell is included in the volume with Cicero's *De Inventione* and *De Optimo Genera Oratorum.*

Stylistics and Criticism: Dionysius, Demetrius, and Longinus

Research in classical rhetoric, and particularly in the interrelationships among the canons of rhetoric, has prompted an interest in the theoretical presuppositions grounding treatises on style and criticism. Fortunately, excellent English sources are available for such study. A clear example of this sort of work is the W. Rhys Roberts translation (1910) of the *De Compositione Verborvm* of Dionysius of Halicarnassus (fl. 30 B.C.). The *De Compositione Verborvm* (ca. 20–10 B.C.) is a detailed statement on literary composition that will be of interest not only to historians of rhetoric but to historical linguists and grammarians as well. The Roberts edition is an excellent source for the English reader because the Greek text is included with the translation, an introduction, notes, a glossary, and appendixes on such subjects as word order and pronunciation. Similarly, Stephen Usher's translation of critical essays by Dionysius of Halicarnassus in the Loeb Classical Library series (1974) provides valuable but indirect evidence of the theoretical standards implicit in such models of eloquence as Lysias and Demosthenes.

Inexpensive and lucid translations of Demetrius' *On Style* (first century A.D.) and Longinus' *On the Sublime* (ca. A.D. 40) are more readily available than the writings of Dionysius and are included with other, related classical texts. Demetrius' *On Style* includes examples from historians and poets as well as orators. The text also discusses letter-writing, which would become a popular subject for rhetoric in the Middle Ages and Renaissance. Two English editions are available. The Loeb Classical Library series provides a translation by W. Rhys Roberts (revised 1932), who devoted much of his scholarly career to translating and explicating treatises in classical rhetoric. This volume also includes Longinus' *On the Sublime* and Aristotle's *Poetics*. Another acceptable, and more easily available, English edition of Demetrius' *On Style* was published by Everyman's Library (1963). While this edition does not offer the Greek text, as does the Loeb Classical Library series, it includes editions of Aristotle's *Poetics* and Longinus' *On the Sublime*. Although the Everyman edition cannot be recommended for research, it does provide students with an inexpensive copy of important treatises on style and criticism.

Longinus' *On the Sublime* is commonly seen as one of the major texts in classical literary criticism. While *On the Sublime* is frequently discussed in rhetoric more as a point of departure from the pedantic rhetorical exercises that characterized much of the history of rhetoric in the first century A.D., the accessibility of English editions and the work's impact in the history of rhetoric warrant its attention. In addition to the editions mentioned in the preceding paragraph, the Penguin Classics series offers an inexpensive translation of Longinus' *On the Sublime* (1965); T. S. Dorsch's edition is easy to read (the Roberts translation is used), and his introduction provides a brief but broad overview of classical literary criticism.

Rhetoric and Roman Education: Seneca (The Elder) and Quintilian

Rhetoric thrived during the Roman Imperial period not so much for its political and forensic utility—which characterized the Ciceronian age—but because of its indisputable contributions to higher education in the ancient world. Until 1974, however, readers of English had to limit their study of Roman declamation to secondary sources. Michael Winterbottom's two-volume translation of the Elder Seneca's *Oratorum Senteniae Divisiones Colores* (ca. A.D. 37) in the Loeb Classical Library series (1974) provides a thesaurus of illustrations on the rhetorical exercises of *controversiae* and *suasoriae* that educated Romans. Unlike other treatises of rhetoric discussed in this section, Seneca's collection can be used as a reference for illustrating common topics in deliberative and forensic issues, since theoretical presuppositions driving the exercises are presented indirectly.

The most comprehensive and important statement of rhetoric in higher education is Quintilian's *Institutio oratoria* (ca. A.D. 94–95). The end product of a career of distinguished instruction, Quintilian's twelve-book treatise on the moral education of youth, and the concern for an ethical grounding to rhetoric, has established the *Institutio oratoria* as a landmark in the history of rhetoric. Researchers in the history of rhetoric stress the importance of this work not only for the moral plea for rhetoric—illustrated most pointedly in book 12—but also because Quintilian's compendious work provides important primary references on the history of rhetoric in Greece and Rome. Quintilian's enduring popularity has prompted English editions for several years. Unfortunately, many have become dated or have been so stringently edited that only the H. E. Butler translation in the Loeb Classical Library series (1920–1922) can be recommended. The value of this translation is enhanced by the synopsis of the books in the respective volumes, a summary of the life of Quintilian, and a letter from Trypho, his publisher.

Commentators and Historians of Rhetoric

Even in Antiquity, scholars were beginning to realize the value of preserving and recording the history of rhetoric. Plutarch's *Vitae Parallelae* (ca. A.D. 50–120) illustrates his attempts to record the deeds of prominent historical figures, many of whom helped to shape the history of rhetoric. Primary examples of such writings are his comparative accounts of the lives of Demosthenes and Cicero. B. Perrin's translation in the Loeb Classical Library series (1919) is a dated, but standard, reference for readers of English. It should also be noted that, although not strictly dealing with rhetorical theory, the popularization of the ten Attic orators in [Plutarch], *Vitae decem oratorum*, helped to establish a standard for excellence throughout much of the history of rhetoric and was particularly popular in periods where rhetorical proficiency was taught not through the mastery of theory but through the study of models. The tenth volume of H. N. Fowler's translation of Plutarch's *Moralia* (1936) offers an introduction to the Attic orators that is too brief for the importance they had in the history of rhetoric, but it does offer a readable translation of the text.

Other historians of the period who earned their lasting recognition in other writings also commented on rhetoric. Tacitus, most famous for his *Annales,* presented an attack on the practices and objectives of rhetorical training during his own time and glorified Cicero and the orators of preceding generations in the *Dialogus* (ca. A.D. 84–85). M. Winterbottom's revision of W. Peterson's translation of the *Dialogus* (1970) is recommended; the Bobbs-Merrill edition (1967), which does provide an inexpensive text for students of the history of rhetoric, is not suggested for research.

Similar to Tacitus, Suetonius took time from his historical writing to chronicle the emergence of rhetoric as a formal discipline in Rome. Suetonius' treatise *De Rhetoribus* (ca. A.D. 106 –113) provides a wealth of information about the periods when the teaching of rhetoric was outlawed in Rome and the use of stock declamations. Two English versions of this treatise are available. J.C. Rolfe's translation of Suetonius' writings in the Loeb Classical Library series (1914) provides a readable text but with virtually no commentary. Readers who wish to understand the *De Rhetoribus* within its historical context are advised to consult the Richard Leo Enos translation of *De Rhetoribus* (1972), which does include an extensive commentary.

Two additional documents are of interest to historians of rhetoric. Philostratus' *Vitae Sophistarum* (ca. A.D. 230–238) and Eunapius' *Vitae Sophistarum* (ca. A.D. 396) provide important information about the First and Second Sophistic. Illustrations of declamations along with invaluable references to sophists such as Gorgias help to provide a unique perspective to the history of rhetoric. Both of these important statements are available in English in the Loeb Classical Library series (1921), and, although dated, the translation by Wilmer C. Wright makes for clear reading.

Minucian and Hermogenes

The second century A.D. produced not only chroniclers of rhetoric's history but also theoreticians who elaborated and extended the notions of rhetoric established during the classical period. Minucian's *On Epicheiremes* (second century A.D.) presents the systemic structuring of argument that complements the enthymeme. The translation by Prentice A. Meador, Jr. (1964) provides one of the few editions on the subject. Similarly, recent advances in neoclassical rhetoric have made apparent the importance of *stasis*. The writings of Hermogenes of Tarsus (second century A.D., fl. ca. A.D. 150) are one of the most important contributions on the subject, ranking with Hermagoras of Temnos (second century B.C.). Ray Nadeau's translation of Hermogenes' *On Stasis* (1964) is highly recommended. Nadeau not only presents a careful translation of a highly technical subject but also provides an introduction and advances observations that are of value to serious historians of rhetoric.

Secondary Works

Reviews

It is only proper that any statement concerning a review of research acknowledge previous efforts. Although dated, two reviews of research in classical rhetoric continue to be beneficial. Charles S. Rayment's "A Current Survey of Ancient Rhetoric" (1958) provides a review of research. Similarly, for many years the volume *Fifty Years (and Twelve) of Classical Scholarship* (ed. Maurice Platnauer, 1968) has been a standard reference for researchers in classical rhetoric. Platnauer's edited volume contains specific sections on Greek and Roman rhetoric, but much of the research reviewed is from British and Continental sources with virtually no recognition of American contributions.

George A. Kennedy's 1975 review of research in *Classical Philology* will be very helpful to readers of English. Not only does Kennedy, himself a recognized authority on ancient rhetoric, synthesize European with American research, but he also directs the reader to needed areas of research. The utility of his review is demonstrated by the number of times it is cited in research as justification for an area of inquiry. Particularly useful is his commentary on George Kustas's study of Byzantine rhetoric (1973), which is available to American researchers only with extraordinary difficulty.

Those interested in a review of research that examines classical rhetoric within the larger framework of rhetorical theory are encouraged to consult Michael C. Leff's excellent essay, "In Search of Ariadne's Thread: A Review of the Recent Literature on Rhetorical Theory" (1978). The value of this statement is Leff's ability to track a common theme, the epistemology of rhetoric, across a range of areas. Consequently, although classical research is not emphasized, the compatibility of topics with other domains makes apparent relationships that might otherwise be missed.

Reference Works and Bibliographies

Students and researchers of classical rhetoric require easily available sources for referring to the variety of concepts, individuals, and issues that are subsumed under the study of classical rhetoric. Three works are readily available to readers of English. The *Oxford Classical Dictionary* (2d ed., 1970) is an invaluable source for quick and reliable information. The brief overviews of Greek and Latin rhetoric are synoptic, but accurate, and make for an excellent opening assignment to a new student of classical rhetoric. Several technical subjects are treated, and a list of sources often accompanies each entry; it is quite common to see this work by the desk of any researcher of classical rhetoric. On a much smaller scale, the publication of *Ancient Greek and Roman Rhetoricians: A Bibliographical Dictionary* (Bryant et al., 1968) offers an overview of prominent rhetoricians. While not recommended as a final source for researchers, it does provide a clear, readable accounting of prominent theorists; the discussion of Plato by Everett Lee Hunt is especially helpful. Lastly, the recent contribution of sources in the history of rhetoric under the editorship of Winifred Bryan Horner, *Historical Rhetoric: An Annotated Bibliography of Selected Sources in English* (1980), is intended for those who wish to have a thorough reference and introduction to the area. "The Classical Period," offered by Richard Leo Enos, was composed to respond to the revitalized interest in classical rhetoric, and particularly the emergence of neoclassical theorists of rhetoric and composition. While many works stress invention, the constraints of the publisher limited other entries and the length of discussion. Nonetheless, the work is recommended as a source specifically directed to readers of English.

A detailed discussion of bibliographical studies for classical rhetoric must be limited here to general sources, but a specific collection of recommended works is provided in the Bibliography section at the end of this essay. Those who wish to keep abreast of philological research in rhetoric are encouraged to consult *L'Année Philologeque,* which regularly publishes references to classical rhetoric. Similarly, references to studies in classical rhetoric growing out of communication studies in America are available in Ronald J. Matlon's *Index to Journals in Communication Studies Through 1979.* In addition, the *Rhetoric Society Quarterly* regularly publishes bibliographies in classical rhetoric, and the *Rhetoric Newsletter* of the International Society for the History of Rhetoric annually updates its members on current research among colleagues in the organization.

Historical Studies: General, Specific, and Pedagogical

Many readers of English were introduced to the history of rhetoric through the pioneer efforts of Charles Sears Baldwin's *Ancient Rhetoric and Poetic* (1959). However, Baldwin's work is less a history than a summary and digest of ancient authors and was replaced as the essential secondary source by George Kennedy's *The Art of Persuasion in Greece* (1963). It is through Kennedy's efforts that many readers of English were widely exposed to the rich history of classical rhetoric. In fact, it is not too much to say that Kennedy's *The Art of Persuasion in Greece* and Edward P. J. Corbett's *Classical Rhetoric for the Modern Student* (1965) did more to encourage the neoclassical movement in rhetoric for readers of English than any two other works. In testimony to his efforts, Kennedy's work, which is still widely used, is being expanded and modified by subsequent research—much of which his work helped to promote. While other works, such as Werner Jaeger's *Paideia: The Ideals of Greek Culture* (1945), J. W. H. Atkins's *Literary Criticism in Antiquity* (1934), Albin Lesky's *A History of Greek Literature* (1966), and Rudolf Pfeiffer's *History of Classical Scholarship from the Beginnings to the End of the Hellenistic Age* (1968), provide a larger framework to examine rhetoric, Kennedy's *The Art of Persuasion in Greece* has yet to be replaced for its central emphasis on rhetoric.

It should also be noted, however, that interest in specialized studies focusing on periods and cultures is developing. Robert W. Smith's excellent study, *The Art of Rhetoric in Alexandria: Its Theory and Practice in the Ancient World* (1974), provides insight to the impact of classical rhetoric in Greco-Roman Egypt from 300 B.C. to A.D. 400. Similar attention is being paid to

Byzantine studies. While Kennedy again should be cited for his excellent article on rhetoric and philosophy in the Byzantine period ("Later Greek Philosophy and Rhetoric" [1980]), the only comprehensive study is George Kustas's *Studies in Byzantine Rhetoric* (1973). As indicated earlier, Kustas's work, although written in English, was published in Greece and is extremely difficult to obtain in the United States.

George A. Kennedy's scholarly dominance in the history of Greek rhetoric is paralleled, to a somewhat lesser extent, in Roman rhetoric. For many years only works such as Martin L. Clarke's *Rhetoric at Rome* (1953), J. F. D'Alton's *Roman Literary Theory and Criticism* (1962), and J. Wright Duff's two-volume work on the literary history of Rome (1964, 1967) served as the basic histories for English readers. Kennedy's *The Art of Rhetoric in the Roman World: 300 B.C.–A.D. 300* (1972) provides the comprehensive statement on rhetoric welcomed by historians of the discipline. While *The Art of Rhetoric in the Roman World* has not gained the popularity of his *The Art of Persuasion in Greece*, the volume is regarded as a standard source by researchers, and the section on Cicero (discussed later in this essay) is well worth reading. Those interested in Roman rhetoric, however, are strongly encouraged to read the excellent treatise by A. D. Leeman, *Orationis Ratio: The Stylistic Theories and Practice of the Roman Orators, Historians and Philosophers* (1963). Leeman's two-volume work is a carefully prepared and thoroughly documented source that will frequently aid researchers.

Several histories of rhetoric have emphasized education and the preservation of rhetorical traditions that grew out of antiquity. H. I. Marrou's *A History of Education in Antiquity* (1964), Donald Lemen Clark's *Rhetoric in Greco-Roman Education* (1957), and Aubrey Gwynn's *Roman Education from Cicero to Quintilian* (1926) are the most well known of these works. There are also studies that do not stress new scholarly research but attempt to acquaint students to the field through a review of the history of classical rhetoric. James J. Murphy's edition *A Synoptic History of Classical Rhetoric* (1972) and James L. Golden, Goodwin F. Berquist, and William E. Coleman's *The Rhetoric of Western Thought* (2d ed., 1978) are illustrations of such introductory textbooks on the history of rhetoric that advance no claims beyond acquainting new students with an overview of rhetoric's sources of social and intellectual power. The newest, and possibly the most provocative, of these historical statements is George Kennedy's *Classical Rhetoric and Its Christian and Secular Tradition from Ancient to Modern Times* (1980). While the scope of this work—as evidenced by the title—and the consistency of its quality across periods are still being evaluated by reviewers, there should be little surprise that the early chapters on the Greek and Roman periods have been well received. Kennedy's discussion of *letteraturizzazione,* or the transformation of rhetoric from its primary function of oral persuasion to its secondary function of written literary expression, is important for understanding the relationship between oral and written expression. For those who wish to have an inexpensive textbook on the history of rhetoric, Kennedy's book is one to consider seriously.

Rhetoricians

Perhaps the most difficult and constraining task of this review is to select those studies from the scores of excellent research on the most prominent figures in the history of rhetorical theory. Such a task immediately omits research on the Attic orators and such distinguished efforts as Richard C. Jebb's *The Attic Orators from Antiphon to Isaeos* (1962). Moreover, the limitations of this inquiry call not only for passing over contemporary research but also for omitting rhetorical theorists who, while making noteworthy contributions to the history of rhetoric, are not directly relevant to the objectives of this study. With these caveats and apologies in mind, it is appropriate to make a chronological examination of the most important figures.

Many scholars are interested in the proto-history of rhetoric; that is, evidence of the development of notions about the structuring of discourse long before rhetoric emerged as an established discipline. Although not strictly considered statements on rhetoric, the philological research of Milman Parry (1932, 1971), G. S. Kirk (1976), and Berkley Peabody (1975) have made an excellent case for continued examination of rhetorical techniques in the earliest Greek literature and indirectly refute the claim of D. A. G. Hinks (1940) that studies of rhetoric prior to Corax and Tisias are irrelevant to the discipline. Examples of studies that have emphasized the proto-history of rhetoric are Richard Leo Enos's "The Hellenic Rhapsode" (1978) and "Emerging Notions of Heuristic, Eristic, and Protreptic Rhetoric in Homeric Discourse: Proto-Literate Conniving, Wrangling and Reasoning" (1981). Readers who are interested in examining the impact of writing on the oral basis of Greek expression are encouraged to read Eric A. Havelock's *The Literate Revolution in Greece and Its Cultural Consequences* (1982). This coherent edition brings together Havelock's research on literacy over his career with an insightful, synthetic introduction.

A considerable amount of research has resulted from the debate over the legitimacy and province of rhetoric as a discipline. Studies emphasizing Plato's views most helpful to readers of English are Everett Lee Hunt's essay "Plato and Aristotle on Rhetoric and Rhetoricians" (1920), which endures as required reading for students of classical rhetoric. W. K. C. Guthrie's *Socrates* (1971) also provides a perspective on Plato's dialogue character. For provocative interpretations of Plato's views on rhetoric, however, readers are encouraged to consult Edwin Black's (1958) and David Kaufer's (1978) interpretations of Plato's philosophical and epistemological position toward rhetoric. An excellent, but expensive, collection about Plato's position on rhetoric is Keith V. Erickson's *Plato: True and Sophistic Rhetoric* (1979).

In addition to the well-regarded commentaries on Aristotle's *Rhetorica* by Edward M. Cope (1867), Cope and John Edwin Sandys (1877), and William M. A. Grimaldi (1980) discussed earlier, several other noteworthy contributions to explicating Aristotle's views on rhetoric are available to readers of English. One of the best collections of scholarship on Aristotelian rhetoric is the volume edited by Keith V. Erickson, *Aristotle: The Classical Heritage of Rhetoric* (1974). The advantage of the Erickson collection is that it draws together some of the foremost essays on the subject from scholars in various disciplines. All of the essays in the collection merit attention, but readers will find the essay by Friedrich Solmsen, "The Aristotelian Tradition in Ancient Rhetoric," to be a fine historical statement and a good overview of the main points of the *Rhetorica*. Also included in this collection are important studies on the enthymeme (Lloyd Bitzer), the example (Gerard A. Hauser), and *topoi* (William M. A. Grimaldi and Donovan J. Ochs).

An extensive collection of studies on Aristotelian rhetoric is also available in Winifred Bryan Horner's *Historical Rhetoric: An Annotated Bibliography of Selected Sources in English* (1980), but two studies are particularly worthy of note. William M. A. Grimaldi's "Studies in the Philosophy of Aristotle's *Rhetoric*" (1972) is a comprehensive monograph that provides a detailed analysis of Aristotle's notion of the enthymeme in particular and rhetorical argument in general. Wilbur Samuel Howell's "Aristotle and Horace on Rhetoric and Poetics" (1968) is one of the clearest statements on the differences between rhetoric and poetics and explicates the distinctions that established them as separate disciplines.

Cicero is commonly acknowledged by historians of rhetoric as the most dominant figure in the Latin-speaking West, and the amount of research devoted to his works testifies to his contributions. Unlike Plato and Aristotle, however, no anthology of research is readily available for Ciceronian rhetoric. A series of essays edited by T. A. Dorey in *Cicero* (1965) comes closest to a set of readings, but the work is dated and not all the essays deal directly with rhetoric. As indicated earlier, the best overview of Cicero's contributions is found in George A. Kennedy's *The Art of Rhetoric in the Roman World* (pp. 103–300). Kennedy not only provides a readable account of Cicero as a theoretician and practitioner of rhetoric but also establishes perspective by presenting his discussion in the context of the forces and figures shaping the period. While much has been written about Cicero as an advocate, far fewer studies have been devoted to his theoretical work. The summer 1978 issue of the *Central States Speech Journal*, however, is primarily devoted to either discussing aspects of Cicero's theoretical views on rhetoric or explicating his view of the relationship between theory and practice. Lastly, the introduction to the Latin edition of Cicero's *De Oratore* by Augustus S. Wilkins (1965) presents a fine overview of Cicero and his works.

George A. Kennedy presents a needed biographical profile of Quintilian in his *Quintilian* (1969) and integrates this information within his *The Art of Rhetoric in the Roman World* (1972). A brief but informative sketch of Quintilian also appears in the *Oxford Classical Dictionary* (2d ed., 1970). Much of the research on Quintilian is devoted more to his impact throughout the history of rhetoric than to the particular contributions inherent in his *Institutio oratoria*, but Keith V. Erickson's excellent bibliography on Quintilian in the *Rhetoric Society Quarterly* (1981) provides a valuable collection of difficult to locate studies. Two available works do provide treatment of Quintilian's theoretical position. Marsh H. McCall, Jr., discusses Quintilian's views on style in *Ancient Rhetorical Theories of Simile and Comparison*

(1969), and A. D. Leeman analyzes Quintilian's views in *Orationis Ratio: The Stylistic Theories and Practice of the Roman Orators, Historians and Philosophers* (1963). It is clear, however, that readers of English are in need of additional studies of a theorist whose impact extends throughout the history of rhetoric.

A discussion of research on the sophists and the sophistic movement is extremely difficult to isolate, and it is impossible to fix the sophists to a specific point in the history of rhetoric because of the pervasiveness and endurance of their impact. Excellent research on the First Sophistic is available to readers of English. Mario Untersteiner's *The Sophists* (1954) is commonly, and correctly, regarded as the most authoritative statement on the early sophists. Untersteiner's meticulous attention to detail and thoroughness of citation make this a superior study. W. K. C. Guthrie's *The Sophists* (1971) is also worthy of praise, and both works deserve to be read carefully.

Everett Lee Hunt's synoptic essay "On the Sophists" (1965) directed attention to the important role sophists played in the history of rhetoric. Recently, however, in-depth treatment of individual sophists has become increasingly popular, with particular emphasis on Gorgias of Leontini. Studies by C. P. Segal (1962), Bruce E. Gronbeck (1972), Richard A. Engnell (1973), and Richard Leo Enos (1976) have all stressed the contributions of Gorgias as a serious thinker of rhetoric. An interesting comparison of Gorgias with Plato and Aristotle is offered in Jacqueline de Romilly's *Magic and Rhetoric in Ancient Greece* (1975). It is also clear, however, that much more work is needed on the individual sophists who are now seen as little more than straw men for Socrates in Plato's dialogues.

The 105th annual meeting of the American Philological Association in 1973 witnessed a strong interest in research of the Second Sophistic, sometimes called the "Greek Renaissance." The coordinator of this effort was G. W. Bowersock, whose excellent book *Greek Sophists in the Roman Empire* (1969) is a fine statement about the place of the Second Sophistic within the Roman world. Out of the American Philological Association meeting came a monograph entitled *Approaches to the Second Sophistic* (1974). Unfortunately, this valuable collection of papers by such scholars as George Kennedy is virtually unavailable today. It is, nonetheless, strongly recommended as an excellent introduction to the period; excluding the works mentioned above, the only other such introduction available is Charles

Sears Baldwin's dated account in *Medieval Rhetoric and Poetic (to 1400): Interpreted from Representative Works* (1959). More specialized studies on the sophists within their historical context are in I. Avotins's "The Holders of the Chairs of Rhetoric at Athens" (1975) and Richard Leo Enos's "The Effects of Imperial Patronage on the Rhetorical Tradition of the Athenian Second Sophistic" (1977). Lastly, although these works do not deal directly with the Second Sophistic, readers interested in comparing the Greek techniques for declamation with their Roman counterparts are encouraged to consult S. F. Bonner's excellent *Roman Declamation in the Late Republic and Early Empire* (1949), Harry Caplan's "The Decay of Eloquence at Rome in the First Century" (1944), and A. F. Sochatoff's "Basic Rhetorical Theories of the Elder Seneca" (1939).

Specialized Concepts

Although many of the concepts and heuristic processes central to rhetoric are subsumed, and have been discusssed, in earlier sections, there are several works worthy of attention and even repetition. The concept of *stasis*, for example, has occupied the attention of rhetoricians for much of the classical period. Fortunately, the excellent article by Otto A. L. Dieter, *"Stasis"* (1950), although difficult to read because of the density of the material and thoroughness of treatment, persists as one of the most important essays in classical rhetoric. Studies following Dieter's essay have helped to explain the notion of *stasis*, the most beneficial of which are presented by Ray Nadeau in his two *Speech Monographs* essays (1958, 1959) and his excellent survey of classical systems of *stases* in *Greek, Roman and Byzantine Studies* (1959). After Dieter and Nadeau, research on *stasis* becomes much more specialized, as is apparent in the writings of James C. Backes (1960), Wayne N. Thompson (1972), and the thoroughly documented study by Ray D. Dearin (1976); in fact, the Dearin essay itself provides a fine review of research on *stasis*.

The argumentative structures of enthymeme, epicheireme, and example have been discussed in earlier sections. Particular reference is again paid to William M. A. Grimaldi's (1972) and James A. McBurney's (1936) studies on the enthymeme. Similarly, studies by David A. Church and Robert S. Cathcart (1965) and Gary Cronkhite (1966) on the epicheireme provide important, and needed, information. Studies on the example by

Gerard Hauser (1968) and William Lyon Benoit (1980) are helpful interpretations of Aristotle's views, but the most valuable statement on paradigmatic reasoning in classical rhetoric is made by William M. A. Grimaldi in the appendix to his commmentary on Aristotle's *Rhetorica* (1980). As discussed earlier, Grimaldi's studies on the example, enthymeme, *pistis*, and *topoi* should be required reading for all serious students of classical rhetoric. Lastly, the concept of *topoi* is embedded in many of the works discussed earlier, but readers will find the statements of William M. A. Grimaldi (1974, 1980) and Donovan J. Ochs (1969, 1982) the most helpful of all those discussed. It is clear, however, that a considerable amount of research on heuristic processes is still required if the merits of classical rhetoric are to be fully realized.

Needed Areas for Future Research

There are several areas of research that merit attention. First, very little has been done on the proto-history of rhetoric; that is, studies that examine the emergence of rhetorical techniques in oral and written literature prior to rhetoric's canonization as a formal discipline. Second, much more work needs to be done in the epistemology generating classical rhetorical theories, particularly with understanding sophistic rhetoric and the interaction of heuristic processes. Although such topics have recently been discussed in several articles, continued study is required before the presuppositions grounding ancient views on the relationship between thought and discourse can be realized. Third, much of the evidence of classical rhetoric is still in need of collection, analysis, and synthesis. Such work will require not only proficiency in textual analysis and philological research but also "fieldwork" in libraries and archaeological sites. This need is particularly serious both in the study of literary fragments of sophists and in the collection and analysis of such nontraditional, but invaluable, evidence as epigraphical sources. Fourth, as Kennedy correctly indicates in his review article (1975), the impact of classical rhetoric across cultures and through time is still in need of study. It is known, for example, that classical rhetoric was influential, and in some cases even preserved by the Byzantine Empire and Arab world, yet relatively little is known about these phenomena. Lastly, the theories of classical rhetoric have survived throughout our history in part because of their utility. The resurgence of classical rhetoric in departments of English is an illustration of the power of these theories. One of the most important tasks for historians and theoreticians of classical rhetoric is to introduce, refine, and possibly modify the heuristic and stylistic processes of classical rhetorical theory for the resolution of contemporary communication problems so that the benefits of rhetoric, which have been evident for centuries, can continue to be made apparent through scholarly research.[1]

Bibliography

This bibliography is intended to provide full citations for works referred to in the essay. For the sake of coherence, the references listed will be divided into three categories: primary works, secondary works, and selected bibliographies. The "Primary Works" section will adhere as closely as possible to the chronology and order of presentation of primary sources mentioned in the essay. The "Secondary Works" section will list works in alphabetical order. The "Selected Bibliographies" section will provide a sampling of collections for further study. In a few cases, additional studies have been listed that, while not the focus of specific commentary in the essay, are recommended to the reader. Hopefully, this bibliography will be both a sampling and a foundation upon which further reading and research can be based.

Primary Works

Pre-Socratic Philosophers and Sophists:
Homeric to ca. the Peloponnesian War

Ancilla to the Pre-Socratic Philosophers. Edited by Kathleen Freeman. Oxford: Basil Blackwell, 1971.

Artium scriptores: Reste der voraristotelischen Rhetorik. Edited by Ludwig Radermacher. Vienna: Rudolf M. Rohrer, 1951.

Die Fragmente der Vorsokratiker. Edited by Hermann Diels and Walther Kranz. 2 vols. Dublin: Weidmann, 1972.

The Older Sophists. Edited by Rosamond Kent Sprague. Columbia: University of South Carolina Press, 1972.

The Pre-Socratic Philosophers: A Companion to Diels, Fragmente der Vorsokratiker. Edited by Kathleen Freeman. 2d ed. Oxford: Basil Blackwell, 1966.

The Presocratic Philosophers: A Critical History with a Selection of Texts. Edited by G. S. Kirk and J. E. Raven. Cambridge: Cambridge University Press, 1973.

Plato

Plato: Euthyphro—Apology—Crito—Phaedo—Phaedrus. Translated by H. N. Fowler. The Loeb Classical Library. Cambridge: Harvard University Press, 1914.

Plato: Gorgias—A Revised Text with Introduction and Commentary. Edited by E. R. Dodds. Oxford: Clarendon Press, 1959.

Plato: Lysis—Symposium—Gorgias. Translated by W. R. M. Lamb. The Loeb Classical Library. Cambridge: Harvard University Press, 1925.

Plato's Phaedrus: *Translated with an Introduction and Commentary.* Translated by R. Hackforth. Cambridge: Cambridge University Press, 1972.

Aristotle

(Anaximenes.) *Rhetorica ad Alexandrum.* Translated by H. Rackham (Preceded by *Problems, Books XXII–XXXVIII.* Translated by W. S. Hett.) The Loeb Classical Library. Cambridge: Harvard University Press, 1937.

The "Art" of Rhetoric. Translated by J. H. Freese. The Loeb Classical Library. Cambridge: Harvard University Press, 1926.

Rhetoric and Poetics of Aristotle. Translated by W. Rhys Roberts and Ingram Bywater. Introduction and notes by Friedrich Solmsen. New York: Modern Library, 1954.

The Rhetoric of Aristotle. Edited by Edward M. Cope and John Edwin Sandys. 3 vols. Cambridge: Cambridge University Press, 1877.

The Rhetoric of Aristotle. Translated by Lane Cooper. New York: Appleton-Century-Crofts, 1960.

Cicero

(Cicero.) *Ad C. Herennium de Ratione Dicendi (Rhetorica ad Herennium).* Translated by Harry Caplan. The Loeb Classical Library. Cambridge: Harvard University Press, 1954.

Brutus. Translated by G. L. Hendrickson. *Orator.* Translated by H. M. Hubbell. The Loeb Classical Library. Cambridge: Harvard University Press, 1952.

Cicero on Oratory and Orators. Translated by J. S. Watson. Edited by Ralph A. Micken. Carbondale: Southern Illinois University Press, 1970.

De Inventione—De Optimo Genere Oratorum—Topica. Translated by H. M. Hubbell. The Loeb Classical Library. Cambridge: Harvard University Press, 1949.

De Oratore. Books I–II. Translated by E. W. Sutton and H. Rackham. The Loeb Classical Library. Cambridge: Harvard University Press, 1942. Revised, 1948.

De Oratore. Book III. De Fato—Paradoxoa Stoicorum—De Partitione Oratoria. Translated by H. Rackham. The Loeb Classical Library. Cambridge: Harvard University Press, 1942.

M. Tulli Ciceronis De Oratore Libri Tres. Edited by Augustus S. Wilkins. Hildesheim: Georg Olms Verlag, 1965.

Stylistics and Criticism: Dionysius, Demetrius, and Longinus

Dionysius of Halicarnassus: The Critical Essays. Translated by Stephen Usher. Vol. 1. The Loeb Classical Library. Cambridge: Harvard University Press, 1974.

Dionysius of Halicarnassus: On Literary Composition. Edited with an introduction, translation, notes, glossary, and appendixes by W. Rhys Roberts. London: Macmillan and Co., 1910.

(Aristotle), *The Poetics and Longinus, On the Sublime.* Translated by W. Hamilton Fyfe. *Demetrius, On Style.* Translated by W. Rhys Roberts. The Loeb Classical Library. Rev. ed. Cambridge: Harvard University Press, 1932.

Aristotle's Poetics, Demetrius on Style, Longinus on the Sublime. Introduction by John Warrington. Translated by John Warrington, T. A. Moxon, and H. L. Havell. London and New York: Everyman's Library, 1963.

Aristotle, Horace, Longinus: Classical Literary Criticism. Translated by T. S. Dorsch. London: Penguin, 1965.

Rhetoric and Roman Education: Seneca (The Elder) and Quintilian

Seneca: Controversiae, I–VI. Translated by Michael Winterbottom. Vol. 1. The Loeb Classical Library. Cambridge: Harvard University Press, 1974.

Seneca: Controversiae, VII–X. Suasoriae. Translated by Michael Winterbottom. Vol. 2. The Loeb Classical Library. Cambridge: Harvard University Press, 1974.

The Institutio oratoria of Quintilian. Translated by H. E. Butler. 4 vols. The Loeb Classical Library. Cambridge: Harvard University Press, 1920–1922.

Commentators and Historians of Rhetoric

Plutarch: Moralia [Lives of the Ten Orators]. Translated by H. N. Fowler. Vol. 10. The Loeb Classical Library. Cambridge: Harvard University Press, 1936.

Plutarch: Parallel Lives; Demosthenes and Cicero—Alexander and Caesar. Translated by B. Perrin. The Loeb Classical Library. Cambridge: Harvard University Press, 1919.

Tacitus: Agricola. Translated by M. Hutton, revised by R. M. Ogilvie. *Germania.* Translated by M. Hutton, revised by E. H. Warmington. *Dialogus.* Translated by Wm. Peterson, revised by Michael Winterbottom. The Loeb Classical Library. Cambridge: Harvard University Press, 1970.

Tacitus: Agricola, Germany, Dialogue on Orators. Translated with an introduction and notes by Herbert W. Benario. Indianapolis: The Bobbs-Merrill Co., 1967.

Suetonius: The Lives of the Caesars (continued), The Lives of Illustrious Men. Translated by J. C. Rolfe. Vol. 2. The Loeb Classical Library. Cambridge: Harvard University Press, 1914.

(Suetonius.) Enos, Richard Leo. "When Rhetoric Was Outlawed in Rome: A Translation and Commentary of Suetonius's Treatise on Early Roman Rhetoricians." *SM* 39 (March 1972): 37–45.

Philostratus: Lives of the Sophists. Eunapius: Lives of the Philosophers and Sophists. Translated by Wilmer C. Wright. The Loeb Classical Library. Cambridge: Harvard University Press, 1921.

Minucian and Hermogenes

(Minucian.) Meador, Prentice A., Jr. "Minucian, *On Epicheiremes:* An Introduction and Translation." *SM* 31 (March 1964): 54–63.

(Hermogenes.) Nadeau, Ray. "Hermogenes's *On Stasis*: A Translation with an Introduction and Notes." *SM* 31 (November 1964): 361–424.

Secondary Works

Arnhart, Larry. *Aristotle on Political Reasoning: A Commentary on the "Rhetoric."* DeKalb: Northern Illinois University Press, 1981.

Atkins, J. W. H. *Literary Criticism in Antiquity: A Sketch of Its Development.* 2 vols. Cambridge: Cambridge University Press, 1934.

Avotins, I. "The Holders of the Chairs of Rhetoric at Athens." *HSCP* 79 (1975): 313–24.

Backes, James C. "Aristotle's Theory of *Stasis* in Forensic and Deliberative Speech in the *Rhetoric.*" *CSSJ* 12 (Autumn 1960): 6–8.

Baldwin, Charles Sears. *Ancient Rhetoric and Poetic.* Gloucester, Mass.: Peter Smith, 1959.

———. *Medieval Rhetoric and Poetic (to 1400): Interpreted from Representative Works.* Gloucester, Mass.: Peter Smith, 1959.

Benoit, William Lyon. "Aristotle's Example: The Rhetorical Induction." *QJS* 66 (April 1980): 182–92.

Bitzer, Lloyd. "Aristotle's Enthymeme Revisited." *QJS* 45 (December 1959): 399–408.

Black, Edwin. "Plato's View of Rhetoric." *QJS* 44 (December 1958): 361–74.

Bonner, S. F. *Roman Declamation in the Late Republic and Early Empire.* Liverpool: Liverpool University Press, 1949.

Bowersock, G. W., ed. *Approaches to the Second Sophistic.* Ephrata, Pa.: Science Press, 1974.

———. *Greek Sophists in the Roman Empire.* Oxford: Clarendon Press, 1969.

Brandes, Paul D. "Evidence in Aristotle's *Rhetoric.*" *SM* 28 (March 1961): 21–28.

Bryant, Donald C., Robert W. Smith, Peter D. Arnott, Erling B. Holtsmark, and Galen O. Rowe, eds. *Ancient Greek and Roman Rhetoricians: A Bibliographical Dictionary.* Columbia, Mo.: The Artcraft Press, 1968.

Caplan, Harry. "The Decay of Eloquence at Rome in the First Century." In *Studies in Speech and Drama in Honor of Alexander M. Drummond,* edited by Herbert A. Wichlens, pp. 295–325. Ithaca: Cornell University Press, 1944.

Church, David A., and Robert S. Cathcart. "Some Concepts of the Epicheireme in Greek and Roman Rhetoric." *WS* 29 (Summer 1965): 140–47.

Clark, Donald Lemen. *Rhetoric in Greco-Roman Education*. New York: Columbia University Press, 1957.

Clarke, Martin L. *Rhetoric at Rome*. London: Cohen & West, 1953.

Cope, Edward M. *An Introduction to Aristotle's Rhetoric: With Analysis, Notes and Appendices*. London: The Macmillan Co., 1867.

Corbett, Edward P. J. *Classical Rhetoric for the Modern Student*. New York: Oxford University Press, 1965.

Cronkhite, Gary. "The Enthymeme as Deductive Rhetorical Argument." *WS* 30 (Spring 1966): 129–34.

D'Alton, J. F. *Roman Literary Theory and Criticism*. New York: Russell and Russell, 1962.

Dearin, Ray D. "The Fourth *Stasis* in Greek Rhetoric." In *Rhetoric and Communication*, edited by Jane Blankenship and Hermann G. Stelzner, pp. 3–16. Urbana: University of Illinois Press, 1976.

de Romilly, Jacqueline. *Magic and Rhetoric in Ancient Greece*. Cambridge: Harvard University Press, 1975.

Dieter, Otto A. L. "*Stasis*." *SM* 17 (August 1950): 345–69.

Dobson, John F. *The Greek Orators*. Freeport, N.Y.: Books for Libraries Press, 1971.

Dorey, T. A., ed. *Cicero*. New York: Basic Books, 1965.

Duff, J. Wright. *A Literary History of Rome: From the Origins to the Close of the Golden Age*. Edited by A. M. Duff. London: Ernest Benn, 1967.

———. *A Literary History of Rome in the Silver Age: From Tiberius to Hadrian*. Edited by A. M. Duff. 3d ed. London: Ernest Benn, 1964.

Ehninger, Douglas W. "The Classical Doctrine of Invention." *Gavel* 39 (March 1957): 59–62, 70.

———. "On Systems of Rhetoric." *PR* 1 (Summer 1968): 131–44.

Engnell, Richard A. "Implications for Communication of the Rhetorical Epistemology of Gorgias of Leontini." *WS* 37 (Summer 1973): 175–84.

Enos, Richard Leo. "The Effects of Imperial Patronage on the Rhetorical Tradition of the Athenian Second Sophistic." *Communication Quarterly* 25 (Spring 1977): 3–10.

———. "Emerging Notions of Heuristic, Eristic, and Protreptic Rhetoric in Homeric Discourse: Proto-Literate Conniving, Wrangling and Reasoning." In *Selected Papers from the 1981 Texas Writing Research Conference*, edited by Maxine C. Hairston and Cynthia L. Selfe, pp. 44–64. Austin: The University of Texas at Austin, 1981.

———. "The Epistemological Foundation for Cicero's Litigation Strategies." *CSSJ* 26 (Summer 1975): 207–14.

———. "The Epistemology of Gorgias's Rhetoric: A Re-examination." *SSJ* 42 (Fall 1976): 35–51.

———. "The Hellenistic Rhapsode." *WS* 42 (Spring 1978): 134–43.

Erickson, Keith V. "The Lost Rhetorics of Aristotle." *SM* 43 (August 1976): 229–37.

———. *Plato: True and Sophistic Rhetoric*. Amsterdam: Editions Rodopi, 1979.

Erickson, Keith V., ed. *Aristotle: The Classical Heritage of Rhetoric.* Metuchen, N.J.: Scarecrow Press, 1974.

Golden, James L., Goodwin F. Berquist, and William E. Coleman. *The Rhetoric of Western Thought.* 2d ed. Dubuque, Iowa: Kendall/Hunt Publishing Co., 1978.

Grimaldi, William M. A., S. J. "The Aristotelian *Topics.*" In *Aristotle: The Classical Heritage of Rhetoric,* edited by Keith V. Erickson, pp. 176–93. Metuchen, N.J.: Scarecrow Press, 1974.

———. *Aristotle,* Rhetoric *I: A Commentary.* Bronx, N.Y.: Fordham University Press, 1980.

———. "Rhetoric and Truth: A Note on Aristotle, *Rhetoric,* 1355a." *PR* 11 (Summer 1978): 173–77.

———. "Studies in the Philosophy of Aristotle's *Rhetoric.*" *Hermes: Zeitschrift für klassische Philologie* 25 (1972): 1–151.

Gronbeck, Bruce E. "Gorgias on Rhetoric and Poetic: A Rehabilitation." *SSJ* 38 (Fall 1972): 27–38.

Guthrie, W. K. C. *Socrates.* Cambridge: Cambridge University Press, 1971.

———. *The Sophists.* Cambridge: Cambridge University Press, 1971.

Gwynn, Aubrey. *Roman Education from Cicero to Quintilian.* Oxford: Oxford University Press, 1926.

Hammond, N. G. L., and H. H. Scullard, eds. *The Oxford Classical Dictionary.* 2d ed. Oxford: Clarendon Press, 1970.

Hauser, Gerard A. "The Example in Aristotle's *Rhetoric*: Bifurcation or Contradiction?" *PR* 1 (Spring 1968): 78–90.

Havelock, Eric A. *The Literate Revolution in Greece and Its Cultural Consequences.* Princeton: Princeton University Press, 1982.

Hendrickson, G. L. "The Origin and Meaning of the Ancient Characters of Style." *AJP* 26 (1905): 249–90.

Hinks, D. A. G. "Tisias and Corax and the Invention of Rhetoric." *Classical Quarterly* 34 (April 1940): 61–69.

Howell, Wilbur Samuel. "Aristotle and Horace on Rhetoric and Poetics." *QJS* 54 (December 1968): 325–39.

Hunt, Everett Lee. "On the Sophists." In *The Province of Rhetoric,* edited by Joseph Schwartz and John A. Rycenga, pp. 69–84. New York: The Ronald Press Co., 1965.

———. "Plato and Aristotle on Rhetoric and Rhetoricians." *QJS* 6 (June 1920): 35–56.

Jaeger, Werner. *Paideia: The Ideals of Greek Culture.* Translated by Gilbert Highet. 3 vols. New York: Oxford University Press, 1945.

———. "The Rhetoric of Isocrates and Its Cultural Ideal." In *The Province of Rhetoric,* edited by Joseph Schwartz and John A. Rycenga, pp. 84–111. New York: The Ronald Press Co., 1965.

Jebb, Richard C. *The Attic Orators from Antiphon to Isaeos.* 2 vols. New York: Russell and Russell, 1962.

Kaufer, David S. "The Influence of Plato's Developing Psychology on His Views of Rhetoric." *QJS* 64 (February 1978): 63–78.

Kennedy, George A. *The Art of Persuasion in Greece*. Princeton: Princeton University Press, 1963.

———. *The Art of Rhetoric in the Roman World: 300 B.C.–A.D. 300*. Princeton: Princeton University Press, 1972.

———. *Classical Rhetoric and Its Christian and Secular Tradition from Ancient to Modern Times*. Chapel Hill: The University of North Carolina Press, 1980.

———. "Later Greek Philosophy and Rhetoric." *PR* 13 (Summer 1980): 181–97.

———. *Quintilian*. New York: Twayne Publishers, 1969.

———. "Review Article: The Present State of the Study of Ancient Rhetoric." *CP* 70 (December 1975): 278–82.

Kirk, G. S. *Homer and the Oral Tradition*. Cambridge: Cambridge University Press, 1976.

Kustas, George. *Studies in Byzantine Rhetoric*. Salonika, Greece: Patriarchal Institute for Patristic Studies, 1973.

Leeman, A. D. *Orationis Ratio: The Stylistic Theories and Practice of the Roman Orators, Historians and Philosophers*. 2 vols. Amsterdam: Adolf M. Hakkert, 1963.

Leff, Michael C. "In Search of Ariadne's Thread: A Review of the Recent Literature on Rhetorical Theory." *CSSJ* 29 (Summer 1978): 73–91.

Lesky, Albin. *A History of Greek Literature*. Translated by James Willis and Cornelis de Heer. London: Methuen, 1966.

Lundy, Susan Ruth, and Wayne N. Thompson. "Pliny, A Neglected Roman Rhetorician." *QJS* 66 (December 1980): 407–17.

McBurney, James A. "The Place of the Enthymeme in Rhetorical Theory." *SM* 3 (1936): 49–74.

McCall, Marsh H., Jr. *Ancient Rhetorical Theories of Simile and Comparison*. Cambridge: Harvard University Press, 1969.

Marrou, H. I. *A History of Education in Antiquity*. Translated by George Lamb. New York: New American Library, 1964.

Meador, Prentice A., Jr. "The Classical Epicheireme: A Re-Examination." *WS* 30 (Summer 1966): 151–55.

Mudd, Charles. "The Enthymeme and Logical Validity." *QJS* 45 (December 1959): 409–14.

Murphy, James J., ed. *A Synoptic History of Classical Rhetoric*. Berkeley: University of California Press, 1972.

Nadeau, Ray. "Classical Systems of *Stases* in Greek: Hermagoras to Hermogenes." *Greek, Roman and Byzantine Studies* 2 (January 1959): 51–71.

———. "Hermogenes on 'Stock Issues' in Deliberative Speaking." *SM* 25 (March 1958): 59–66.

———. "Some Aristotelian and Stoic Influences on the Theory of *Stasis*." *SM* 26 (November 1959): 248–54.

Ochs, Donovan J. "Aristotle's Concept of Formal Topics." *SM* 36 (November 1969): 419–25.

———. "Cicero's *Topica*: A Process View of Invention." In *Explorations in Rhetoric: Studies in Honor of Douglas Ehninger,* edited by Ray E. McKerrow, pp. 107–18. Glenview, Ill.: Scott, Foresman and Co., 1982.

Parry, Adam, ed. *The Making of Homeric Verse: The Collected Papers of Milman Parry.* Oxford: Clarendon Press, 1971.

Parry, Milman. "Studies in the Epic Technique of Oral Verse-Making, II. The Homeric Language as the Language of Oral Poetry." *HSCP* 43 (1932): 1–50.

Peabody, Berkley. *The Winged Word: A Study in the Technique of Ancient Greek Oral Composition as Seen Principally through Hesiod's* Works and Days. Albany: State University of New York Press, 1975.

Pfeiffer, Rudolf. *History of Classical Scholarship from the Beginnings to the End of the Hellenistic Age.* Oxford: Clarendon Press, 1968.

Platnauer, Maurice, ed. *Fifty Years (and Twelve) of Classical Scholarship.* 2d ed. Oxford: Basil Blackwell, 1968.

Rayment, Charles S. "A Current Survey of Ancient Rhetoric." *The Classical World* 52 (December 1958): 75–91.

Roberts, W. Rhys. *Greek Rhetoric and Literary Criticism.* New York: Longmans, Green & Co., 1928.

Sattler, William M. "Conceptions of *Ethos* in Ancient Rhetoric." *SM* 14 (1947): 55–65.

———. "Some Platonic Influences in the Rhetorical Works of Cicero." *QJS* 35 (April 1949): 164–69.

Segal, C. P. "Gorgias and the Psychology of the *Logos*." *HSCP* 66 (1962): 99–155.

Smith, Robert W. *The Art of Rhetoric in Alexandria: Its Theory and Practice in the Ancient World.* The Hague: Martinus Nijhoff, 1974.

Sochatoff, A. F. "Basic Rhetorical Theories of the Elder Seneca." *CJ* 34 (March 1939): 345–54.

Solmsen, Friedrich. "The Aristotelian Tradition in Ancient Rhetoric." *AJP* 62 (1941): 35–50, 169–90. See also Keith V. Erickson, ed., *Aristotle: The Classical Heritage of Rhetoric,* pp. 278–309.

Sumner, G. V. *The Orators in Cicero's* Brutus: *Prosopography and Chronology.* Toronto: University of Toronto Press, 1973.

Thompson, Wayne N. "*Stasis* in Aristotle's *Rhetoric*." *QJS* 58 (April 1972): 134–41.

Thonssen, Lester, and A. Craig Baird. "Cicero and Quintilian on Rhetoric." In *The Province of Rhetoric,* edited by Joseph Schwartz and John A. Rycenga, pp. 137–57. New York: The Ronald Press Co., 1965.

Untersteiner, Mario. *The Sophists.* Translated by Kathleen Freeman. New York: Philosophical Library, 1954.

Wagner, Russell H. "The Rhetorical Theory of Isocrates." In *Readings in Rhetoric*, edited by Lionel Crocker and Paul A. Carmack, pp. 169–83. Springfield, Ill.: Charles C. Thomas, 1965.

Wilkinson, L. P. *Golden Latin Artistry.* Cambridge: Cambridge University Press, 1963.

Yates, Frances Amelia. *The Art of Memory.* London & Chicago: Routledge and University of Chicago Press, 1966.

Selected Bibliographies

Allen, Walter. "A Survey of Selected Ciceronian Bibliography, 1939–1953." *Classical World* 47 (1953–1954): 129–39.

Benoit, William L. "A Brief Bibliography of Sources on Isocrates in English." *RSQ* 11 (Fall 1981): 263–64.

Caplan, Harry. "Bibliography." In [*Cicero*]. *Ad C. Herennium de Ratione Dicendi (Rhetorica ad Herennium)*, translated by Harry Caplan, pp. xli–xliv. The Loeb Classical Library. Cambridge: Harvard University Press, 1954.

Enos, Richard Leo. "The Classical Period." In *Historical Rhetoric: An Annotated Bibliography of Selected Sources in English*, edited by Winifred Bryan Horner, pp. 1–41. Boston: G. K. Hall, 1980.

———. "Early Concepts of Greek Rhetoric and Discourse: A Selected Bibliography." *RSQ* 10 (Winter 1980): 49–50.

———. "Epigraphical Sources for the History of Hellenic Rhetoric." *RSQ* 9 (Summer 1979): 169–76.

Enos, Richard Leo, and Dean N. Constant. "A Bibliography of Ciceronian Rhetoric." *RSQ* 6 (Spring 1976): 21–28.

Enos, Richard Leo, and Honora Mary Rockar. "General Works on the Development of Writing and Scripts." *RSQ* 10 (Fall 1980): 263–65.

Enos, Richard Leo, and Howard E. Sypher. "A Bibliography for the Study of Classical Invention." *RSQ* 7 (Spring 1977): 53–57.

Erickson, Keith V. "Plato's Philosophy of Rhetoric: A Research Guide." *RSQ* 7 (Summer 1977): 78–90.

———. "Quintilian's *Institutio oratorio* and *Pseudo-Declamationes*." *RSQ* 11 (Winter 1981): 45–62.

Lentz, Tony M. "The Oral Tradition in Transition: A Bibliography Relevant to the Study of Reading in Hellenic Greece." *RSQ* 8 (Spring 1978): 82–98.

Matlon, Ronald J. *Index to Journals in Communication Studies Through 1979.* Annandale, Va.: Speech Communication Association, 1980.

2

THE MIDDLE AGES
James J. Murphy

Scholarship to 1942

Serious attempts to understand the medieval mind are of fairly recent origin. In the sixteenth century Edmund Spenser referred to Chaucer as a literary diamond in a dung heap of an age, while nineteenth-century figures like William Morris and Alfred Lord Tennyson who overly romanticized the middle ages perpetuated an equal though different sense of unreality. Medieval rhetoric long shared the same fate.

The first major change in attitude toward rhetoric of that period came in Germany in the 1850s and 1860s, when scholars began to realize that certain "historical" documents—letters, contracts, formulas—were in fact not records of real events but models or even teaching exercises for medieval students of the *ars dictaminis*, or art of letter-writing. This discovery led to the publication in 1863 of a landmark collection of Latin texts: Ludwig Rockinger, *Briefsteller und Formelbücher des eilften bis vierzehnten Jahrhunderts*. Rockinger's introduction is not very pertinent today, but his set of eighteen texts, which include both letter-writing manuals and model letter collections, is still quite useful, and the book was in fact reprinted in 1961.

In 1868, M.C. Thurot, "Notices et extraits de divers manuscrits latins pour servir a l'histoire des doctrines grammaticales au moyen âge," was published in a special issue of *Notices et Extraits*. Thurot's set of studies, lists, and text excerpts is still extremely valuable, and the book was reprinted in 1964.

James J. Murphy is professor and chairman of the department of rhetoric as well as a professor in the separate department of English at the University of California, Davis. His many works include *Rhetoric in the Middle Ages: A History of Rhetorical Theory from Saint Augustine to the Renaissance* (University of California Press, 1974) and *Medieval Rhetoric: A Select Bibliography* (University of Toronto Press, 1971). In addition, he is currently the editor of *Rhetorica*, a new journal in the history of rhetoric that began publication in 1983.

The next major advance came in a different rhetorical field, and some six decades later, with the publication in 1924 of Edmond Faral's *Les arts poétiques du XIIᵉ et du XIIIᵉ siècles*. Faral furnishes the Latin texts or summaries of six major *artes poetriae*, with brief biographies of their authors, together with a useful analysis of their basic doctrines and a brief chapter on the medieval use of the tropes and figures of the pseudo-Ciceronian *Rhetorica ad Herennium*. Faral's book triggered a wave of interest in the literary influences of the *artes*, especially the *Poetria nova* of Geoffrey of Vinsauf; a key article by John M. Manly ("Chaucer and the Rhetoricians," 1926) was among the first of more than fifty such studies. *Les arts poétiques* was reprinted in 1958.

The first major modern study of medieval preaching theory appeared at almost the same time as Faral's book, in 1926. By the Cambridge don Gerald R. Owst, this work was *Preaching in Medieval England: An Introduction to Sermon Manuscripts of the Period, c. 1350-1450*. This marvelously detailed study of both theory and practice remains a standard. Then, in a remarkable scholarly coincidence, three extremely important guides to the study of medieval preaching theory appeared within three years of each other. Harry Caplan's *Mediaeval Artes Praedicandi: A Hand-List* came out in 1934. Then in 1936 Father Th.-M. Charland's *Artes praedicandi: contribution à l'histoire de la rhétorique au moyen âge* was published, the same year as Caplan's *Supplement* to his basic 1934 handlist. Caplan and Charland between them listed some three hundred treatises of the *ars praedicandi*, or art of preaching, many anonymous, and almost all still in manuscript. Today, nearly five decades later, only about twenty-five are available in any printed form. Charland's book includes an excellent summary of theory, the biographies of known authors, lists of manuscripts, and the Latin texts of two preaching manuals by Thomas Waleys and Robert of Basevorn. Like Faral and Rockinger, Charland remains indispensable for any serious study of rhetoric in the middle ages.

Meanwhile, in 1928 Charles S. Baldwin had produced *Medieval Rhetoric and Poetic*, with useful summaries of some medieval treatises; he pays little attention to developments in rhetoric after the thirteenth century, however, and stresses unduly the role of dialectic. The "Poetic" in his title is largely Chaucerian. (Four years earlier he had completed another volume on the same plan, *Ancient Rhetoric and Poetic*.) Moreover, since the work of Charland and Caplan had not yet been done,

Baldwin paid comparatively little detailed attention to preaching theories.

By the time of World War II it was clear that, in addition to the long-documented survival of ancient rhetorical texts (especially those of Cicero), there was considerable interest during the middle ages in rhetorical theories developed by medieval writers in the three fields of letter-writing, verse-writing, and sermon-making. Taking together the three basic collections of Latin treatises—those by Rockinger, Faral, and Charland—there was ample text material in hand for further study.

Richard McKeon's landmark monograph, "Rhetoric in the Middle Ages" (1942), was an effort at a synthesis of what had been learned to that point. McKeon used the relations between the three arts of the medieval *Trivium*—grammar, rhetoric, and dialectic—to place the rhetorical forms of the middle ages in an understandable context. Although the article is still cited frequently and does contain some valuable citations and other information, it is densely, even obscurely written and over-emphasizes the influence of dialectic on medieval rhetorical theory. Nevertheless, many readers may find it worth the careful reading that its sometimes murky prose will require.

The Present State of Scholarship

Basic Resources

In some respects the medieval period is one of the best covered, since we now have in print a general bibliography and a partial one, two collections of translations in addition to a number of individual translations, a volume of essays dealing with medieval rhetoric, a number of key studies, and finally a one-volume history of rhetoric for the period from Saint Augustine to the Renaissance. All of these have appeared within the past two decades.

Besides these publications specifically relating to medieval rhetoric, there are also two important encyclopedic projects under way that will include many items relating to the subject. The first fascicles of *Lexikon des Mittelalters* began to appear in 1978; the German-language *Lexikon* is published by Artemis & Winkler of Munich, West Germany, and is planned for five volumes and an index volume. Articles are generally short, with emphasis on summary rather than detail, and have brief bibliographies at the end. Excellent articles appear in the first volume on *Ars dictaminis* (Hans Martin Schaller) and *Ars praedicandi* (Franz Quadlbauer), though the article on *Ars poetica, ars versificatoria* (R. Düchting) is less satisfactory in its omission of most scholarship of the last twenty years.

The other encyclopedia, *Dictionary of the Middle Ages*, began publication alphabetically in 1982, with completion of its ten volumes expected by 1984. The project is under the direction of a committee headed by the well-known historian Joseph R. Strayer and is edited under the auspices of the American Council of Learned Societies. Publisher is Charles Scribner's Sons of New York. In contrast to the brevity of the *Lexikon*, the *Dictionary of the Middle Ages* will publish articles ranging up to ten thousand words on major subjects; "Western European Rhetoric," for instance, will have eight thousand words in an article by James J. Murphy, while separate essays will be devoted to Arabic, Persian, and Hebrew rhetoric (Andras Hamori and Jerome Clinton) and to Byzantine rhetoric (Robert Browning). The *Dictionary* will also include articles on dialectic, grammar, and a number of important rhetorical authors like Boethius and Geoffrey of Vinsauf. A short bibliography will accompany each essay.

A major advantage of an encyclopedic entry, of course, is that it usually represents a distillation of the major elements in a subject by an expert in the field. (Paradoxically, this is less true of the treatment of medieval rhetoric in the latest edition of *The Encyclopedia Britannica*, where the article on "Rhetoric" by Thomas O. Sloane takes a broad and conceptual view of the subject that may be of less value to one interested specifically in rhetoric of the middle ages.)

Bibliographies

The standard bibliography for medieval rhetoric remains James J. Murphy, *Medieval Rhetoric: A Select Bibliography* (1971), containing 531 citations arranged under eight headings: Background Works, The Transitional Period (A.D. 400–1050), Transmission of Classical Rhetorical Traditions, Grammar (*Ars grammatica*), the Art of Letter-Writing (*Ars Dictaminis*), the Art of Preaching (*Ars praedicandi*), the University Disputation (*Disputatio*), and Miscellaneous. Many items are annotated. A listing of twenty-six key books concludes the volume. Each item has a double coding: a letter indicating its field and its number within that field (thus, P7 is Charles Smyth's *The Art of Preaching: A Practical Survey of Preaching in the Church of England, 747–1939*, which is number 7 in the Preaching section). A second edition is in preparation.

A bibliography of more limited scope that may be useful for beginning the study of medieval rhetoric is that of Luke Reinsma, "The Middle Ages," in Winifred Bryan Horner, ed., *Historical Rhetoric: An Annotated Bibliography of Selected Sources in English* (1980). All 235 primary and secondary sources are annotated; Reinsma points out that he has concentrated on the more recent of the secondary works (30 percent of them since 1970), with special attention to "liberally documented" sources whose notes can facilitate further study. He also notes that nearly half of his citations are not in the Murphy bibliography. The Reinsma bibliography lists primary sources chronologically and secondary sources alphabetically by author rather than by field or chronological period; while some readers may find this a disadvantage, the extensive annotation may be of assistance. (Additional remarks on bibliography may be found below in the section on Journals and Series.)

Translations

Two collections of translations are now available. The first to appear was *Three Medieval Rhetorical Arts* (1971), edited by Murphy. This set of original translations includes the editor's rendering of Anonymous of Bologna, *The Principles of Letter-Writing* (1135)—still the only *ars dictaminis* so far rendered into English—Geoffrey of Vinsauf, *The New Poetics* (ca. 1210), translated by Jane Baltzell Kopp; and Robert of Basevorn, *The Form of Preaching* (1322), translated by Father Leopold Krul O.S.B. The three works are essentially complete. An appendix includes excerpts from the two works of Aristotle used in medieval universities for training in *disputatio*, his *Topics* and *On Sophistical Refutations*. An introduction (pp. vii–xxiii) outlines the place of the three translated texts in the "preceptive tradition" of the middle ages.

The second collection, while more extensive in some respects (thirty-six authors are named), is more difficult to assess because it includes items at three levels: complete translations, translations of excerpts, and nine "commentaries" of a page or two that cite translations available elsewhere. This collection is Joseph M. Miller, Michael H. Prosser, and Thomas W. Benson, eds., *Readings in Medieval Rhetoric* (1973). Some of the translations included were first published elsewhere; Father Joseph Miller is the sole translator of the original renderings in the volume. A few of the works translated may strike some readers as trivial—for instance, Hildebert of Lavardin's Second Sermon for Pentecost—but the volume also presents for the first time in English some extremely valuable texts for the history of medieval rhetoric; especially noteworthy are texts of the excerpts from Priscian, Martianus Capella, Isidore of Seville, Rabanus Maurus, Walafrid Strabo, Alberic of Monte Cassino, Alain de Lille, Giles of Rome, and Thomas of Todi. Nevertheless, the reader might well have a mixed reaction to the items gathered in this collection.

Other translations of individual works will be of interest. A number of key texts of the *ars poetriae* are now available in English. One of the most important is Traugott Lawler's *The Parisiana Poetria of John of Garland* (1974). John of Garland was a prominent early thirteenth-century grammar master who undertook to prepare a single book that could give the reader everything he needed to know about composing prose, quantitative verse, or rhymed syllabic verse. As John says in his prologue, "the art of composition is here channeled in a short stream." Lawler's work contains the Latin text facing the English. With its careful and extensive notes giving frequent cross-references to other works of the time (especially those of Geoffrey of Vinsauf), this volume can be an invaluable introduction to the whole relationship of grammar and rhetoric in the late twelfth and early to mid thirteenth century.

The *Poetria nova* and *Documentum* of Geoffrey of Vinsauf have both been translated—the *Poetria nova* three times—and further editions and commentaries are in preparation. One translation of the *Poetria nova* has already been noted above (Murphy, *Three Arts*, 1971). Another with some unique features is that of Ernest A. Gallo, *The Poetria nova and Its Sources in Early Rhetorical Doctrine* (1971); Gallo provides a Latin text (basically Faral's), a facing prose translation, and then devotes a hundred pages (133–236) to a discussion of the poem's ancient rhetorical sources. The doctrine of *amplificatio* gets special attention. Gallo uses the method of parallel passages to argue derivation from Horace's *Ars poetica*, Cicero's *De inventione*, and the pseudo-Ciceronian *Rhetorica ad Herennium*, though his parallels to the *Institutio oratoria* of Quintilian are less convincing.

The most highly regarded translation of Vinsauf's work, however, has been that of Margaret F. Nims, *The Poetria Nova of Geoffrey of Vinsauf* (1967). A crisp translation close to the flavor of the difficult Latin text, coupled with economical yet revealing notes, has made this by far the preferred version of the poem's text, though some readers may prefer a translation with a more extensive introduction.

Vinsauf's prose *Documentum de modo et arte dictandi et versificandi*, which presents substantially the same doctrine as his hexameter *Poetria nova*, has been translated by Roger Parr as *Instruction in the Method and Art of Speaking and Versifying* (1968).

The *Ars versificatoria* of the twelfth-century author Matthew of Vendôme has been translated twice. The earlier, partial version is by Ernest Gallo, "Matthew of Vendôme: Introductory Treatise on the Art of Poetry" (1974); Gallo summarizes some sections instead of offering a direct translation. A complete rendering is found in *Matthew of Vendôme: the Art of Versification*, translated by Aubrey E. Gaylon (1980). Of the two, Gallo's may be better for the general background of the treatise, Gaylon's better for the sense of the text itself. Eberhard the German's *Laborintus* was translated as a Cornell Master's thesis by Evelyn Carlson in 1930.

One other major Latin work in this tradition, Gervase of Melkley's *Ars versificaria*, is not yet available in English. Faral offers only a summary, but it was later edited in Germany by Hans-Jurgen Gräbner under the title *"Ars poetica"* in *Forschungen zur romantischen Philologie* 17 (1965).

Translations are more plentiful when one turns to the *ars praedicandi*, or preaching manual, but here it must be noted that fewer than a dozen of the three-hundred-odd known treatises are available in English—while editions of the Latin texts still number only about twenty. Details of the Latin texts may be secured in the Murphy bibliography for such authors as Francis Eiximenis, Hugh of St. Victor, or Martin of Cordova. The *Ars componendi sermones* of Ranulph Higden, edited by Margaret Jennings, will be published in Leiden in 1983. The Miller-Prosser-Benson collection discussed above includes translated excerpts from the manuals of Alain de Lille, Rabanus Maurus, Guibert of Nogent, Humbert of Romans, and Thomas of Todi. In addition, both Murphy and Reinsma in their bibliographies list translations of Simon Alcock, Thomas Waleys, Henry of Hesse, and Pseudo-Aquinas. One of the longest (and in the eyes of one historian of the subject, most "typical") treatises is the *Form of Preaching* (1322) of Robert of Basevorn, translated by Leopold Krul in Murphy's *Three Arts*. One rendering not listed in either the Reinsma or Murphy bibliography is Harry C. Hazel, Jr., "Translation, with Commentary, of the Bonaventuran *Ars concionandi*," Ph.D. dissertation, Washington State University, 1972; this work was at one time erroneously attributed to Saint Bonaventure. Harry Caplan's *Of Eloquence* (1970) reprints his earlier journal translations of "Henry of Hesse" and "Pseudo-Aquinas."

As was noted earlier, only one *ars dictaminis* or letter-writing manual has so far appeared in English; this is the so-called Anonymous of Bologna, *Principles of Letter-Writing*, in the Murphy collection *Three Arts*. However, some interesting aspects of the tradition may be seen in Charles H. Haskins, "The Life of Medieval Students as Illustrated by Their Letters" (1929).

Most of the foundational works of the late classical period and the early middle ages are now available in some kind of English version and will generally repay the reading—Saint Augustine, Martianus Capella, Priscian, Isidore of Seville, Cassiodorus, Boethius, Bede, Rabanus Maurus, and Alcuin. For details see the bibliography at the end of this essay.

Surveys and General Studies

Since World War II a number of surveys or extensive studies have attempted to place in perspective the larger number of medieval rhetorical treatises that have come to light. Some older works were still in use, such as Paul Abelson's *The Seven Liberal Arts* (1906) and Louis J. Paetow's *The Arts Course at Medieval Universities with Special Reference to Grammar and Rhetoric* (1910). Then in 1943 John W. H. Atkins wrote *English Literary Criticism: The Medieval Phase*, whose lengthy analysis of Geoffrey of Vinsauf and other authors of the *artes poetriae* sparked another wave of journal articles dealing with rhetoric in literature.

The most useful book of the immediate postwar period, however, proved to be Ernst R. Curtius, *European Literature and the Latin Middle Ages* (1953), translated from the original 1948 German version. The basic thesis of the book is that *topoi* or rhetorical topics can be used to analyze the impact of rhetoric on medieval habits of literary development; with examples from several national literatures as well as from Latin, Curtius popularized for a time the search for "themes" as well as rhetorical figures in medieval literary works. The book is so richly documented that it is well worth studying today. It was reprinted in 1967.

Another provocative general study worth perusal is Erich Auerbach, *Literary Language and Its Public in Late Latin Antiquity and in the Middle Ages* (1965). As its title indicates, this book raises some useful generic questions about communication in the middle ages.

As the titles of Atkins's, Curtius's, and Auerbach's works indicate, a literary approach to the study of medieval rhetoric seemed for a time to be dominant among scholars. Meanwhile, however, a number of parallel studies were going on relating to such diverse subjects as preaching, Italian humanism, the *ars dictaminis*, medieval grammar, the *disputatio* in universities, the *trivium*, and medieval commentaries on the rhetoric of Cicero. See in the bibliography at the end of this essay the entries under Harry Caplan, Charles H. E. Smyth, Woodburn O. Ross, Paul O. Kristeller, Jerrold Seigel, Charles B. Faulhaber, M. C. Thurot, R. H. Robins, Reginald J. O'Donnell, James J. Murphy, Mary Dickey, and John O. Ward. Space does not permit a detailed listing here, but the important point about this array of names is that it represents a widespread and continuing set of investigations into what is increasingly regarded as a very complex subject. The first attempt at a survey bibliography appeared in 1962 (*Speech Monographs*, vol. 29), with two hundred items; a plan for a survey history had been published the previous year in vol. 23 of *Medieval Studies*.

The "standard history of medieval rhetoric" (to use Reinsma's term) appeared in 1974 with the publication of Murphy's *Rhetoric in the Middle Ages: A History of Rhetorical Theory from Saint Augustine to the Renaissance*. Its preface declares that it traces the medieval history of the "preceptive rhetorical tradition"—the fundamental concept of order and plan in discourse—first laid down in ancient Greece and then transmitted to the middle ages through Roman writers. The book is divided into six chapters and an epilogue. The first three chapters deal with ancient rhetorical theory and its continuations: the ancient traditions, Saint Augustine and the age of transition (to A.D. 1050), and the medieval survival of classical traditions. The second set of three chapters discusses three medieval "genres" of verse-writing, letter-writing, and preaching. An epilogue describes the fifteenth-century rediscovery of the complete texts of Quintilian's *Institutio* and Cicero's *De oratore*.

Rhetoric in the Middle Ages argues that Greek and Roman rhetoric was committed to the discovery of precepts that could be used to plan and present future discourse. These discoveries were amalgamated into books like Aristotle's *Rhetoric* or Cicero's *De inventione*. Roman education, built around rhetorical preparation for civic life, systematically applied the Isocratean trilogy of Talent, Education, and Practice to devise a complex training program of great efficiency. Both grammatical and rhetorical precepts were employed. This educational program outlasted the culture that gave it birth, transmitting Roman rhetorical educational practices directly into the middle ages. Early medieval writers like Saint Augustine defended the values of Roman rhetorical training in the face of Christian distrust of pagan ideas, and the so-called encyclopedists (Martianus Capella, Isidore of Seville, and Cassiodorus) digested basic rhetorical doctrines as part of their surveys of ancient learning. Thus men of the high middle ages—A.D. 1050–1400—inherited both a respect for Roman rhetoric and a set of texts (mainly Ciceronian) presenting its theory. Commentary writers of the twelfth and thirteenth centuries further popularized these ideas. Medieval rhetoric to a great extent then became a series of adaptations of Ciceronian rhetoric to particular needs of the times, with applications to problems of letter-writing, verse-writing, and preaching. In the universities, however, the basic communicative methodology remained the *disputatio* derived from principles of Aristotelian dialectic. *Rhetoric in the Middle Ages* was reissued as a paperback in 1981.

A recent general survey of rhetorical history with a segment on the middle ages is George A. Kennedy, *Classical Rhetoric and Its Christian and Secular Tradition from Ancient to Modern Times* (1980). Kennedy, already well known for *The Art of Persuasion in Greece* (1963) and *The Art of Rhetoric in the Roman World* (1972), sets out in this book "to define classical rhetoric and its tradition by examining the various strands of thought which are woven together in different ways at different times" (p. 3). He includes an interesting chapter on Judeo-Christian rhetoric, and another on Greek rhetoric in the middle ages; he devotes twenty pages to Latin rhetoric in the period, covering fourteen topics very briefly. The reader should remember, though, that Kennedy's purpose is to seek traces of the later history of classical rhetoric, not to write a history of every period.

An equally brief but more significant treatment of medieval rhetòric may be found in Paul O. Kristeller, "Philosophy and Rhetoric from Antiquity to the Renaissance" (1979). Kristeller's notes alone would be worth the reading. His reflections on the developmental role of *dictamen* are particularly valuable. (For a parallel view about the importance of the medieval *ars dictaminis* in terms of later Renaissance humanism, see Jerrold Seigel, *Rhetoric and Philosophy in Renaissance Humanism: the Union of Eloquence and Wisdom, Petrarch to Valla* [1968], especially chapter 7, "From the *dictatores* to the Humanists.")

Readers interested in a more inductive approach to the various facets of medieval rhetoric may be interested in a collection of fourteen essays edited by Murphy under the title *Medieval Eloquence: Studies in the Theory and Practice of Medieval Rhetoric* (1978). Part 1 includes six essays on rhetorical theory: Michael Leff on Boethius, John O. Ward on Ciceronian commentaries, Ernest Gallo on Geoffrey of Vinsauf, Charles B. Faulhaber on Guido Faba's *dictamen*, Margaret Jennings on Ranulph Higden's preaching manual, and M. B. Parkes on the rhetorical uses of punctuation. Part 2 contains eight examinations of rhetoric as applied to various literatures: Calvin Kendall on Bede's Latin, Jackson J. Campbell on Old English literature, Murphy on an early Middle English poem, Douglas Kelly on Old French literature, Aldo Scaglione on Dante, Robert O. Payne on Chaucer, Samuel Jaffe on Gottfried von Strassburg, and Josef Purkart on Boncompagno of Signa. Taken together, these essays with their notes and other references can provide an illuminating introduction to the subject.

Journals and Series

Most humanistic journals will consider articles dealing with the history of rhetoric. Even a rapid scan of the bibliography at the end of this essay will show that significant items dealing with medieval rhetoric have appeared in such journals as *Speculum, Medium Aevum, Studi Medievali, Medieval Studies, Medievalia et Humanistica,* and *Review of English Studies*. Articles from these and similar journals are indexed in the annual *MLA Bibliography*.

For journals in the speech/communication field there is now a useful index covering publications through 1979: Ronald J.

Matlon, *Index to Journals in Communication Studies Through 1979* (1980). Among the journals indexed are several that have carried numerous relevant articles: *Quarterly Journal of Speech, Communication Monographs* (formerly *Speech Monographs*), *Western Speech Communication Journal* (formerly *Western Speech*), *Southern Speech Journal,* and *Central States Speech Journal.* Cross-references in the Matlon volume permit searches for subjects and periods as well as for authors and titles.

Perhaps the most important new resource is the twice-yearly *Rhetorica: A Journal of the History of Rhetoric*, published by the University of California Press for the International Society for the History of Rhetoric. The first issue will appear in March 1983. Information about the journal may be secured from the periodicals editor, University of California Press.

An important but so far little known series is the *Cahiers de l'Institut du Moyen-Âge Grec et Latin* (1969 –) begun at the University of Copenhagen under the general editorship of the late Jan Pinborg. (See in the bibliography the entries for Karin M. Fredborg.) The *Cahiers* include texts and studies relating to the middle ages.

This brief overview cannot of course offer complete coverage of the many studies that European and American scholars have devoted to medieval rhetoric over the past several decades. The bibliography at the end of this essay—itself necessarily highly selective—can point to additional resources. What is heartening, however, is that after centuries of comparative neglect there is now a strong interest in exploring medieval ideas of communication. The next section will examine the frontiers of our present knowledge and suggest some possible new lines of inquiry.

Six Issues for Future Scholarship

I. *Texts.* Some textual problems occur in any field, but in a field as comparatively uncharted as medieval rhetoric there is a need for the publication of the medieval texts that can provide evidence for our assessment of the subject. There are at least three hundred unedited *artes praedicandi* or preaching manuals; there are perhaps four hundred unedited *artes dictaminis*—Emil Polak of Queensborough Community College has been touring Europe the past several years uncovering hitherto unknown treatises by the score. It is not only a deep interest in medieval literature, certainly, that has produced so many studies relating to the *ars poetriae*; it must be remembered that Faral's basic Latin texts have been in print for almost sixty years. So far we lack that kind of textual control for preaching manuals, or letter-writing treatises and commentaries, or school texts. Without numerous texts to compare, the average scholarly reader is at the mercy of the summarizer and survey-writer.

Somewhat the same thing can be said in this decreasingly Latinic age about the value of translations. The Latin-less reader is also at the mercy of the summarizer, unless he or she has a readable version of the texts to compare with what the surveyor alleges. Directors of theses and dissertations might well bear this need in mind when counseling their students about making a "contribution to knowledge."

Jacques Maritain once remarked that the history of philosophy was not the same as the history of its books. The same is no doubt true of medieval rhetoric, but at the same time the written record of ideas and their applications over the centuries of the middle ages can surely be of immense assistance to us in trying to understand that period.

II. *The educational background:* This may be treated under two headings:

A. *The history of education.* Insofar as rhetoric deals with a basic and essential social ability—the power to speak or to write—it has been closely related to education since the days of Plato, Isocrates, and Aristotle. It was imbedded in the whole Roman approach to education. All evidence points to this continued relation of rhetoric to education even into our own times.

Yet we have barely begun to approach this question for the middle ages. The rough outlines of medieval educational history have long been in place, in the works of such writers as Henri Marrou, Hastings Rashdall, Foster Watson, Louis Paetow, Theodore Haarhoff, Lynn Thorndike, Arthur F. Leach, Pearl Kibre, and Lowrie Daly. (For details see the Murphy bibliography.) More lately there have been studies of medieval elementary education: by Cora E. Lutz (1977), by Nicholas Orme (1973, 1976), and by Murphy (1967, 1980). Rashdall's *The Universities of Europe in the Middle Ages* (1936) has been supplemented and in some cases surpassed by Gordon Leff, *Paris and Oxford Universities in the Thirteenth and Fourteenth Centuries* (1968), and especially by what is probably the most perceptive treatment, A. B. Cobban, *The Medieval Universities: Their Development and*

Organization (1970). Cobban's publisher (Methuen) has declined to reprint the book, now out of print. Cobban's masterful correlation of the diverse forces in medieval university life, from student power to theological controversy, makes this book indispensable for anyone wishing to study the relation of rhetoric to other arts in that particular educational environment.

Nevertheless, what would be gratefully received today would be a definitive study of the place of rhetoric in both university and nonuniversity education of the middle ages. The question of whether the "Seven Liberal Arts" ever actually functioned as a unit in medieval education might then find an answer. The changing roles of *dialectica* and *grammatica* would then be easier to assess. The relative worth of the rhetoric of Cicero, of Aristotle, and of Quintilian at different times could be analyzed. Arabic and Greek influences could be studied. Above all, the precise contributions of commentaries—so typically an adjunct of a teaching situation—might be more carefully understood.

Once the educational history of the middle ages is well charted, with or without direct studies of the place of rhetoric, it will be easier to grasp the pervasive influence that the educational backgrounds of medieval writers must surely have had on their ways of thinking, their modes of composition, and even their choices of word patterns.

B. *Educational biographies*. A good start in the direction of a history of medieval education might well be made by systematically investigating the educational biographies of major writers. As John Baldwin has shown so well in his *Masters, Princes and Merchants* (1970), the influence of even one teacher like Peter the Chanter can spread like ripples from a rock thrown in a pond. Helene Wieruszowski's study of Arezzo (1953) shows the influence of the schools of one town. Studies of the dictaminal writer Guido Faba by Ernst H. Kantorowicz (1941–1943), Virgilio Pini (1956), and Charles Faulhaber (1978) demonstrate how much of the *ars* or theory of a master can be gleaned from careful study of his antecedents. Edith Rickert's landmark essay on "Chaucer at School" (1931) offers a model for such studies in relation to a literary figure.

Much could be learned from intensive study of, for instance, the Thomas Chabham who seems to have been the first or at least a very early writer of an *ars praedicandi* outlining the so-called thematic sermon. Writing about A.D. 1200, he was clearly conversant with Horace, Sedulius, Aristotle, Cicero, Peter Lombard, Abelard, Peter the Chanter, and half a dozen other authors and capable of comparing Cicero's *orationes* to the sermons of the Church Fathers. Who taught him? Where? In what way? And what impelled him to chart what proved to be a new course for sermon-making? In this case we do know the rudiments of his biography, and perhaps with more study the connections can be made. But we need many such.

There now prove to have been many more schools in medieval France, England, Italy, and Germany than once was thought. Who attended them, and what effect if any did they have on the theory and practice of rhetoric in the middle ages?

III. *Definition and scope of medieval rhetoric.* There seem to be two quite different understandings of the nature of "rhetoric" regardless of the historical period under study. One says that rhetoric is a certain definable body of principles, usually embodied in texts, and applied in various ways as times and circumstances change; the other says that rhetoric is always culture-bound and is substantially different in each time and place. (These are of course the extremes, and most scholarship partakes of both.) While this difference may seem merely an abstraction of little importance to the historian, it does have practical consequences in terms of the evidence that scholars are willing to accept in respect to medieval rhetoric. A case in point is the early history of the study of the *ars dictaminis*: some scholars (for example Paetow, C. S. Baldwin) saw it as a theory and often simply equated it with the whole of medieval rhetoric, while others (for example Atkins) dismissed it as merely a medieval habit or practice with no theoretical aspect. The first view saw it as an application in the middle ages of ancient Roman ideas, while the other view saw it as a mere practice, limited to a time and place.

This general problem will need resolution as research uncovers more and more examples of rhetorical practice—poems, letters, sermons, histories—to assess against the *scientia* or *ars* of the theoretical treatises of the middle ages. There may be no immediate solution to the problem, short of improving our whole concept of the historiography of medieval rhetoric, but in this writer's view it remains an important bar to a consensus as to the nature and scope of the subject.

In this connection the student of medieval rhetoric would do well to examine carefully some of the excellent general studies of medieval culture that have lately appeared: see in the bibliography, for instance, items by Judson B. Allen, Marcia L. Colish, Peter Dronke, J. Olivet, Robert O. Payne, and Winthrop Wetherbee.

IV. *The role of dictamen*. There are two scholarly debates in progress in this area, one about the origins of the *ars dictaminis* and another about its outcomes. There seems to be general agreement about the midlife of *dictamen*, as Kristeller points out: "The body of literature that belongs to *dictamen* and its related enterprises is very large indeed, and exceeds by far in bulk anything comparable that has been preserved from classical antiquity, and anything else remotely rhetorical, such as the rhetorical commentaries on Cicero, produced in the Middle Ages" ("Philosophy and Rhetoric from Antiquity to the Renaissance," p. 241).

While there is less agreement about its beginnings, the matter is in part one of definition (as noted above). Typical of one point of view is the 1971 article by Murphy titled "Alberic of Monte Cassino: Father of the Medieval *Ars dictaminis*," discussing the first known theoretical treatises in the genre. On the other hand, William Patt ("The Early 'Ars dictaminis' as Response to a Changing Society," 1978), among others, has pointed to the practice of tenth-century writers composing letters according to the five parts of the standard *ars dictaminis*. Was Alberic's work, then, merely the confirmation of an existing practice, or did it instead analyze a current tendency and elevate it to a theoretical level? Implicit in this issue is the question of "art" versus "practice" mentioned earlier. It could well be that both sides of the issue are correct. In any case further investigation can only benefit our general understanding.

There is still a great deal of work to be done to assess the influence of the *ars dictaminis* during the high middle ages—not only on chancery affairs but also on letters in general including the vernacular—but of great interest also is the history of the *ars dictaminis* toward the end of the middle ages. Renaissance humanists often looked to classical models for letter composition, and the controversy over "Ciceronianism" enhanced such movements; certainly by the sixteenth century there was available a new epistolography that turned away from medieval patterns. Yet Lidia Winniczuk has shown that some of the medieval manuals continued to be printed into the sixteenth century. Meanwhile, it seems clear that the *ars dictaminis* as a genre allowed Italian writers (as well as some French and English) a form in which to include new ideas of literary theory; for that matter Kristeller and Seigel among others have shown how individual *dictatores* used their dictaminal talents to introduce "humanist" ideas. Guido Faba and Justus Lipsius were both interested in letters: how do they differ? A history of ideas about letter-writing for, say, the period 1450–1650 might provide a highly illuminating perspective on that period.

V. *The relation of rhetoric and grammar to the ars poetriae*. When Edmond Faral completed his *Les arts poétiques* in 1924 he not only pointed to Ciceronian influences but actually organized his summaries of works like Vinsauf's *Poetria nova* under the five Roman rhetorical canons of Invention, Arrangement, Style, Memory, and Delivery. Those elements are certainly visible in the Faral texts; in fact many of the subsequent studies simply refer to those writers as "rhetoricians." Beginning in 1964, however, Murphy ("A New Look at Chaucer and the Rhetoricians") argued that this line of reasoning was leading scholars to overlook the contributions to the *ars poetriae* by principles of the medieval *ars grammatica*. This argument did not win universal acceptance, especially in the absence of a definitive history of medieval grammar; perhaps the strongest single rebuttal appeared in a 1968 article by Richard J. Schoeck titled "On Rhetoric in Fourteenth-Century Oxford." (The title reflects the fact that it is intended as a reply to a 1965 article by Murphy titled "Rhetoric in Fourteenth-Century Oxford.") Schoeck objects to placing the *ars poetriae* within a grammatical tradition, saying that to do so would be a distortion of the meaning of grammar. In Murphy's *Rhetoric in the Middle Ages* (1974) a chapter is devoted to a brief history of medieval grammar and analysis of the six *artes poetriae*, with the added argument that all the authors of these *artes* were in fact teachers of grammar who regarded grammar as their main subject and used Ciceronian rhetoric only to supplement it in forming "preceptive grammar."

The issue is one both of definition and of principle, with implications for our understanding of medieval attitudes toward language use. Did it make any difference to Geoffrey of Vinsauf what his precepts were called? We know that the fourteenth-century preaching theorist Robert of Basevorn did consciously call on the preacher to use interchangeably the lores of rhetoric, of grammar, and of dialectic, pointing as well to models like Saint Bernard who might be imitated regardless of precepts. Was that attitude also prevalent a century earlier? Was it prevalent among grammar teachers? In the first Christian century, Quintilian had warned that grammarians would try to take over the province of rhetoricians: was this still a problem in the age of Vinsauf? The difficulty, in other words, is that we need to distinguish between what we wish to call things today and what medieval writers may or may not have called things. Perhaps Vinsauf would not have cared one way or another, given the pragmatic tendencies of medieval usage that employed anything from any period or from any art if it seemed useful. On the other hand, given the jurisdictional problems of medieval education, the title of a master or of a book might have made a good deal of difference.

The definitive history of medieval grammar (and of rhetoric, and of dialectic) that might illuminate these questions is still in the future. Meanwhile the issue itself is worth keeping in mind when we soberly give modern names to medieval phenomena.

VI. *Sermons and sermon theory*. We do not yet know enough to make a sure judgment about whether the theory of the "thematic sermon" preceded or followed the widespread making of such sermons. The genesis of the treatises offering this sermon theory itself is now fairly clear, datable almost precisely to A.D. 1200 in the works of Alexander Ashby and Thomas Chabham. (For details see Murphy, *Rhetoric in the Middle Ages*, chapter 6.) The proliferation of the *artes praedicandi* shortly afterward is well documented by Caplan, Charland, Ross, Smyth, and Roth, with several hundred now identified. Yet a question remains, not unlike one posed in relation to the *ars dictaminis*: do Ashby and Chabham in effect offer a rationale for existing practice, or does the proposed thematic plan represent a breakthrough? Some careful examination of surviving twelfth-century sermons might provide the beginnings of an answer to that question.

There is also a broader problem in connection with the study of this whole area: Who is best equipped to study medieval sermons? Literary historians seeking influences on medieval writers often pick over the texts of sermons looking for passages; cultural historians look for social implications; theologians look for doctrinal matters; biographers sometimes count sermons of their subjects the way they would list book titles. By and large, rhetoricians have not taken up the challenge of looking at sermons holistically, the way they look at orations or speeches of other ages—that is, as whole oral compositions delivered in a certain time and place for a given reason. Audience analysis, as a result, is almost entirely neglected.

The whole matter of deciding *how* to study medieval sermons remains to be settled. Some attention to this problem would surely pay immense dividends, especially now that more and more sermon texts are becoming available. (In this respect it is heartening to see the establishment of the *Medieval Sermon Studies Newsletter*, edited by Gloria Cigman, Department of English, Warwick University, Coventry, England.)

A final note. What runs through all the works cited here, and resides in the six issues raised here, is the conviction on the part of hundreds of twentieth-century scholars that medieval theories of communication are worth the study. The more we learn, the more we see what needs to be learned. What is involved is a thousand years of human interest in one of the most complex activities of mankind—the ability to translate thought into speech or writing. Our study of that past might well illuminate our own future.

Bibliography

Since there are specialized bibliographies available for medieval rhetoric, no attempt is made here to list every item that might be of interest. Nevertheless, this bibliography is self-sufficient—that is, it does include the major citations necessary to undertake a study of the subject. All books and articles cited in the text are described here more fully. For convenience, basic modern studies, bibliographies, collections of texts and translations, and recent studies are grouped together in separate sections.

Basic Modern Studies

Since modern studies of medieval rhetoric have proliferated to a bewildering degree, the following list is provided as a basic selection of works useful for understanding the subject. Most are books, but the reader is cautioned that much of the recent work on the medieval arts of discourse continues to appear in journal articles rather than in books.

Abelson, Paul. *The Seven Liberal Arts: A Study in Mediaeval Culture*. Columbia University Teachers' College Contributions to Education, no. 11. New York: Teachers' College, Columbia University, 1906. Reprinted: New York: AMS Press, 1972.

Arbusow, Leonid H. N. *Colores rhetorici: Eine Auswahl rhetorischer Figuren und Gemeinplätze als Hilfsmittel für akademische Übungen an mittelalterlichen Texten*. Göttingen: Vandenhoeck & Ruprecht, 1948. 2d ed. edited by Helmut Peters, 1963. Reprinted: Geneva: Slatkine Reprints, 1974.

Artes libéraux et philosophie au moyen âge. Actes du Quatrième Congrès International de Philosophie Médiévale. Montreal: Institut d'Études Médiévales; Paris: J. Vrin, 1969.

Atkins, John W. H. *English Literary Criticism: The Medieval Phase*. New York: The Macmillan Co.; Cambridge: Cambridge University Press, 1943. Reprinted: London: Methuen; New York: Peter Smith, 1952.

Auerbach, Erich. *Literary Language and Its Public in Late Latin Antiquity and in the Middle Ages*. Translated by Ralph Manheim. Bollingen Series, no. 74. New York: Pantheon Books; Princeton: Princeton University Press, 1965.

Baldwin, Charles S. *Medieval Rhetoric and Poetic (to 1400) Interpreted from Representative Works*. New York: The Macmillan Co., 1928. Reprinted: Gloucester, Mass.: Peter Smith, 1959; St. Clair Shores, Mich.: Scholarly Press, 1976.

Caplan, Harry. *Of Eloquence: Studies in Ancient and Mediaeval Rhetoric*. Edited by Anne King and Helen North. Ithaca: Cornell University Press, 1970.

Charland, Th.-M. *Artes praedicandi: Contribution à l'histoire de la rhétorique au moyen âge*. Publications de l'Institut d'Études Médiévales d'Ottowa, 7. Paris: J. Vrin; Ottawa: Institut d'Études Médiévales, 1936.

Curtius, Ernst R. *European Literature and the Latin Middle Ages*. Translated by Willard R. Trask. Bollingen Series, no. 36. New York: Pantheon Books, 1953. Reprinted: Princeton: Princeton University Press, 1967.

Dargan, Edwin C. *A History of Preaching*. 2 vols. New York: A. C. Armstrong & Son, 1905–1912. Reprinted: Burt Franklin Research and Source Works Series, no. 177. New York: Burt Franklin, 1968.

Denholm-Young, Noël. "The Cursus in England." In *Oxford Essays in Medieval History Presented to Herbert Edward Salter*, pp. 68–103. Oxford: Clarendon Press, 1934. Reprinted: Freeport, N.Y.: Books for Libraries Press, 1968. Reprinted in Denholm-Young, *Collected Papers on Mediaeval Subjects*, pp. 26–55. Oxford: B. Blackwell, 1946. Reprinted with revisions in Denholm-Young, *Collected Papers of N. Denholm-Young*, pp. 42–73. Cardiff: University of Wales Press, 1969.

Faral, Edmond. *Les Arts Poétiques du XIIᵉ et du XIIIᵉ siècles: Recherches et documents sur la technique littéraire du moyen âge*. Bibliothéque de l'École des Hautes Etudes. Paris: Champion, 1924, 1962.

Kennedy, George A. *Classical Rhetoric and Its Christian and Secular Tradition from Ancient to Modern Times*. Chapel Hill: University of North Carolina Press, 1980.

Lausberg, Heinrich. *Handbuch der literarischen Rhetorik*. 2 vols. Munich: M. Hueber, 1960.

McKeon, Richard. "Rhetoric in the Middle Ages." *Speculum* 17 (1942): 1–32. Reprinted with revisions in *Critics and Criticism: Ancient and Modern*, edited by R. S. Crane, pp. 260–96. Chicago: University of Chicago Press, 1952, 1975. Reprinted from Crane in Joseph Schwartz and John A. Rycenga, eds. *The Province of Rhetoric*, pp. 172–212. New York: The Ronald Press Co., 1965.

Murphy, James J. *Rhetoric in the Middle Ages: A History of Rhetorical Theory from Saint Augustine to the Renaissance*. Berkeley, Los Angeles, and London: University of California Press, 1974, 1981.

Murphy, James J., ed. *Medieval Eloquence: Studies in the Theory and Practice of Medieval Rhetoric*. Berkeley, Los Angeles, and London: University of California Press, 1978.

Owst, Gerald R. *Preaching in Medieval England: An Introduction to Sermon Manuscripts of the Period, c. 1350–1450*. Cambridge Studies in Medieval Life and Thought. Cambridge: Cambridge University Press, 1926. Reprinted: New York: Russell & Russell, 1965.

Paetow, Louis J. *The Arts Course at Medieval Universities with Special Reference to Grammar and Rhetoric*. University Studies of the University of Illinois, nos. 3, 7. Champaign: University of Illinois Press, 1910. Reprinted: Dubuque, Iowa: Wm. C. Brown Reprint Library, n.d.

Robins, R. H. *Ancient & Mediaeval Grammatical Theory in Europe with Particular Reference to Modern Linguistic Doctrine*. London: G. Bell & Sons, 1951. Reprinted: Port Washington, N.Y., and London: Kennikat Press, 1971.

Smyth, Charles H. E. *The Art of Preaching: A Practical Survey of Preaching in the Church of England, 747–1939*. London: S.P.C.K.; New York: The Macmillan Co., 1940. Reprinted: London: S.P.C.K., 1953.

Thurot, M. C. "Notices et extraits de divers manuscrits latins pour servir à l'histoire des doctrines grammaticales au moyen âge." *Notices et Extraits des Manuscrits de la Bibliothèque Impériale*, no. 22, 2. Paris: Imprimerie Impériale, 1868. Reprinted: Frankfurt-am-Main, 1964.

Ward, John O. "*Artificiosa Eloquentia* in the Middle Ages: The Study of Cicero's *De inventione*, the *Ad Herennium* and Quintilian's *De institutione oratoria* from the early Middle Ages to the Thirteenth Century, with special reference to the schools of northern France." 2 vols. Ph.D. diss., University of Toronto, 1972.

Bibliographies

General Bibliographies of Rhetoric for All Periods

Doctoral Dissertations on Rhetoric and Rhetorical Criticism. Selected and edited by James J. Murphy. London and Ann Arbor: University Microfilms International, 1977.

Erickson, Keith V., ed. *Aristotle's Rhetoric: Five Centuries of Philological Research*. Metuchen, N.J.: Scarecrow Press, 1975.

Horner, Winifred Bryan, ed. *Historical Rhetoric: An Annotated Bibliography of Selected Sources in English*. Boston: G. K. Hall, 1980.

Matlon, Ronald J., ed. *Index to Journals in Communication Studies Through 1979*. Falls Church, Va.: Speech Communication Association, 1980.

Rhetoric Newsletter. 1978–. International Society for the History of Rhetoric. Centre for Renaissance Studies, ETH-Zentrum, CH 8092 Zurich, Switzerland; or Department of Rhetoric, University of California, Davis, CA 95616.

Rhetoric Society Quarterly. 1968–. Rhetoric Society of America. Department of Philosophy, St. Cloud State University, St. Cloud, Minnesota.

Vickers, Brian. "Bibliography of Rhetoric Studies, 1970–1980." In *Comparative Criticism: A Yearbook, 3*, pp. 316–22. Cambridge: Cambridge University Press, 1981.

Specialized Medieval Bibliographies

Caplan, Harry. *Medieval Artes praedicandi: A Hand-list*. Cornell Studies in Classical Philology, 24. Ithaca: Cornell University Press, 1934. *Supplement*, 1936.

Faulhaber, Charles. "Rétoricas clásicas y medievales en bibliotecas castellanas." *Abaco* 4 (1973): 151–300.

Murphy, James J. *Medieval Rhetoric: A Select Bibliography*. Toronto Medieval Bibliographies, 3. Toronto: University of Toronto Press, 1971.

Reinsma, Luke. "The Middle Ages." In *Historical Rhetoric: An Annotated Bibliography of Selected Sources in English*, edited by Winifred Bryan Horner, pp. 45–108. Boston: G. K. Hall, 1980.

Scaglione, Aldo D. "The Historical Study of *Ars Grammatica:* A Bibliographic Survey." In his *Ars Grammatica: A Bibliographic Survey, Two Essays on the Grammar of the Latin and Italian Subjunctive, and a Note on the Ablative Absolute*, pp. 11–43. Janua Linguarum, Series Minor, no. 77. The Hague and Paris: Mouton, 1970.

Schneyer, Johann Baptist. *Repertorium der leteinischen Sermones des Mittelalters für die Zeit von 1150–1350*. Beiträge zur Geschichte der Philosophie des Mittelalters, 43. 7 vols. Münster: Aschendorff, 1969–1976.

See also, under Basic Modern Studies (above), Charland, *Artes praedicandi*; Denholm-Young, "The Cursus in England"; Faral, *Les Arts Poétiques*; and Ward, "*Artificiosa Eloquentia* in the Middle Ages," esp. vol. 2.

The Educational Background

Rhetoric has been deeply involved with schools since the earliest times, and in the middle ages the changing relationships among grammar, rhetoric, and dialectic in the set of arts called the *trivium* make it even more important for modern readers to understand the place of rhetoric in medieval education. These relationships changed greatly from time to time and place to place. The history of both elementary and university education is involved. No single standard history of medieval education has yet appeared, though the following works can provide a good deal of information about the subject.

Baldwin, John W. *Masters, Princes, and Merchants: The Social Views of Peter The Chanter and His Circle*. Princeton: Princeton University Press, 1970.

Bernstein, Alan E. *Pierre d'Ailly and the Blanchard Affair: University and Chancellor of Paris at the Beginning of the Great Schism*. Leiden: E. J. Brill, 1978.

Bliese, John. "The Study of Rhetoric in the Twelfth Century." *QJS* 63 (1977): 364–83.

Cobban, A. B. *The Medieval Universities: Their Development and Organization*. London: Methuen, 1970.

Contreni, John. *The Cathedral School of Laon from 850 to 930: Its Manuscripts and Masters*. Münchener Beiträge zur Mediävistik und Renaissance-Forschung, 29. Munich: Arbeo-Gessellschaft, 1978.

History of Universities. Edited by Charles B. Schmitt. Amershan, Eng.: Avebury Publishing Co., 1981–.

Leff, Gordon. *Paris and Oxford Universities in the Thirteenth and Fourteenth Centuries: An Institutional and Intellectual History*. New Dimensions in History: Essays in Comparative History. New York, London, and Sydney: John Wiley & Sons, 1968. Reprinted: Huntington, N.Y.: R. E. Krieger Publishing Co., 1975.

Lutz, Cora E. "Remigius' Ideas on the Classification of the Seven Liberal Arts." *Traditio* 12 (1956): 65–86.

———. *Schoolmasters of the Tenth Century*. Hamden, Conn.: Archon Books, 1977.

Murphy, James J. "Literary Implications of Instruction in the Verbal Arts in Fourteenth Century England." *Leeds Studies in English* n.s. 1 (1967): 119–35.

———. "The Teaching of Latin as a Foreign Language in the Twelfth Century." *Historiographia Linguistica* 7, nos. 1/2 (1980): 159–75.

O'Donnell, J. Reginald. "The Liberal Arts in the Twelfth Century with Special Reference to Alexander Nequam (1157–1217)." In *Arts libéraux et philosophie au moyen âge*, pp. 127–35. Actes du Quatriéme Congrès International de Philosophie Médiévale. Montreal: Institut d'Études Médiévales; Paris: J. Vrin, 1959.

Orme, Nicholas I. *English Schools in the Middle Ages*. London: Methuen, 1973.

———. *Education in the West of England, 1066–1548*. Exeter: University of Exeter Press, 1976.

Rashdall, Hastings. *The Universities of Europe in the Middle Ages*. 3 vols. 2d ed., rev. by F. M. Powicke and A. B. Emden. Oxford: Clarendon Press, 1936.

Riché, Pierre. *Education and Culture in the Barbarian West from the Sixth through the Eighth Century*. 3d ed. Translated by John J. Contreni. Columbia: University of South Carolina Press, 1978.

———. *Les Écoles et l'enseignement dans l'Occident chrétien de la fin du Ve siècle au milieu du XIe siècle*. Paris: Aubier Montaigne, 1979.

Scaglione, Aldo. "Aspetti della arti del trivio fra medioevo e rinascimento." *Medioevo Romanza* 3 (1976): 265–91.

Siraisi, Nancy G. *Arts and Sciences at Padua: The Studium of Padua before 1350*. Pontifical Institute of Mediaeval Studies, Studies and Texts, no. 25. Toronto: Pontifical Institute of Mediaeval Studies, 1973.

Stump, Eleonore. "Dialectic in the Eleventh and Twelfth Centuries: Garlandus compotista." *History and Philosophy of Logic* 1 (1980): 1–18.

Thorndike, Lynn. *University Records and Life in the Middle Ages*. New York: Columbia University Press, 1944. Reprinted: New York: Norton, 1975.

Weisheipl, James A. "Curriculum of the Faculty of Arts at Oxford in the early Fourteenth Century." *MS* 26 (1964): 143–85.

———. "Developments in the Arts Curriculum at Oxford in the Early Fourteenth Century." *MS* 28 (1966): 151–75.

———. "The Parisian Faculty of Arts in Mid-Thirteenth Century: 1240–1270." *ABR* 25 (1974): 200–217.

Wieruszowski, Helene. "Arezzo as a Center of Learning and Letters in the Thirteenth Century." *Traditio* 9 (1953): 321–91. Reprinted in *Politics and Culture in Medieval Spain and Italy*, pp. 387–474. Storia e Letteratura, Raccolta di Studi e Testi, no. 121. Rome: Edizioni de Storia e Letteratura, 1971.

———. *The Medieval University: Masters, Students, Learning*. Princeton: Van Nostrand Reinhold, 1966.

Translations and Recent Editions of Primary Sources

This too is a selective list, designed to be representative rather than exhaustive.

It should be noted that an edition of a text may be very valuable even for readers unfamiliar with Latin or other medieval languages, since such works may often have extensive introductions that explain the relevance of the text and thus place it within the context of medieval culture. Two good examples may be seen below in Polak's book on Jacques de Dinant, with its English commentary as well as Latin text, and in the Thomson/Murphy edition of Ventura da Bergamo, which relates the edited text to the genre of the *ars dictaminis*.

Details of other medieval texts published prior to 1970 may be found in Murphy, *Medieval Rhetoric*, and usually also in Reinsma, "The Middle Ages" (with some supplementary data on certain works), listed above under Specialized Medieval Bibliographies.

A. Collections of Two or More Works

Caplan, Harry. *Of Eloquence: Studies in Ancient and Medieval Rhetoric*. Edited by Anne King and Helen North. Ithaca: Cornell University Press, 1970. "Pseudo-Aquinas," *Treatise on the Art and True Method of Preaching*. "Henry of Hesse," *Tractatulus . . . de arte praedicandi*.

Miller, Joseph M., Michael H. Prosser, and Thomas W. Benson, eds. *Readings in Medieval Rhetoric*. Bloomington: Indiana University Press, 1973.

Martianus Capella, "The Book of Rhetoric" (*De nuptiis Philologiae et Mercurii*, V)

Pseudo-Augustine, *On Rhetoric*

Emporius the Orator, *Concerning Ethopeia*

Rufinus of Antioch, *Verses . . . On the Word Arrangement and Metres in Oratory*

Priscian the Grammarian, *Fundamentals Adapted from Hermogenes*

Anicius M. S. Boethius, *An Overview of the Structure of Rhetoric*

Cassiodorus Senator, "On Rhetoric" (*Institutiones divinarum et saecularium litterarum* II.2)

Isidore of Seville, "Concerning Rhetoric" (*Etymologies* II. 1–15)

Venerable Bede, *Concerning Figures and Tropes*

Rabanus Maurus, *On the Training of the Clergy*, III. 19

Walafrid Strabo, *Verse on the Five Parts of Rhetoric*

Alberic of Monte Cassino, *Flowers of Rhetoric*

Guibert of Nogent, *A Book about the Way a Sermon Ought To Be Given*

Philip of Harveng, *On the Training of the Clergy*

Alain de Lille, *A Compendium on the Art of Preaching*

Brunetto Latini, *Li Livres dou Tresor*, III. 60–65

Giles of Rome, *On the Difference between Rhetoric, Ethics and Politics*, Part 1.

Thomas of Todi, *The Art of Giving Sermons and of Preparing Conferences* (excerpts).

(The book also includes brief excerpts from other texts.)

Murphy, James J., ed. *Three Medieval Rhetorical Arts*. Berkeley: University of California Press, 1971.

Anonymous of Bologna, *The Principles of Letterwriting*

Geoffrey of Vinsauf, *The New Poetics*

Robert of Basevorn, *The Form of Preaching*

Preminger, Alex, O. B. Hardison, Jr., and Kevin Kerrane, eds. *Classical and Medieval Literary Criticism: Translations and Interpretations*. New York: Frederick Ungar, 1974.

Evanthius, *On Drama*

Donatus, *On Comedy*

Proclus, *On the More Difficult Questions in "The Republic": The Nature of Poetic Art*

Fulgentius, *The Exposition of the Content of Vergil "According to Moral Philosophy"*

Averroës, *The Middle Commentary on the Poetics of Aristotle*

Geoffrey of Vinsauf, from *Poetria nova*

Dante, *De vulgari eloquentia*

Boccaccio, *Genealogy of the Gods*, from XIV, XV.

Rockinger, Ludwig, ed. *Briefsteller und Formelbücher des eilften bis vierzehnten Jahrhunderts*. 2 vols. Quellen und Erörterungen zur bayerischen und deutschen Geschichte, 9. Munich, 1863–1864. Reprinted (in one volume): New York: Burt Franklin, 1961.

Nine Latin texts of the *ars dictaminis* and *ars notaria*, with some texts of formularies

Faral, *Les arts poétiques*, and Charland, *Artes praedicandi* (listed above under Basic Modern Studies) also include Latin texts of *artes poetriae* and *artes praedicandi* respectively.

B. Individual Translations or Recent Editions

This list concentrates on translations, regardless of their age, but cites only recent Latin or other editions not found in the Murphy or Reinsma bibliographies, listed above.

(The reader is also cautioned that more than thirty other translations are listed above under Collections of Two or More Works.)

Alain of Lille. *Anticlaudianus, or the Good and Perfect Man*. Translated by James J. Sheridan. Toronto: Pontifical Institute of Mediaeval Studies, 1973.

———. Alverny, M.–Th. d'. *Alain de Lille. Textes inédits avec une introduction sur sa vie et ses oeuvres*. Paris: J. Vrin, 1965.

Alcock, Simon. "Simon Alcock on Expanding the Sermon." Translated by Mary F. Boynton. *Harvard Theological Review* 34 (1941): 201–16.

Alcuin. *The Rhetoric of Alcuin & Charlemagne; a Translation, with an Introduction, the Latin Text, and Notes*. Edited and translated by Wilbur S. Howell. Princeton: Princeton University Press, 1941. Reprinted: New York: Russell & Russell, 1965.

Alexandre de Villedieu. *Das Doctrinale des Alexander de Villa-Dei: Kritischexegetische Ausgabe mit Einleitung, Verzeichniss der Handschriften und Drucke nebst Registern*. Edited by Dietrich Reichling. Monumenta Germaniae Paedagogica, no. 12. Berlin: A. Hoffmann & Comp., 1893.

Al-Farabi. *Deux ouvrages inédits sur la rhétorique*. Edited by J. Langlade and P. Grinaschi. Beirut, 1971.

Alfonso d'Alpraox. "El 'Ars praedicandi' de Fr. Alfonso d'Alprao O.F.M.: Aportacion al estudio de la teoría de la predicacion en la Península Ibérica." Edited by Albert G. Hauf. *AFM* 72 (1979): 233–329.

d'Andeli, Henri. *The Battle of the Seven Arts: A French Poem by Henri d'Andeli, Trouvère of the Thirteenth Century*. Edited and translated by Louis J. Paetow. Memoirs of the University of California, no. 4, 1. Berkeley: University of California Press, 1914. Reprinted as pt. 1 of Paetow's *Two Medieval Satires on the University of Paris*. Berkeley: University of California Press, 1927.

Augustine. *On Christian Doctrine*. Translated by D. W. Robertson. Library of Liberal Arts, 80. New York: Bobbs-Merrill, 1958.

Averroes' Three Short Commentaries on Aristotle's "Topics," "Rhetoric," and "Poetics." Edited and translated by Charles E. Butterworth. Albany: State University of New York Press, 1977.

Boethius. *Boethius's De topicis differentiis: Translated, with Notes and Essays on the Text*. Edited by Eleonore A. Stump. Ithaca and London: Cornell University Press, 1978.

Buridan, John. Fredborg, Karin M. "Buridan's *Quaestiones super Rhetoricam Aristotelis*." In *The Logic of John Buridan: Acts of the 3rd European Symposium on Medieval Logic and Semantics, Copenhagen 16.–21. November 1975*, edited by Jan Pinborg, pp. 47–59. Copenhagen: Museum Tusculanum, 1976.

Capella, Martianus. *Martianus Capella and the Seven Liberal Arts*. Vol. 2: *The Marriage of Philology and Mercury*. Translated by William H. Stahl, Richard Johnson, and E. L. Burge. Columbia University Records of Civilization, Sources and Studies, no. 84. New York: Columbia University Press, 1977.

Cassiodorus Senator. *An Introduction to Divine and Human Readings by Cassiodorus Senator; Translated with an Introduction and Notes*. Translated by Leslie W. Jones. Columbia University Records of Civilization, Sources and Studies, no. 40. New York: Columbia University Press, 1946. Reprinted: New York: W. W. Norton & Co., 1969.

Dybinus, Nicholas. Jaffe, Samuel P. *Nicolaus Dybinus' "Declaratio Oracionis de Beata Dorothea": Studies and Documents in the History of Late Medieval Rhetoric*. Wiesbaden: Steiner, 1974.

Eberhard the German. "The *Laborintus* of Eberhard rendered into English with Introduction and Notes." Translated by Evelyn Carlson. Master's thesis, Cornell University, 1930.

Geoffrey of Vinsauf. *The Poetria Nova of Geoffrey of Vinsauf*. Translated by Margaret F. Nims. Toronto: Pontifical Institute of Mediaeval Studies, 1967.

———. "The New Poetics." Translated by Jane Baltzell Kopp. In Murphy, *Three Medieval Rhetorical Arts*, pp. 29–108. Berkeley: University of California Press, 1971.

———. Gallo, Ernest A. *The* Poetria nova *and Its Sources in Early Rhetorical Doctrine*. De Proprietatibus Litterarum, Series Maior, no. 10. The Hague and Paris: Mouton, 1971.

———. *Documentum de modo et arte dictandi et versificandi (Instruction in the Method and Art of Speaking and Versifying)*. Translated by Roger P. Parr. Mediaeval Philosophical Texts in Translation, no. 17. Milwaukee: Marquette University Press, 1968.

Hugh of St. Victor. *The* Didascalicon *of Hugh of St. Victor: A Medieval Guide to the Arts; Translated from the Latin with an Introduction and Notes*. Translated by Jerome Taylor. Columbia University Records of Civilization, Sources and Studies, no. 64. New York and London: Columbia University Press, 1961.

Humbert of Romans. *Treatise on Preaching by Humbert of Romans*. Translated by Dominican Students, Province of St. Joseph. Edited by Walter M. Conlon. Westminster, Md.: Newman Press, 1951. Reprinted: London: Blackfriars Publications, 1955.

Isidore of Seville. "The Rhetoric and Dialectic of Isidorus of Seville: A Translation and Commentary." Translated by Dorothy V. Cerino. Master's thesis, Brooklyn College, 1938.

Jacques de Dinant. Polak, Emil J. *A Textual Study of Jacques de Dinant's "Summa dictaminis."* Études de philologie et d'histoire, 28. Geneva: Droz, 1975.

John of Garland. *The* Parisiana Poetria *of John of Garland; Edited with Introduction, Translation, and Notes*. Edited and Translated by Traugott Lawler. Yale Studies in English, no. 182. New Haven and London: Yale University Press, 1974.

John of Salisbury. *The Metalogicon of John of Salisbury: A Twelfth-Century Defense of the Verbal and Logical Arts of the Trivium; Translated with an Introduction & Notes*. Translated by Daniel D. McGarry. Berkeley and Los Angeles: University of California Press, 1955, 1971.

Juan Gil de Zamora. *Dictaminis Epithalamium*. Edited by Charles Faulhaber. Biblioteca degli Studi Mediolatini e Volgari, n.s. 2. Pisa: Pacini, 1978.

Latini, Brunetto. "Book Three of Brunetto Latini's *Tresor*: An English Translation and Assessment of its Contribution to Rhetorical Theory." Translated by James R. East. Ph.D. diss., Stanford University, 1960.

Matthew of Vendôme. " Matthew of Vendôme: Introductory Treatise on the Art of Poetry." Translated by Ernest Gallo. *PAPS* 118 (1974): 51–92.

————. *"Matthew of Vendôme: The Art of Versification*. Translated by Aubrey E. Gaylon. Ames: Iowa State University Press, 1980.

Pseudo-Bonaventure. "Translation, with Commentary, of the Bonaventuran *Ars concionandi*." Translated by Harry C. Hazel, Jr. Ph.D. diss., Washington State University, 1972.

Siguinus, Magister. *Ars lectoria: Un Art de lecture à haute voix du onzième siècle*. Edited by C. H. Kneepkeus and H. F. Reijnders. Leiden: E. J. Brill, 1979.

Ventura da Bergamo. "Dictamen as a Developed Genre: The *Brevis doctrina* of Ventura da Bergamo." Edited by David Thomson and James J. Murphy. *Studi Medievali* 3d ser. 23 (1982): 361–86.

Waleys, Thomas. "Thomas Waleys' *De modo componendi sermones* Rendered into English." Translated by Dorothy E. Grosser. Master's thesis, Cornell University, 1949.

Some Recent Studies

Allen, Judson B. *The Ethical Poetic of the Later Middle Ages*. Toronto: University of Toronto Press, 1981.

————. "Hermann the German's Averroistic Aristotle and Medieval Poetic Theory." *Mosaic* 9 (1976): 67–81.

Bagni, Paolo. *La Costituzione della poesia nell artes del XII–XIII secolo*. Università degli Studi di Bologna facoltà di lettere e filosofia: Studi e Richerche, n.s. 20. Bologna: Zanichelli Editore, 1968.

Banker, James R. "The *Ars dictaminis* and Rhetorical Textbooks at the Bolognese University in the Fourteenth Century." *M&H*, n.s. 5 (1974): 153–68.

————."Giovanni di Bonandrea and Civic Values in the Context of the Italian Rhetorical Tradition." *Manuscripta* 18 (1974): 3–20.

Benson, Robert. "Proto-humanism and Narrative Technique in Early Thirteenth-Century Italian 'Ars dictaminis.'" In *Boccaccio: Secoli di vita. Atti del Congresso Internationale: Boccaccio 1975*, pp. 31–50. Acura di Marga Cottino-Jones e Edward F. Tuttle. Los Angeles: Center for Medieval and Renaissance Studies; Ravenna: Longo, 1979.

Beyer, Heinz-Jürgen. "Die Frühphase der 'Ars dictandi.'" *Studi medievali* 18 (1977): 19–43.

Boggess, William F. "Aristotle's *Poetics* in the Fourteenth Century." *Studies in Philology* 67 (1970): 278–94.

———."Hermannus Alemannus's Rhetorical Translations." *Viator* 2 (1971): 227–50.

Bolgar, Robert R., ed. *Classical Influences on European Culture*, A.D. 500– 1500. Cambridge: Cambridge University Press, 1971.

Bonebakker, S. A. *Materials for the History of Arabic Rhetoric*. Naples: 1975.

Brehaut, Ernest. *An Encyclopedist of the Dark Ages: Isidore of Seville*. Columbia University Studies in History, Economics, and Public Law, no. 48. New York: Columbia University; London: P. S. King & Son, 1912. Reprinted: Burt Franklin Research & Source Works Series, no. 107. New York: Burt Franklin, 1964.

Bursill-Hall, G. L. *Speculative Grammars of the Middle Ages: The Doctrine of* Partes orationis *of the Modistae*. Approaches to Semiotics, no. 11. The Hague and Paris: Mouton, 1971.

Camargo, Martin. "The English Manuscripts of Bernard of Meung's *Flores dictaminum*." *Viator* 12 (1981): 197–219.

Caplan, Harry. "Classical Rhetoric and the Mediaeval Theory of Preaching." *CP* 28 (1933): 73–96. Revised in *Historical Studies of Rhetoric and Rhetoricians*, edited by Raymond F. Howes, pp. 71–89. Ithaca: Cornell University Press, 1961. Reprinted in Caplan, *Of Eloquence: Studies in Ancient and Mediaeval Rhetoric*, edited by Anne King and Helen North, pp. 247–70. Ithaca and London: Cornell University Press, 1970.

———. "A Mediaeval Commentary on the *Rhetorica ad Herennium*." In his *Of Eloquence: Studies in Ancient and Mediaeval Rhetoric*, edited by Anne King and Helen North, pp. 247–70. Ithaca and London: Cornell University Press, 1970.

———. "Rhetorical Invention in Some Mediaeval Tractates on Preaching." *Speculum* 2 (1927): 284–95. Reprinted in Caplan, *Of Eloquence: Studies in Ancient and Mediaeval Rhetoric*, edited by Anne King and Helen North, pp. 79–92. Ithaca and London: Cornell University Press, 1970.

Christ, Winfried. *Rhetorik und Roman: Untersuchungen zu Gottfrieds von Strassburg "Tristan und Isold."* Deutsche Studien, 31. Meisenheim: Hain, 1977.

Clanchy, M. T. *From Memory to Written Record: England, 1066–1307*. Cambridge: Harvard University Press, 1979.

Colish, Marcia L. *The Mirror of Language: A Study in the Medieval Theory of Knowledge*. New Haven: Yale University Press, 1968.

Constable, Giles. *Letters and Letter-Collections*. Turnhout, 1976.

———. "The Structure of Medieval Society According to the *Dictatores* of the Twelfth Century." In *Law, Church, and Society: Essays in Honor of Stephan Kuttner*, edited by Kenneth Pennington and Robert Sommerville, pp. 253–67. Philadelphia: University of Pennsylvania Press, 1977.

Dalzell, Ann. "The *forma dictandi*: Attributed to Albert of Morra and Related Texts." *MS* 39 (1977): 440–65.

Dickey, Mary. "Some Commentaries on the *De inventione* and *Ad Herennium* of the Eleventh and Early Twelfth Centuries." *MARS* 6 (1968): 1–41.

Dronke, Peter. "Mediaeval Rhetoric." In *Literature and Western Civilization*, edited by David Daiches and A. Thorlby, 2:315–45. London: Aldus, 1973.

East, James R. "Brunetto Latini's Rhetoric of Letter Writing." *QJS* 54 (1968): 241–46.

Faulhaber, Charles B. "Las Retóricas hispanolatinas medievales siglos XIII–XV." *Repertorio de Historia de las ciencias Eclesiásticas en España* 7 (1979): 11–64.

———. *Latin Rhetorical Theory in Thirteenth and Fourteenth Century Castile*. University of California Publications in Modern Philology, no. 103. Berkeley, Los Angeles, and London: University of California Press, 1972.

Frank, Roberta. "Some Uses of Paronomasia in Old English Scriptural Verse." *Speculum* 47 (1972): 207–26.

Fredborg, Karin M. "The Commentaries on Cicero's *De inventione* and *Rhetorica ad Herennium* by William of Champeaux." *Cahiers* 17 (1976): 1–39.

———. "Petrus Helias on Rhetoric." *Cahiers* 13 (1974): 31–41.

Gallick, Susan. "*Artes Praedicandi*: Early Printed Editions." *MS* 39 (1977): 477–89.

Gatch, Milton McC. *Preaching and Theology in Anglo-Saxon England: Aelfric and Wulfstan*. Toronto: University of Toronto Press, 1977.

Green-Pedersen, Niels-Jørgen. "The Doctrine of 'maxima propositio' and 'locus differentia' in Commentaries from the 12th Century on Boethius' 'Topics.'" *Studia Mediewistyczne* 18 (1977): 126–63.

———. "On the Interpretation of Aristotle's *Topics* in the Thirteenth Century." *Cahiers* 9 (1973): 1–46.

———. "William of Champeaux on Boethius' *Topics* according to Orléans Bibl. Mun. 266." *Cahiers* 13 (1974): 13–30.

Gronbeck-Tedesco, John L. "An Application of Medieval Rhetorical Invention to Dramatic Composition: Matthew of Vendôme's *Ars versificatoria* and *Milo*." *Theatre Journal* 32 (1980): 235–47.

Haskins, Charles H. "The Early *Artes dictandi* in Italy." In his *Studies in Mediaeval Culture*, pp. 170–92. New York: Frederick Ungar; Oxford: Clarendon Press, 1929. Reprinted: New York: Frederick Ungar, 1965.

————. "The Life of Medieval Students as Illustrated by Their Letters." *American Historical Review* 3 (1897–1898): 203–29. Revised and expanded in his *Studies in Mediaeval Culture*, pp. 1–35. New York: Frederick Ungar; Oxford: Clarendon Press, 1929. Reprinted: New York: Frederick Ungar, 1965.

Hazel, Harry C. "The Bonaventuran 'Ars concionandi.'" *WS* 36 (1972): 241–50.

Hill, Sidney R., Jr. "*Dictamen*: That Bastard of Literature and Law." *CSSJ* 24 (1973): 17–24.

Holtz, Louis. *Donat et la tradition de l'enseignement grammatical*. Paris: Centre national de la recherche scientifique, 1981.

Isola, Antonio. "*Il De schematibus et tropis* di Beda in rapporto al *De doctrina christiana* di Agostino." *Romanobarbarica* 1 (1976): 71–82.

Janson, Tore. *Prose Rhythm in Medieval Latin from the 9th to the 13th Century*. Acta Universitatis Stockholmiensis, Studia Latina Stockholmiensia, no. 20. Stockholm: Almqvist & Wiskell International, 1975.

Kane, Peter E. "*Dictamen*: The Medieval Rhetoric of Letter-Writing." *CSSJ* 21 (1970): 224–30.

Kantorowicz, Ernst H. "An 'Autobiography' of Guido Faba." *Mediaeval and Renaissance Studies* 1 (1941–1943): 253–80. Reprinted in his *Selected Studies*, pp. 194–212. Locust Valley, N.Y.: J. J. Augustin, 1965.

Karaus, S. M. J. "Selections from the Commentary of Bartolinus de Benincasa de Canulo on the *Rhetorica ad Herennium*. Ph.D. diss., Columbia University, 1970.

Kelly, Douglas. *Medieval Imagination: Rhetoric and the Poetry of Courtly Love*. Madison: University of Wisconsin Press, 1978.

————. "Theory of Composition in Medieval Narrative: Poetry and Geoffrey of Vinsauf's *Poetria nova*." *MS* 31 (1969): 117–48.

————. "The Scope of the Treatment of Composition in the Twelfth- and Thirteenth-Century Arts of Poetry." *Speculum* 41 (1966): 261–78.

Kristeller, Paul O. "Matteo de'Libri, Bolognese Notary of the Thirteenth Century and His *Artes dictaminis*." In *Miscellanea Giovanni Galbiati*, 2: 283–320. Fontes Ambrosiani, 26. Milan, 1951.

————. "Philosophy and Rhetoric from Antiquity to the Renaissance." Part 5 (pp. 211–60, notes pp. 312–27) in *Renaissance Thought and Its Sources*, edited by Michael Mooney. New York: Columbia University Press, 1979.

Kuhn, Sherman M. "Cursus in Old English: Rhetorical Ornament or Linguistic Phenomenon?" *Speculum* 47 (1972): 188–206. See also Smedick, "*Cursus* in Middle English," below.

Lanham, Carol D. Salutatio *Formulas in Latin Letters to 1200: Syntax, Style, and Theory*. Münchener Beiträge zur Mediävistik und Renaissance—Forschung, no. 22. Munich: Arbeo-Gesellschaft, 1975.

Leff, Michael C. "Boethius and the History of Medieval Rhetoric." *CSSJ* 25 (1974): 134–41.

Licitra, Vicenzo. "Il mito di Alberico di Montecassino iniziatore dell' 'Ars dictaminis.'" *Studi medievali* 18 (1977): 609–27.

Longère, Jean. *Oeuvres oratoires de maitres parisiens au XIIe siècle. Étude historique et doctrinale.* 2 vols. Paris: Etudes Augustiniennes, 1975.

Lubienski-Bedenhami, H. "The Origins of the Fifteenth-Century View of Poetry as 'seconde rhétorique.'" *MLR* 74 (1979): 26–38.

McKeon, Richard. "Poetry and Philosophy in the Twelfth Century: The Renaissance of Rhetoric." *MP* 43 (1946): 217–34. Reprinted in *Critics and Criticism: Ancient and Modern*, edited by R. S. Crane, pp. 297–318. Chicago: University of Chicago Press, 1952, 1975.

Manly, John M. "Chaucer and the Rhetoricians." Warton Lecture on English Poetry. *PBA* 12 (1926): 95–113. Reprinted in *Chaucer Criticism, the Canterbury Tales: An Anthology*, edited by Richard J. Schoeck and Jerome Taylor, pp. 268–90. Notre Dame: University of Notre Dame Press, 1960. See also Murphy, "A New Look at Chaucer and the Rhetoricians," below.

Marshall, J. H. "Observations on the Sources of the Treatment of Rhetoric in the *Leys d'Amors.*" *MLR* 64 (1969): 39–52.

Monfasani, John. *George of Trebizond: A Biography and a Study of His Rhetoric and Logic.* Columbia Studies in the Classical Tradition, 1. Leiden: E. J. Brill, 1976.

Murphy, James J. "Alberic of Monte Cassino: Father of the Medieval *Ars dictaminis.*" *ABR* 22 (1971): 129–46. See also Patt, "The Early 'Ars dictaminis' as Response to a Changing Society," below.

———. "A New Look at Chaucer and the Rhetoricians." *RES*, n.s. 15 (1964): 1–20. See also Manly, "Chaucer and the Rhetoricians," above.

———. "Rhetoric in Fourteenth-Century Oxford." *MAE* 34 (1965): 1–20. See also Schoeck, "On Rhetoric in Fourteenth-Century Oxford," below.

Nims, Margaret F. "*Translatio*: 'Difficult Statement' in Medieval Poetic Theory." *UTQ* 43 (1974): 215–30.

O'Donnell, James J. *Cassiodorus.* Berkeley: University of California Press, 1979.

O'Donnell, J. Reginald. "The Commentary of Giles of Rome on the Rhetoric of Aristotle." In *Essays in Medieval History Presented to Bertie Wilkinson*, edited by Thayron A. Sandquist and Michael R. Powicke, pp. 139–56. Toronto: University of Toronto Press, 1969.

———. "The Liberal Arts in the Twelfth Century with Special Reference to Alexander Nequam (1157–1217)." In *Arts libéraux et philosophie au moyen âge*, pp. 127–36. Montreal and Paris, 1969.

———. "The *Rhetorica Divina* of William of Auvergne: A Study in Applied Rhetoric." In *Images of Man in Ancient and Medieval Thought: Studia Gerardo Verbeke ab amicis et collegiis dicata*, edited by F. Bossier et al., pp. 323–33. Louvain: Louvain University Press, 1976.

Olivet, J. *Arts du langage et theologie chez Abelard.* Paris: J. Vrin, 1969.

Owst, Gerald R. *Literature and Pulpit in Medieval England: A Neglected Chapter in the History of English Letters & of the English People.* Cambridge: Cambridge University Press, 1933. 2d ed. New York: Barnes & Noble; Oxford: Basil Blackwell, 1961, 1966.

Patt, William D. "The Early 'Ars dictaminis' as Response to a Changing Society." *Viator* 9 (1978): 133–35. See also Murphy, "Alberic of Monte Cassino," above.

Patterson, Linda M. *Troubadours and Eloquence.* Oxford: Clarendon Press, 1975.

Payne, Robert O. "Chaucer and the Art of Rhetoric." In *Companion to Chaucer Studies,* edited by Beryl Rowland, pp. 42–64. Rev. ed. Toronto, New York, and London: Oxford University Press, 1979.

———. *The Key of Remembrance: A Study of Chaucer's Poetics.* New Haven and London: Yale University Press, 1963. Reprinted: Westport, Conn.: Greenwood Press, 1973.

Pini, Virgilio. "La *Summa de vitiis et virtutibus* di Guido Faba." *Quadrivium* 1 (1956): 41–152.

Press, Gerald A. "The Subject and Structure of Augustine's *De doctrina christiana.*" *Augustinian Studies* 11 (1980): 99–124.

Reinsma, Luke. "Rhetoric in England: The Age of Aelfric, 970–1020." *CM* 44 (1977): 390–403.

Ricket, Edith. "Chaucer at School." *MP* 29 (1931): 257–74.

Roberts, Phyllis B. *Stephanus de Lingua-Tonante: Studies in the Sermons of Stephen Langton.* Studies and Texts, 16. Toronto: Pontifical Institute for Mediaeval Studies, 1968.

Robinson, I. S. "The 'colores rhetorici' in the Investiture Contest." *Traditio* 32 (1976): 209–38.

Ross, Woodburn O. *Middle English Sermons: Edited from British Museum MS. Royal 18 B. xxiii.* Early English Text Society, o.s. no. 209. London: Oxford University Press, 1940. Reprinted: London, New York, and Toronto: Oxford University Press, 1960.

Roth, Dorothea. *Die mittelterliche Predigttheorie und das Manuale curatorum des Johann Ulrich Surgant.* Basler Beiträge zur Geschichtswissenschaft, 58. Basil and Stuttgart, 1956.

Rouse, Richard, and Mary Rouse. "Biblical Distinctions in the Thirteenth Century." *Archives d'Histoire Doctrinale et Littéraire du Moyen Âge* 41 (1974): 27–37.

Scaglione, Aldo D. *The Classical Theory of Composition from Its Origins to the Present: A Historical Survey.* University of North Carolina Studies in Comparative Literature, no. 53. Chapel Hill: University of North Carolina Press, 1972.

Schaller, Hans Martin. "Dichtungslehren und Briefsteller." In *Die Renaissance der Wissenschaften im 12. Jahrhundert,* edited by Peter Weimar, pp. 249–71. Zurcher Hochschulforum, 2. Zurich and Munich: Artemis Verlag, 1981.

Schoeck, Richard J. "On Rhetoric in Fourteenth-Century Oxford." *MS* 30 (1968): 214–25. See also Murphy, "Rhetoric in Fourteenth-Century Oxford," above.

Seigel, Jerrold. *Rhetoric and Philosophy in Renaissance Humanism: The Union of Eloquence and Wisdom, Petrarch to Valla*. Princeton: Princeton University Press, 1968.

Sitzmann, Marion. "Lawrence of Aquileja and the Origins of the Business Letter." *ABR* 28 (1977): 180–87.

Smedick, Lois K. "*Cursus* in Middle English: *A Talking of De Love of God* Reconsidered." *MS* 37 (1975): 387–406. See also Kuhn, "Cursus in Old English," above.

Speer, Richard. "John of Salisbury: Rhetoric in the *Metalogicon*." *CSSJ* 20 (1969): 92–96.

Stump, Eleonore A. "Boethius's Work on the Topics." *Vivarium* 12 (1974): 77–93.

Tedesco, John L. "Theology in Two Medieval Tractates on Preaching: A Comparative Study." *SSJ* 41 (1976): 177–88.

Wailes, Stephen. "The Composition of Vernacular Sermons by Berthold von Regensburg." *Michigan Germanic Studies* 5 (1979): 1–24.

Wallach, Luitpold. *Alcuin and Charlemagne: Studies in Carolingian History and Literature*. Cornell Studies in Classical Philology, no. 32. Ithaca: Cornell University Press, 1959.

Ward, John O. "The Date of the Commentary on Cicero's *De inventione* by Thierry of Chartres (c. 1095–1160?) and the Cornifician Attack on the Liberal Arts." *Viator* 3 (1972): 219–73.

Wetherbee, Winthrop. *Platonism and Poetry in the Twelfth Century: The Literary Influence of the School of Chartres*. Princeton: Princeton University Press, 1972.

Widhalm, Gloria-Maria. *Die rhetorische Elemente in der Regula Benedicti*. Regula Benedicti Studia, Supplementa, 2. Hildesheim, 1974.

Winniczuk, Lidia. *Epistolografia*. Biblioteka Meandra, 19. Warsaw, 1952.

Witt, Ronald. "Medieval 'Ars dictaminis' and the Beginnings of Humanism: A New Construction of the Problem." *RQ* 35 (1982): 1–35.

Zink, Michel. *La Prédication en langue Romane avant 1300*. Paris: J. Vrin, 1976.

Zumthor, Paul. "Rhétorique médiévale et poétique." *Poetics* 1 (1971): 46–82.

THE RENAISSANCE

Don Paul Abbott

In his *English Literature in the Sixteenth Century* (Oxford: Clarendon Press, 1954), C. S. Lewis offers the following confession to his readers:

> Rhetoric is the greatest barrier between us and our ancestors. If the Middle Ages had erred in their devotion to that art, the *renascentia*, far from curing, confirmed the error. In rhetoric, more than in anything else, the continuity of the old European tradition was embodied. . . . Nearly all our older poetry was written and read by men to whom the distinction between poetry and rhetoric, in its modern form, would have been meaningless. The "beauties" which they chiefly regarded in every composition were those which we either dislike or simply do not notice. This change of taste makes an invisible wall between us and them. Probably all our literary histories, certainly that on which I am engaged, are vitiated by our lack of sympathy on this point. If ever the passion for formal rhetoric returns, the whole story will have to be rewritten and many judgements may be reversed. (p. 16)

As Lewis may have feared, rhetoric has reasserted itself, and the history of Renaissance literature is being rewritten by individuals more sympathetic to rhetoric than was an earlier generation of scholars. It is increasingly difficult to imagine an account of the arts of Renaissance poetry or drama that does not exhibit a corresponding appreciation of the art of rhetoric. Indeed, a treatment of Renaissance culture that remains oblivious to the rhetorical tradition is almost inconceivable.

The purpose of this essay is not to provide a synoptic history of Renaissance rhetoric; several admirable surveys are available

Don Paul Abbott is an Assistant Professor in the department of rhetoric at the University of California, Davis. His recent publications in Renaissance rhetoric include "La Retórica y el Renacimiento: An Overview of Spanish Theory," in *Renaissance Eloquence*, ed. James J. Murphy (University of California Press, 1983), and "Juan Luis Vives and the Rehabilitation of Rhetoric," in *Paideia*, Special Renaissance issue, 1983.

and are discussed below. Rather, the intent is to detail the "re-writing" or, more accurately, the rediscovery of the primacy of rhetoric in Renaissance art and intellect; to document what has been rediscovered and to suggest in what direction future discoveries might lie.

State of the Primary Texts

James J. Murphy has called Renaissance rhetoric the field of "a thousand and one neglected authors" (*Renaissance Eloquence,* p. 20). While of course not all of these authors are English, enough are that G. P. Mohrmann has identified 267 first editions printed in England in the sixteenth and seventeenth centuries (*Renaissance Eloquence,* pp. 68–83). Rather than attempt to discuss over two hundred works, it is probably more useful and realistic to discuss the availability of certain basic texts. The bibliographies discussed in the following section provide comprehensive listings of Renaissance treatises.

Perhaps the most obvious obstacle to research in sixteenth- and seventeenth-century rhetoric is the scarcity of the original works. For example, only five copies of Henry Peacham's *The Garden of Eloquence* (1577) are extant. Even rarer is Abraham Fraunce's *The Arcadian Rhetorike* (1588), of which only two copies remain. There are, of course, practical alternatives to wandering about widely scattered rare-book rooms. A number of Renaissance treatises are to be found in modern editions and facsimile reprints. The most widely available modern editions are those rhetorical materials included among the collected works of well-known writers. Standard collections of the works of Erasmus, Hobbes, and Bacon all contain important rhetorical documents. Unfortunately, the number of rhetorics included in such collections is quite small. More typically, the works of rhetoricians appear in facsimile form.

Probably the most complete collection of such facsimiles is *English Linguistics 1500–1700,* edited by R. C. Alston and published by Scolar Press. This series comprises facsimile reprints of rhetorics, grammars, logics, dictionaries, and other language books published in England during those three centuries. Rhetorical works in this series include Angel Day, *The English Secretorie* (1586); George Puttenham, *The Arte of English Poesie* (1589); Abraham Fraunce, *The Arcadian Rhetorike* (1588); John Smith, *The Mysterie of Rhetorique Unvail'd* (1657); Thomas Farnaby, *Index Rhetoricus* (1625); Henry Peacham, *The Garden of Eloquence* (1577); Thomas Blount, *The Academie of Eloquence* (1654); Joshua Poole, *Practical Rhetorick* (1663); Richard Rainolde, *The Foundacion of Rhetorike* (1563); and William Dugard, *Rhetorices Elementa* (1648). Each volume in this series is prefaced by a brief note discussing the text chosen for reproduction and describing the general characteristics of the work. The volumes contain no other scholarly apparatus. A similar series, although one containing fewer rhetorics, is *The English Experience: Its Record in Early Printed Books Published in Facsimile*. Relevant titles include Rainolde's *Foundacion of Rhetorike* and Thomas Wilson's *The Arte of Rhetorique* (1553).

There are also a number of nonserial facsimiles, most notable of which is perhaps Leonard Cox, *The Arte or Crafte of Rhetoryke* (1530?), edited with an introduction by Frederick Ives Carpenter (1899). Cox's work, the first English rhetoric, is extremely rare, and unfortunately Carpenter's edition is in danger of becoming so. Other facsimiles with useful introductions include William G. Crane's 1954 edition of Peacham's *The Garden of Eloquence*; Francis R. Johnson's 1945 edition of Rainolde's *The Foundacion of Rhetorike*; and Dudley Fenner's *The Artes of Logike and Rhetorike* (1584) in Robert D. Pepper's *Four Tudor Books on Education* (1966). Facsimile editions of other important works (although with less detailed introductions) include Richard Sherry, *A Treatise of Schemes and Tropes* (1550), and Wilson, *The Arte of Rhetorique*.

In addition to the facsimiles, a small number of modern critical editions of Renaissance rhetorics are available. Of these, Gladys Doige Willcock and Alice Walker's 1936 edition of Puttenham's *The Arte of English Poesie* is prefaced by an especially thorough introduction to a particularly rhetorical poetic. Ethel Seaton's 1950 edition of Fraunce's *The Arcadian Rhetorike* and James W. Cleary's 1974 edition of John Bulwer's *Chirologia. . . . Chironomia* (1644) also include informative introductory material. A few other modern editions exist and are noted in the bibliography.

In addition to facsimiles and modern editions, one nonprint resource must be noted: the microfilm series *British and Continental Rhetoric and Elocution* prepared by the Speech Association of America (now Speech Communication Association) and distributed by University Microfilms. This project consists of 142 rhetorical treatises printed in England and Europe from the fifteenth through the nineteenth century. In addition to providing the work or works of some twenty-five English Renaissance authors, this series makes available the texts of Continental figures influential in Britain. These include Arnauld, Cresol, Lamy, Ramus, Talon, Melanchthon, Vossius, Sturm, Susenbrotus, and Vives. *BCRE* makes possible the examination of a large collection of texts, many of which are unavailable in any form save the original.

This combination of modern editions, facsimiles, and microfilms allows a reasonable review of the primary sources of Renaissance rhetoric. This is not to say that the situation is altogether satisfactory. Many works remain exclusively in rarebook rooms, facsimile editions often lack clarity, and translations from the Latin are few. A considerable improvement in the availability and reliability of these basic resources would surely result in greater quantity and quality of scholarship in Renaissance rhetoric.

Bibliographies

Basic bibliographic resources for the study of Renaissance rhetoric have improved tremendously in recent years. The standard bibliography is James J. Murphy, *Renaissance Rhetoric: A Short Title Catalogue* (1981), which provides both primary and secondary sources for the study of rhetoric from 1455 to 1700. Most notably, the bibliography includes alphabetical entries for an astonishing 867 authors of rhetorical treatises. Each entry provides the author's name, birth and death dates, applicable aliases, a list by short titles of relevant works, and a list of libraries holding these works. While *Renaissance Rhetoric: A Short Title Catalogue* lists works published in Europe as well as Britain, a special index identifies 195 books in English or printed in England. A second edition is in preparation. Professor Murphy has already identified some fifty additional authors to be included in the revision.

A second recent bibliography is Charles Stanford, "The Renaissance," which is less comprehensive than *Renaissance Rhetoric: A Short Title Catalogue*. However, unlike Murphy, Stanford annotates all entries. Forty-one primary and 181 secondary sources compose this useful bibliography.

A third bibliography that deserves mention but is more limited than those of Murphy and Stanford is Richard W. Bailey and Delores M. Burton, *English Stylistics: A Bibliography* (1968). "Stylistics" is interpreted broadly enough to include virtually all major rhetorical treatises of the period. Renaissance entries appear on pp. 15–26 and are arranged first by basic works and commentaries, followed by general secondary sources.

A number of specialized bibliographies are also available, and these will be noted in the appropriate sections below.

Surveys and General Studies

Although this essay is concerned primarily with the state of scholarship in English rhetoric, it is of course impossible to ignore the Continental antecedents. So many English works derive from translations of or appropriations from European writers that British and Continental rhetoric are, to a large extent, inseparable. In assessing this relationship, a convenient starting point is Hanna H. Gray's oft-quoted "Renaissance Humanism: The Pursuit of Eloquence" (1963). In this essay Gray rather neatly synthesizes many of the rhetorical concerns of the Italian and northern humanists, which ultimately appear in English treatises. An essay of greater historical breadth is Paul Oskar Kristeller's "Philosophy and Rhetoric from Antiquity to the Renaissance," in his *Renaissance Thought and Its Sources* (1979). Kristeller attempts to distinguish Renaissance rhetoric from its classical and medieval antecedents and to identify defining characteristics of sixteenth-century rhetoric. Another work that documents the humanistic debt to antiquity is *The Classical Heritage and Its Beneficiaries* by R. R. Bolgar (1954). While this virtually encyclopedic work examines all aspects of the survival of classical culture, rhetoric itself is discussed in detail throughout.

A book more directly about rhetoric is Jerrold Seigel's *Rhetoric and Philosophy in Renaissance Humanism* (1968), in which Seigel demonstrates the pervasiveness of the Ciceronian model as the governing ideal of early Renaissance rhetoric. Nancy S. Struever, in *The Language of History in the Renaissance* (1970), details the close relationship between rhetoric and historiography. These two works on Florentine humanism by Seigel and Struever are essential for an understanding of the Italian origins of Renaissance rhetoric and an appreciation of the humanist influence on English theory.

A number of works attempt to detail the development of rhetoric in England itself. One of the earliest attempts is in Donald Lemen Clark's *Rhetoric and Poetry in the Renaissance* (1922), a study of the influence of classical rhetoric on the criticism of poetry. This work includes a useful explanation of the classical distinction between rhetoric and poetic. Another early survey is Charles Sears Baldwin's *Renaissance Literary Theory and Practice* (1939). Baldwin's preoccupation with the triumph of classical models unfortunately causes him to dismiss any rhetorician who deviates from classicism. As a result, Thomas Wilson is the only English theorist discussed in detail. A work far more sympathetic to a plurality of theoretical positions is William Garrett Crane's *Wit and Rhetoric in the Renaissance* (1937). Chapter 7, "English Rhetorics of the Sixteenth Century," remains one of the best brief introductions to English Renaissance rhetorical treatises. J. W. H. Atkins, in his *English Literary Criticism: The Renascence* (1947), argues that earlier studies exaggerated the assimilation of classical doctrine by English critics and underestimated the influence of the Italian humanists. The work contains very good chapters on "Humanism in England: Colet, Erasmus, Vives" (3) and "The Rhetorical Tradition in England: Jewel, Wilson and Ascham" (6).

In 1956 Wilbur S. Howell's *Logic and Rhetoric in England, 1500–1700* was published and immediately became, and remains, the standard history of English Renaissance rhetoric. The work is based upon the assumption that "logic and rhetoric are the two great arts of communication, and that the complete theory of communication is identified, not with one, not with the other, but with both" (p. 4). Howell further assumes that logic and rhetoric are quite distinct from the third art of communication, poetic. The development of both logic and rhetoric is charted across two centuries. For rhetoric this charting begins with the classically derived "traditional rhetoric," which Howell divides into three patterns: "Ciceronian," "stylistic," and "formulary." The dominance of these traditional approaches was successfully challenged by the arrival of Ramistic rhetoric in the last quarter of the sixteenth century. Howell sees in the writing of seventeenth-century figures such as Descartes and Bacon the portent of a "new rhetoric." *Logic and Rhetoric in England, 1500–1700* is detailed, erudite, and essential reading for any serious student of Renaissance rhetoric. An interesting supplement to this book is Howell's essay "Renaissance Rhetoric and Modern

Rhetoric: A Study in Change" in his *Poetics, Rhetoric, and Logic* (1975). In this essay Howell isolates what he regards as the essential distinctions between the Renaissance conception of rhetoric and the modern formulation of the discipline.

An alternative interpretation of Renaissance rhetoric is advanced by Brian Vickers in *Classical Rhetoric in English Poetry* (1970). Vickers argues here and elsewhere that American historians of rhetoric in general, and Howell in particular, misinterpret Renaissance rhetoric because of a failure to understand the figures of speech. Accordingly, Vickers provides a rationale for the figures, and, in contrast to Howell, denies the separability of rhetoric and poetic. Vickers advances the same argument with greater historical scope in "Rhetorical and Anti-Rhetorical Tropes: On Writing the History of *Elocutio*" (1981).

A different type of general work is *A Handbook of Sixteenth-Century Rhetoric* by Lee A. Sonnino (1968). This is very much a reference work and, unlike the other works discussed thus far, provides little in the way of a narrative account of Renaissance rhetoric. What is provided, primarily, is an alphabetical listing by Latin name of the various figures of rhetoric. For each entry the reader is provided with definitions cited from classical and Renaissance texts followed by examples of the figures, again from primary texts. A shorter section listing figures by Greek terminology is also included. Latin, Greek, and Italian terms are cross-referenced. This handbook simplifies the often complicated task of mastering the multitude of figures so familiar to sixteenth-century rhetoricians.

The most recent survey of the field is *Renaissance Eloquence,* a collection of twenty-three papers edited by James J. Murphy (1983). Essays of particular relevance for the study of English rhetoric include Gerald P. Mohrmann, "Oratorical Delivery and Other Problems in Current Scholarship on English Renaissance Rhetoric" (including the appended "First Edition of Rhetorical Works Printed in Britain to A.D. 1700"); Richard J. Schoeck, "Lawyers and Rhetoric in Sixteenth Century England"; Heinrich F. Plett, "The Place and Function of Style in Elizabethan England"; Thomas O. Sloane, "Reading Milton Rhetorically"; and Brian Vickers, "'The Power of Persuasion': Images of the Orator, Elyot to Shakespeare." This volume also includes essays on virtually all aspects of Renaissance rhetoric by Paul Oskar Kristeller, James J. Murphy, A. Kibedi Varga, Nancy Struever, Charles Trinkaus, John W. O'Malley, Marc

Fumaroli, Hugh Davidson, W. Keith Percival, and others. *Renaissance Eloquence* is probably the most ambitious attempt to examine the totality of Renaissance rhetoric, and as such it will surely become a standard in the field.

The general studies discussed above can provide the reader with a very comprehensive view of rhetoric in the sixteenth and seventeenth centuries. But no survey, however thorough, can detail every aspect of a subject as expansive as Renaissance rhetoric. Specialized studies are, of course, necessary to supplement the surveys, and there is a rather large body of such scholarship. Because rhetoric was so pervasive in Renaissance culture, the special studies will be reviewed in the context of the relation of rhetoric to other disciplines and intellectual pursuits.

Logic and Rhetoric

Logic and rhetoric have always had a rather curious coexistence: a relationship that is at once both cooperative and competitive. Renaissance thinkers expended great energy in efforts to realign the functions of logic and rhetoric in order to make both arts more practical and productive. A historical introduction to these efforts, written from a logician's point of view, is provided by E. J. Ashworth, *Language and Logic in the Post-Medieval Period* (1974). This book includes a comprehensive bibliography of logical treatises published during the Renaissance.

One generally accepted consequence of the Renaissance reform of dialectic is that logic became more "rhetorical," that is, "topical." The basic study of the *topoi* or *loci* is Joan Marie Lechner's *Renaissance Concepts of the Commonplaces* (1962). Lechner sorts out the various definitions of this concept and traces its development from antiquity to the seventeenth century. A work of similar scope and plan is Neal W. Gilbert, *Renaissance Concepts of Method* (1960). Like Lechner, Gilbert discusses the meaning of method, its development from ancient origins, and attempts to explain the Renaissance fascination with it. Taken together these works impart a thorough understanding of two key terms of Renaissance logic and rhetoric.

Rudolph Agricola inspired much of the logical reform of the Renaissance. An article of special relevance to such reforms in England is James R. McNally, "Prima pars dialecticae: The Influence of Agricolan Dialectic Upon English Accounts of Invention" (1968). The Agricolan reform of logic may be said to have culminated in the writings of the Frenchman Pierre de la Ramée, or, as he is known in English, Peter Ramus, and the educational ideology known as Ramism. The dominant interpretation of the Ramist phenomenon is Walter Ong's *Ramus, Method, and the Decay of Dialogue* (1958). This work is a magisterial study of Ramism and its intellectual milieu. Ong offers accounts of the life of Ramus, medieval education, scholastic logic, and Agricola's dialectical reform. And all of this is prefatory to a detailed analysis of Ramism itself, including a chapter devoted to Ramist rhetoric. The work concludes by following the spread of Ramism from France into England, Germany, Switzerland, and even Spain.

Also essential for the serious investigation of Ramism is Ong's *Ramus and Talon Inventory*, published conjointly with *Ramus, Method, and the Decay of Dialogue*. This bibliography lists over eight hundred editions of the works of Ramus and his "literary lieutenant," Omer Talon, as well as nearly four hundred attacks on and apologies for Ramism by a variety of writers. Also included in this volume is a short-title catalogue of editions and printed compendia of Agricola's *Dialectical Invention*.

Several of Ong's essays on rhetorical subjects have been collected in his *Rhetoric, Romance, and Technology* (1971). Articles on Elizabethan rhetoric include "Oral Residue in Tudor Prose Style," "Tudor Writings on Rhetoric, Poetic, and Literary Theory," "Memory as Art," and "Ramist Method and the Commercial Mind."

Perhaps in part because of the admirable scholarship of Howell and Ong, Ramus is widely accepted as the central figure in Renaissance rhetoric. A contrary view is presented in a rather polemical manner by Norman E. Nelson in *Peter Ramus and the Confusion of Logic, Rhetoric, and Poetry* (1947). More recently, Vickers has argued that Ramus has been accorded too much importance in rhetoric (*Classical Rhetoric in English Poetry*, pp. 40–44).

A great deal of research on Ramism has been done since Ong wrote *Ramus, Method, and the Decay of Dialogue*. This research is conveniently and critically summarized by Peter Sharrat in "The Present State of Studies on Ramus" (1972). The most recent edition to the scholarship on Ramism is Peter Ramus, *Arguments in Rhetoric Against Quintilian* (1549), translated by Carole Newlands and James J. Murphy (1983). This work contains an English translation and Latin text on facing pages and a lengthy introduction by Murphy, which offers new information and interpretations of the Ramist phenomenon.

Rhetoric, Poetry, and Drama

Rhetoric and literature are, in the Renaissance, often coterminous; rhetorical precept and literary production are so intertwined as to be virtually inseparable. This inseparability draws in large part from the Renaissance deference to classical authority. Several sources discussed in "Surveys and General Studies" chart the influence of classical rhetoricians on English literature. (See especially the works by Bolgar, Kristeller, and Vickers.) Another effort to assess the Renaissance debt to classical rhetoric is Annabel M. Patterson, *Hermogenes and the Renaissance* (1970). Patterson demonstrates that Hermogenes became, in the sixteenth century, an authority to rival Cicero and Quintilian and the rhetorician most responsible for propagating the concept of decorum of style. While this work is concerned with the influence of Hermogenes throughout Europe, his impact on Elizabethan literature is discussed at length. Considering the pervasiveness of decorum and related stylistic concepts, *Hermogenes and the Renaissance* is a book of broad applicability.

Another broadly applicable book, though one with a very different approach, is Hardin Craig, *The Enchanted Glass: The Elizabethan Mind in Literature* (1936). Craig seeks to show how the "thought" of an age affects the literary products of the same age. Given the scope of such an endeavor, it is not surprising to find rhetoric discussed throughout. Of particular interest is the portrayal of Ramus, whom Craig calls "the greatest master of the short-cut the world has ever known" (p. 143). *The Enchanted Glass* contains, among other things, a relatively early assessment of Ramism and English literature.

A more influential interpretation of the literary consequences of Ramism can be found in Rosemond Tuve, *Elizabethan and Metaphysical Imagery* (1947). Tuve believes that Ramism increased the appeal of logic and the attendant concept of wit, thereby providing much of the impetus for metaphysical poetry. Others have challenged this thesis principally on the grounds that Ramism also promoted the plain style and must thereby be incompatible with metaphysical imagery. A convenient summary of these various interpretations of Ramism vis-à-vis poetry is Jackson I. Cope's "Ramist Implications," a chapter in his *The Metaphoric Structure of Paradise Lost* (1962).

In *Elizabethan and Metaphysical Imagery*, Tuve necessarily devotes considerable attention to figurative language, for it is impossible to study Renaissance rhetoric without encountering the figures of speech. One especially helpful guide to the multitude of figures, Sonnino's *Handbook to Sixteenth-Century Rhetoric*, has been discussed previously. A similar work is Warren Taylor, *Tudor Figures of Rhetoric* (1972). This reprint of Taylor's 1937 doctoral dissertation is less comprehensive than Sonnino's work, but it does offer certain features not found in the *Handbook*. In addition to a typical dictionary of figures, Taylor also supplies "A Guide for Determining the Names of the Figures" that describes the function of the figure and then provides the technical term. Another work largely devoted to the figures is Miriam Joseph's *Rhetoric in Shakespeare's Time* (1947). Joseph presents an overview of Renaissance compositional theories, examines Shakespeare's use of those theories, and concludes with a comparative analysis of the figures and the topics. Joseph contends that figurative rhetoric and topical logic are essentially the same, for the purpose of each is the amplification of meaning. Yet another approach to the figures can be found in Heinrich F. Plett, *Rhetorik der Affekte* (1975). Plett attempts to explicate the psychological principles that in turn explain the appeal of figurative language.

It is in the figures, perhaps, where the commonalities of rhetoric and poetic are most clearly revealed. A number of works attempt to clarify the relationship of these two arts. An early attempt is Herbert David Rix, *Rhetoric in Spenser's Poetry* (1940). To determine Spenser's reliance on rhetoric, Rix first catalogs the figures using terminology from Susenbrotus and Peacham together with examples from Spenser. Based on this inventory, Rix concludes that while Spenser occasionally used the figures for ornamentation, he more often employed them to achieve emotional or persuasive efficacy.

In *Ben Jonson's Poems* (1962), Wesley Trimpi demonstrates that Jonson, too, profited from the conscious use of rhetoric. Jonson, however, is an advocate of the plain style and hence is not heavily reliant on such figurists as Peacham or Puttenham. Rather it is the Spanish humanist Juan Luis Vives who is Jonson's most important source. Trimpi demonstrates that key passages in the *Discoveries* are translated from Vives's *De ratione dicendi.* And it is the *Discoveries* that provides a rationale of the plain style that in turn governs the composition of Jonson's poems.

In *The Enduring Moment* (1962), O. B. Hardison, Jr., explores another aspect of the link between rhetorical theory and literary practice. Of the three genres of classical oratory—forensic, deliberative, and epideictic—Hardison maintains that only the last was fully assimilated into Renaissance literary criticism. This is because the functions of epideictic oratory, praise and blame, are also the end of many poetic genres. Hardison supports this thesis with an analysis of a wide variety of Renaissance poetry, which, among other things, clarifies the correspondence between epic and epideictic.

Just as poetic creation profited from rhetorical theory, the development of Renaissance drama was also guided, in part, by the rhetorical tradition. This development is detailed by Charles O. McDonald in *The Rhetoric of Tragedy* (1966). This work examines the influence of rhetorical instruction on the dramatic creativity of fifth century B.C. Greece, first century A.D. Rome, and sixteenth- and seventeenth-century England. In assessing the impact of rhetoric on tragedy, McDonald considers in detail Shakespeare's *Hamlet*, Marston's *Sophonisba* and *The Malcontent*, Chapman's *Bussy D'Ambois*, Tourneur's [?] *The Revengers Tragedie*, Webster's *The White Devil*, and Ford's *The Broken Heart*. McDonald concludes that these dramas derive their world view and verbal technique from rhetorical instruction. The rhetorical influence on drama is also investigated by Joel B. Altman in *The Tudor Play of the Mind* (1978). Altman contends that the rhetorical *quaestio* and its attendant forms of inquiry inspired a large body of Elizabethan drama. That is to say, plays are questions, or more precisely "fictional realizations of questions" (p. 3). Such a view of drama derives, says Altman, directly from the Elizabethen fondness for formal rhetoric. Drama as rhetorical inquiry applies not only to tragedy but also to comedy, court plays, and all variants of Elizabethan theater. A recent rhetorical interpretation of Renaissance drama is Marion Trousdale, *Shakespeare and the Rhetoricians* (1982). Trousdale's concern is with the interaction of "the assumptions of rhetoric" and dramatic form. According to Trousdale, Agricola's place-logic, Erasmus's amplitude, and Puttenham's figures largely explain dramatic composition; therefore, an understanding of these forces makes possible a more meaningful reading of Shakespeare.

Almost all the works discussed thus far share the assumption that the rhetorical treatises and textbooks of the sixteenth and seventeenth centuries explain the function and form of the literature of those same centuries. Therefore, Renaissance rhetoric provides the most appropriate tool for the criticism of Renaissance poetry and drama. Of course, not all rhetorical studies of Renaissance literature accept this position of historical relativism. Some scholars, rather, choose to explicate sixteenth- and seventeenth-century literature by employing twentieth-century rhetorical methods. Books that, to varying degrees, reflect this approach include Thomas O. Sloan and Raymond B. Waddington, *The Rhetoric of Renaissance Poetry* (1974); Richard A. Lanham, *The Motives of Eloquence* (1976); and William J. Kennedy, *Rhetorical Norms in Renaissance Literature* (1978). These three books demonstrate the variety of scholarly analyses that the term *rhetoric* implies. They are interesting, often highly imaginative, and informative about Renaissance literature, but perhaps less instructive about Renaissance rhetoric than many of the works cited earlier. These volumes should be read not as systematic accounts of the rhetoric of the Renaissance, but more as speculative essays on the rhetorical nature of literature.

Rhetoric and Preaching

Rhetoric began in antiquity as the art of oratory, and while writing may have eclipsed orality in the Renaissance, the oration can hardly be said to have disappeared. And the oratorical genre most characteristic of the Renaissance must surely be the sermon. The logical point of departure for the study of this genre is Alan F. Herr, *The Elizabethan Sermon: A Survey and a Bibliography* (1940). This book begins with an introductory essay placing the sermon within the greater body of Elizabethan prose. Herr documents the popularity of preaching and describes the occasions of presentation, methods of delivery, and structure of the sermon. The second portion of the book is a bibliography of sermons printed in England up to 1610, including about 1,200 sermons printed in 513 separate publications. Herr claims, rather convincingly, that this list includes the great majority of sermons printed in Elizabethan England.

A more detailed study of the sermon is J. W. Blench, *Preaching in England in the Late Fifteenth and Sixteenth Centuries* (1964). Blench devotes successive chapters to the preacher's scriptural interpretation, the form of the sermon, style, classical allusions, preaching themes, and the influence of these themes on poetry and drama. Each chapter is developed chronologically, tracing the particular topic through the sermons of the pre-reformation Catholics, early reformers, preachers of Mary's reign, and concluding with the Elizabethan preachers. Taken together, the works of Herr and Blench present a comprehensive account of preaching in the Elizabethan age.

An account of a later age is presented by W. Fraser Mitchell in *English Pulpit Oratory from Andrewes to Tillotson* (1932). Mitchell first examines the theory of sermonizing, regarding preaching as a branch of rhetoric and a product of the "rhetorical bias" in English education. Mitchell then turns from theory to practice and surveys the preaching of Anglo-Catholics, Anglicans, Cambridge Platonists, Latitudinarians, and preachers of the Restoration. From theory and practice Mitchell proceeds to criticism, arguing that secular criticism was largely responsible for the evolution of preaching in this period. The work has a very thorough bibliography, which includes a forty-page listing of "Representative English Sermons of the Seventeenth Century." *English Pulpit Oratory from Andrewes to Tillotson* remains the standard survey of late Renaissance preaching.

A more recent work on preaching is *Increase and Multiply: Arts-of-Discourse Procedure in the Preaching of Donne*, by John S. Chamberlin (1976). While Donne is the ultimate object of this study, Chamberlin's concerns go well beyond the practice of an individual preacher. He attempts to explain how a preacher elaborates a scriptural text by using all the arts of discourse—grammar, dialectic, and rhetoric. Consequently, Chamberlin devotes a chapter to each of these arts, examining their basic principles and applicability to preaching. The discussion is supported by analyses of sermons by Augustine, Alan of Lille, Bonaventure, and William Perkins. After this survey of medieval and Renaissance theory and practice, Chamberlin is ready to confront the preaching of Donne. He demonstrates in detail how Donne dilates a sermon by consciously drawing on the doctrines of grammar, dialectic, and, of course, rhetoric.

Rhetoric and Education

The conspicuous presence of rhetoric in Renaissance literature is convincing evidence of the efficacy of rhetorical training
in the sixteenth and seventeenth centuries. Preachers, poets,
and playwrights could employ rhetorical techniques with great
skill because they had been taught to do so. While many of the
books discussed in the preceding two sections devote as much
as a chapter each to rhetorical education, more complete treatments are available. An important early work is William H.
Woodward's *Studies in Education in the Age of the Renaissance*
(1906). Woodward describes in detail the pedagogical philosophies and practices of such teachers and rhetoricians as Agricola, Erasmus, Budé, Vives, Melancthon, and many others.
Foster Watson's *The English Grammar Schools to 1660* (1908) is
another early work that retains its usefulness. Because the instructional aim of these schools was the writing and speaking of
Latin, the grammatical was often inseparable from the
rhetorical.

The advantages of a rhetorical education can be most clearly
seen in T. W. Baldwin's *William Shakspere's Small Latine and
Lesse Greeke* (1944). Although Shakespeare may not have actually attended a grammar school, he was, argues Baldwin, inevitably affected by the intellectual environment such schooling
created. In the second volume of this 1,500-page work, seven
chapters are devoted to the rhetorical training Shakespeare
might have received. Baldwin concludes that such training in
large part explains Shakespeare's extraordinary accomplishments with language.

Milton was another careful student of rhetoric, as Donald
Lemen Clark shows in *John Milton at St. Paul's School* (1948). The
goal of this work is to demonstrate the influence of classical
rhetoric on Milton's prose and poetry. To do so Clark recon-
structs the curriculum Milton would have followed at St. Paul's
School, a course of studies that might be described as a Roman
education tinted with Ramism. Clark speculates that Milton's
rhetoric text may have been Talon's *Rhetorica* or a similar work
by Butler or Farnaby and that this early exposure to Ramism
shaped Milton's poetry.

A different educational issue is addressed by Richard J.
Schoeck in "Rhetoric and Law in Sixteenth-Century England"

(1953) and by D. S. Bland in his reply, "Rhetoric and the Law Student in Sixteenth-Century England" (1957). Schoeck discusses the relationship between rhetoric and the ways in which lawyers may have pursued the study of rhetoric. In his more recent "Lawyers and Rhetoric in Sixteenth-Century England" (*Renaissance Eloquence*, pp. 274–91), Schoeck indicates that little is yet known about the rhetorical education at the Inns of Chancery and the Inns of Court. It is abundantly clear, however, that lawyers studied rhetoric, applied it, and contributed to its theoretical advancement.

Rhetoric and Science

The rise of science and its effect on English prose have long been a dominant concern of seventeenth-century rhetorical scholarship. This concern began with the influential work of Morris W. Croll, who argues that about 1600 a new prose style emerged as a result of the "Anti-Ciceronian" movement. Anti-Ciceronianism is seen by Croll as a continuation of the classical plain style, which became, in the seventeenth century, the rhetorical expression of science. This thesis is developed by Croll in a series of essays published between 1914 and 1931 and now collected in *Style, Rhetoric, and Rhythm* (1966). A rather different explanation of this stylistic evolution is presented by Richard F. Jones in several essays written in the thirties and later assembled in *The Seventeenth Century* (1951). Jones dates the emergence of modern prose at about 1660 and believes this change is a direct result of the scientific spirit. Hence modern prose is neither a continuation of the plain style of antiquity nor consistent with Anti-Ciceronianism. In *The Senecan Amble* (1951), George Williamson extends Croll's thesis by arguing that the writings of Seneca provided the model for the new style of the seventeenth century. A more recent account of this problem can be found in Robert Adolph, *The Rise of Modern Prose Style* (1968). Adolph analyzes the debate between Croll and Jones and adopts a position closer to Jones's interpretation. Adolph contends that neither Anti-Ciceronianism nor science was the decisive influence on stylistic development, but rather the "new utilitarianism" of the age was chiefly responsible for the emergence of modern prose.

The key figure in the alliance of science and style was, of course, Sir Francis Bacon. Beginning with Karl R. Wallace's

Francis Bacon on Communication and Rhetoric (1943), there have been numerous books exploring various aspects of Bacon's impact on style. Wallace's work remains the most comprehensive treatment of Bacon as a rhetorical theorist. Drawing on such concepts as the "colors of good and evil," the "anti-theta," the "formulae," and "apothegems," Wallace produces a systematic Baconian theory of rhetoric. Wallace is an admittedly "conservative" scholar and consequently renders Bacon as a rather classical rhetorician. Brian Vickers, in *Francis Bacon and Renaissance Prose* (1968), approaches Bacon as a stylist rather than as a theorist of rhetoric. Vickers believes that the power of Bacon's prose derives largely from his "symmetrical syntax" and his mastery of imagery. In *Francis Bacon: From Magic to Science* (1968), Paolo Rossi examines Bacon's philosophy in light of the cultural and intellectual conditions in which it developed. Fully one-half of Rossi's book deals with logical and rhetorical problems and their relation to scientific method. Lisa Jardine documents Bacon's debt to the dialectical reformation of the sixteenth century in *Francis Bacon: Discovery and the Art of Discourse* (1974). Although the focus of this book is on Bacon as a logician, Jardine does include chapters on "Methods of Communication" and "Bacon's View of Rhetoric." Jardine, in contrast to Wallace, for example, concludes that Baconian rhetoric is essentially ornamental and figurative. James Stephens, in *Francis Bacon and the Style of Science* (1975), examines Bacon's indebtedness to Aristotelian thought. Stephens believes that the Baconian position represents a break with the rhetorical tradition, yet, ironically, Bacon relied on Aristotle to help create a new rhetoric.

Directions for Future Research

James J. Murphy has recently written that "Renaissance rhetoric must surely be one of the most-mentioned and least studied subjects in modern scholarship. The apparatus for study— what economists call the 'infra-structure' of basic equipment— is simply not yet fully available to us" (*Renaissance Eloquence,* p. 29). This lack of an infrastructure is the most immediate difficulty confronting scholars of Renaissance rhetoric. The publication, within the last two years, of Murphy's *Short Title Catalogue* and Stanford's bibliography make clear just how extensive the basic equipment really is. Of the 250 or so titles published in England, only a handful are available to scholars in either facsimile or modern editions. Where now there are only originals in a few libraries, facsimiles are needed; where there are now only facsimiles, modern editions are needed. Seaton's edition of *The Arcadian Rhetorike* and Willcock's and Walker's edition of *The Arte of English Poesie* are the exceptions, whereas they should be the rule.

The situation with regard to vernacular rhetorics, though far from perfect, is certainly better than that of non-English works. Latin treatises published in England and Continental volumes widely circulated in Britain are not easily available. Even a work as widely influential as Agricola's *De inventione dialectica* has been only partially translated by Richard McNally (1967). The Murphy and Newlands translation of Ramus's attack on Quintilian is the first rendering of that work into English and probably the first English translation of a work by Ramus since Roland MacIlmaine in the sixteenth century. This shortage of translations has necessitated, in the case of Ramus, a heavy reliance on the interpretation of Walter Ong. Ong's erudition is, of course, extraordinary, but his conclusions remain one of many possible interpretations.

The paucity of English translations has also made it difficult to fully evaluate the contributions of the northern European humanists to the development of English rhetoric. Comparatively little is known about the writings of Melanchthon, Sturm, Susenbrotus, Vives, or Vossius. Yet all of these writers were influential in England, often to the point of being a principal source of a vernacular rhetoric. If more were known about these men and their ideas, the task of determining the impact of Ramism in England might be less illusive. After all, most of these figures preceded Ramus and spread similar doctrines about rhetoric and logic. Indeed, it might be most appropriate, in the sixteenth century at least, to examine the development of English rhetoric in concert with the study of northern European humanism.

More editions and translations of sixteenth- and seventeenth-century works will certainly generate additional investigations, the direction of which may be difficult to anticipate. Certain courses of research do, however, suggest themselves. The greatest quantity and quality of work have been done in the literary applications of rhetoric. While this is as it should be, and hardly cause for complacency, it does suggest that the investigation of less overtly literary rhetoric could be profitable.

One such approach would be to examine more closely the institutional functions of rhetoric. For despite excellent early studies, relatively little is yet known about rhetoric and education, even less about rhetoric and law, and almost nothing about rhetoric and politics. Yet Hobbes, Wilson, and Bacon were politicians and presumably understood the political uses of rhetoric. Political oratory, and all forms of oratory with the exception of preaching, have yet to receive sufficient attention. Indeed, virtually all aspects of the institutional life of the Renaissance present possibilities for future scholarship.

One goal as yet unmet, but which eventually must be achieved, is a truly comprehensive history of Renaissance rhetoric. Howell's authoritative *Logic and Rhetoric in England, 1500–1700* comes very close to this goal, but even it is incomplete insofar as the literary dimensions of rhetoric are excluded. Nor is there a Continental history that transcends national boundaries and literatures. There is, as yet, no work comparable in scope to George Kennedy's *The Art of Persuasion in Greece* (Princeton: Princeton University Press, 1963) and *The Art of Rhetoric in the Roman World* (Princeton: Princeton University Press, 1972) or to James J. Murphy's *Rhetoric in the Middle Ages* (Berkeley: University of California Press, 1974). Such a comprehensive history, when it comes, will help scholars to see Renaissance rhetoric as an intellectual mosaic, rather than as bits and pieces of arcane information. For if it is true, as many have claimed, that the Renaissance is a "rhetorical culture," it is surely necessary to understand the rhetoric of the age before it is possible to completely comprehend its achievement.

Bibliography

This bibliography is by no means complete. However, the citations are sufficient for a rather thorough introduction to the rhetoric of the Renaissance. For the convenience of the reader, the organization of the bibliography parallels that of the essay. Only those primary sources available in facsimiles or modern editions are listed. Citations for less common works can be found in the bibliographies included in section II. Common sources of facsimile reprints are abbreviated as follows:

SFR: Gainesville, Fla.: Scholars' Facsimiles and Reprints.

EngLing: English Linguistics 1500–1800: A Collection of Facsimile Reprints. Edited by R. C. Alston. Menston, Eng.: Scolar Press.

EngEx: The English Experience: Its Record in Early Printed Books Published in Facsimile. New York: Da Capo Press.

Works identified by these abbreviations are all facsimile reproductions. Other editions are modern imprints.

I. Primary Sources

A. Collected Works

Bacon, Francis. *The Collected Works of Francis Bacon.* Edited by James Spedding, Robert Leslie Ellis, and Douglas Denon Heath. 14 vols. London: Longmans, 1857–1874.

British and Continental Rhetoric and Elocution. Sixteen microfilm reels. Ann Arbor: University Microfilms, 1953.

Erasmus, Desiderius. *Collected Works of Erasmus. Literary and Educational Writings 2: De Copia, De Ratione Studii.* Edited by Craig R. Thompson. Toronto: University of Toronto Press, 1978.

Hobbes, Thomas. *The English Works of Thomas Hobbes of Malmsbury.* Edited by Sir William Molesworth. 11 vols. London: J. Bohn, 1839–1845.

B. Individual Treatises

Blount, Thomas. *The Academie of Eloquence* (1654). EngLing, no. 296, 1971.

Bulwer, John. *Chirologia: or the Natural Language of the Hand (and) Chironomia: or the Art of Manual Rhetoric* (1644). Edited by James W. Cleary. Carbondale: Southern Illinois University Press, 1974.

Cox, Leonard, *The Arte or Craft of Rhetoryke* (1530?). Edited by Frederic Ives Carpenter. Chicago: University of Chicago Press, 1899.

Day, Angel. *The English Secretorie* (1586). Edited by Robert O. Evans. SFR, 1967.

———. EngLing, no. 29, 1967.

Dugard, William. *Rhetorices Elementa* (1648). EngLing, no. 365, 1972.

Hawes, Stephen. *The Pastyme of Pleasure* (1517). Edited by William Edward Mead. London: Oxford University Press, 1928.

Hoskins, John. *Directions for Speech and Style* (1599?). Edited by Hoyt Hudson. Princeton: Princeton University Press, 1935.

Farnaby, Thomas. *Index Rhetoricus* (1625). EngLing, no. 240, 1970.

Fenner, Dudley. *The Artes of Logike and Rhetorike* (1584). In *Four Tudor Books on Education*, edited by Robert D. Pepper, pp. 151–80. SFR, 1966.

Fraunce, Abraham. *The Arcadian Rhetorike* (1588). Edited by Ethel Seaton. Oxford: Basil Blackwell, 1950.

———. EngLing, no. 176, 1969.

Peacham, Henry. *The Garden of Eloquence* (2d ed., 1593). Edited by William G. Crane. SFR, 1954.

———. EngLing, no. 267, 1971.

Poole, Joshua. *Practical Rhetorik* (1663). EngLing, no. 341, 1972.

Puttenham, George. *The Art of English Poesie* (1589). Edited by Gladys Doidge Willcock and Alice Walker. Cambridge: Cambridge University Press, 1936.

———. EngLing, no. 110, 1968.

Rainolde, Richard. *The Foundacion of Rhetorike* (1563). Edited by Francis R. Johnson. SFR (New York), 1945.

———. EngEx, no. 91, 1969.

———. EngLing, no. 347, 1972.

Ramus, Peter. *Arguments in Rhetoric Against Quintilian* (1549). Translated by Carole Newlands and James J. Murphy. DeKalb: University of Northern Illinois Press, 1983.

Sherry, Richard. *A Treatise of Schemes and Tropes* (1550). Edited by Herbert W. Hildebrandt. SFR, 1961.

Smith, John. *The Mysterie of Rhetorique Unvail'd* (1657). EngLing, no. 205, 1969.

Wilson, Thomas. *The Arte of Rhetorique* (1553). Edited by G. H. Mair. Oxford: Clarendon Press, 1909.

———. Edited by Robert Hood Bowers. SFR, 1962.

———. EngEx, no. 206, 1969.

Vives, Juan Luis. *Vives: On Education: A Translation of the De Tradendis Disciplinis* (1531). Translated by Foster Watson, 1913. Totowa, N.J.: Rowman and Littlefield, 1971.

II. Bibliographies

Bailey, Richard W., and Dolores M. Burton. *English Stylistics: A Bibliography.* Cambridge: MIT Press, 1968.

Murphy, James J. *Renaissance Rhetoric: A Short Title Catalogue of Works on Rhetorical Theory from the Beginning of Printing to A.D. 1700, with*

Special Attention to the Holdings of the Bodleian Library, Oxford. With a Select Basic Bibliography of Secondary Works on Renaissance Rhetoric. New York: Garland, 1981.

Stanford, Charles L. "The Renaissance." In *Historical Rhetoric: An Annotated Bibliography of Selected Sources in English,* edited by Winifred Bryan Horner, pp. 111–84. Boston: G. K. Hall, 1980.

III. Surveys and General Studies

Atkins, J. W. H. *English Literary Criticism: The Renascence.* London: Methuen, 1947.

Baldwin, Charles Sears. *Renaissance Literary Theory and Practice: Classicism in the Rhetoric and Poetic of Italy, France, and England, 1400–1600.* Edited with introduction by Donald Lemen Clark. New York: Columbia University Press, 1939.

Bolgar, R. R. *The Classical Heritage and Its Beneficiaries.* Cambridge: Cambridge University Press, 1954.

Clark, Donald Lemen. *Rhetoric and Poetry in the Renaissance: A Study of Rhetorical Terms in English Renaissance Literary Criticism.* New York: Columbia University Press, 1922.

Crane, William Garrett. *Wit and Rhetoric in the Renaissance: The Formal Basis of Elizabethan Prose Style.* New York: Columbia University Press, 1937.

Gray, Hanna H. "Renaissance Humanism: The Pursuit of Eloquence." In *Renaissance Essays from the Journal of the History of Ideas,* edited by Paul O. Kristeller and Philip P. Wiener, pp. 192–216. New York: Harper and Row, 1968.

Howell, Wilbur S. *Logic and Rhetoric in England, 1500–1700.* Princeton: Princeton University Press, 1956.

———. *Poetics, Rhetoric, and Logic: Studies in the Basic Disciplines of Criticism.* Ithaca: Cornell University Press, 1975.

Kristeller, Paul Oskar. *Renaissance Thought and Its Sources.* Edited by Michael Mooney. New York: Columbia University Press, 1979.

Murphy, James J., ed. *Renaissance Eloquence: Studies in the Theory and Practice of Renaissance Rhetoric.* Berkeley: University of California Press, 1983.

Seigel, Jerrold. *Rhetoric and Philosophy in Renaissance Humanism.* Princeton: Princeton University Press, 1968.

Sonnino, Lee A. *A Handbook to Sixteenth-Century Rhetoric.* New York: Barnes and Noble, 1968.

Struever, Nancy S. *The Language of History in the Renaissance: Rhetoric and Historical Consciousness in Florentine Humanism.* Princeton: Princeton University Press, 1970.

Vickers, Brian. *Classical Rhetoric in English Poetry.* New York: Macmillan, St. Martin's Press, 1970.

———. "Rhetorical and Anti-Rhetorical Tropes: On Writing the History of *Elocutio*." In *Comparative Criticism: A Year Book*, edited by E. S. Schaffer, 3:105–32, 316–22. Cambridge: Cambridge University Press, 1981.

Yates, Frances A. *The Art of Memory*. Chicago: University of Chicago Press, 1966.

IV. Specialized Studies

A. Logic and Rhetoric

Ashworth, E. J. *Language and Logic in the Post-Medieval Period*. Boston: D. Reidel, 1974.

Gilbert, Neal W. *Renaissance Concepts of Method*. New York: Columbia University Press, 1960.

Lechner, Sister Joan Marie, O.S.U. *Renaissance Concepts of the Commonplaces: An Historical Investigation of the General and Universal Ideas Used in All Argumentation and Persuasion With Special Emphasis on the Educational and Literary Tradition of the Sixteenth and Seventeenth Centuries*. New York: Pageant Press, 1962.

McNally, J. R. "Prima pars dialecticae: The Influence of Agricolan Dialectic Upon English Accounts of Invention." *RQ* 21 (1968): 166–77.

———. "Rudolph Agricola's *De inventione dialecticae libri tres*: A Translation of Selected Chapters." *SM* 34 (1967): 393–422.

Nelson, Norman E. *Peter Ramus and the Confusion of Logic, Rhetoric, and Poetry*. University of Michigan Contributions in Modern Philology, No. 2. Ann Arbor: University of Michigan Press, April 1947.

Ong, Walter, S.J. *Ramus, Method, and the Decay of Dialogue: From the Art of Discourse to the Art of Reason*. Cambridge: Harvard University Press, 1958.

———. *Ramus and Talon Inventory: A Short-Title Inventory of the Published Works of Peter Ramus (1515–1572) and of Omer Talon (ca. 1510–1562) in their Original and in their Variously Altered Forms with Related Material: 1. The Ramist Controversies: A Descriptive Catalogue. 2. Agricola Check List: A Short-Title Inventory of Some Printed Editions and Printed Compendia of Rudolph Agricola's "Dialectical Invention" ("De inventione dialectica")*. Cambridge: Harvard University Press, 1958.

———. *Rhetoric, Romance, and Technology: Studies in the Interaction of Expression and Culture*. Ithaca: Cornell University Press, 1971.

Sharrat, Peter. "The Present State of Studies on Ramus." *Studi Francesi*, no. 47–48 (1972): 201–13.

B. Rhetoric, Poetry, and Drama

Altman, Joel B. *The Tudor Play of the Mind: Rhetorical Inquiry and the Development of Elizabethan Drama*. Berkeley: University of California Press, 1978.

Cope, Jackson I. "Ramist Implications." In his *The Metaphoric Structure of Paradise Lost,* pp. 27–49. Baltimore: Johns Hopkins University Press, 1962.

Craig, Hardin. *The Enchanted Glass: The Elizabethan Mind in Literature.* New York: Oxford University Press, 1936.

Hardison, O. B., Jr. *The Enduring Moment: A Study of the Idea of Praise in Renaissance Literary Theory and Practice.* Chapel Hill: University of North Carolina Press, 1962.

Joseph, Sister Miriam, C.S.C. *Rhetoric in Shakespeare's Time: Literary Theory of Renaissance Europe.* 1947. Reprint: New York: Harcourt, Brace & World, 1962.

Kennedy, William J. *Rhetorical Norms in Renaissance Literature.* New Haven: Yale University Press, 1978.

Lanham, Richard A. *The Motives of Eloquence: Literary Rhetoric in the Renaissance.* New Haven: Yale University Press, 1976.

McDonald, Charles O. *The Rhetoric of Tragedy: Form in Stuart Drama.* Amherst: University of Massachusetts Press, 1966.

Patterson, Annabel M. *Hermogenes and the Renaissance: Seven Ideas of Style.* Princeton: Princeton University Press, 1970.

Plett, Heinrich F. *Rhetorik der Affekte: Englische Wirkungsasthetik im Zeitalter der Renaissance.* Studien zur Englischen Philologie, n.s. 18. Tubingen: Max Niemeyer, 1975.

Rix, Herbert David. *Rhetoric is Spenser's Poetry.* Pennsylvania State College Studies, no. 7. State College: Pennsylvania State College, 1940.

Sloan, Thomas O., and Raymond B. Waddington, eds. *The Rhetoric of Renaissance Poetry from Wyatt to Milton.* Berkeley: University of California Press, 1974.

Taylor, Warren. *Tudor Figures of Rhetoric.* Whitewater, Wis.: Language Press, 1972.

Trimpi, Wesley. *Ben Jonson's Poems: A Study of the Plain Style.* Palo Alto: Stanford University Press, 1962.

Trousdale, Marion. *Shakespeare and the Rhetoricians.* Chapel Hill: University of North Carolina Press, 1982.

Tuve, Rosemond. *Elizabethan and Metaphysical Imagery: Renaissance Poetic and Twentieth-Century Critics.* Chicago: University of Chicago Press, 1947.

C. Rhetoric and Preaching

Blench, J. W. *Preaching in England in the Late Fifteenth and Sixteenth Centuries: A Study of English Sermons 1450–c. 1600.* Oxford: Basil Blackwell, 1964.

Chamberlin, John S. *Increase and Multiply: Arts-of-Discourse Procedure in the Preaching of Donne.* Chapel Hill: University of North Carolina Press, 1976.

Herr, Alan F. *The Elizabethan Sermon: A Survey and a Bibliography.* New York: Octagon Books, 1969.

Mitchell, W. Fraser. *English Pulpit Oratory from Andrewes to Tillotson*: *A Study of Its Literary Aspects*. 1932. Reprint: New York: Russell & Russell, 1962.

D. Rhetoric and Education

Baldwin, T. W. *William Shakspere's Small Latine and Lesse Greeke*. 2 vols. Urbana: University of Illinois Press, 1944.
Bland, D. S. "Rhetoric and the Law Student in Sixteenth-Century England." *SP* 54 (1957): 506–8.
Clark, Donald Lemen. *John Milton at St. Paul's School*: *A Study of Ancient Rhetoric in English Renaissance Education*. New York: Columbia University Press, 1948.
Schoeck, Richard J. "Rhetoric and Law in Sixteenth-Century England." *SP* (1953): 110–27.
Watson, Foster. *The English Grammar Schools to 1660: Their Curriculum and Practice*. 1908. Reprint: London: Frank Cass, 1968.
Woodward, William H. *Studies in Education during the Age of the Renaissance 1400–1600*. 1906. Reprint: Cambridge: Cambridge University Press, 1924.

E. Rhetoric and Science

Adolph, Robert. *The Rise of Modern Prose Style*. Cambridge: MIT Press, 1968.
Croll, Morris W. *Style, Rhetoric, and Rhythm*: *Essays by Morris W. Croll*. Edited by J. Max Patrick and Robert O. Evans, with John M. Wallace and R. J. Schoeck. Princeton: Princeton University Press, 1966.
Hannah, Robert. "Francis Bacon, the Political Orator." In *Studies in Rhetoric and Public Address in Honor of James Albert Winans*, pp. 91–132. New York: Century, 1925.
Jardine, Lisa. *Francis Bacon*: *Discovery and the Art of Discourse*. Cambridge: Cambridge University Press, 1974.
Jones, Richard Foster. *Ancients and Moderns*: *A Study of the Battle of the Books*. Washington University Studies—New Series. Language and Literature—no. 6. St. Louis: 1936.
———. *The Seventeenth Century*: *Studies in the History of English Thought and Literature from Bacon to Pope*. Palo Alto: Stanford University Press, 1951.
———. *The Triumph of the English Language*: *A Survey of Opinions Concerning the Vernacular from the Introduction of Printing to the Restoration*. Palo Alto: Stanford University Press, 1953.
Rossi, Paolo. *Francis Bacon*: *From Magic to Science*. Translated by Sacha Rabinovitch. London: Routledge and Kegan Paul, 1968.
Stephens, James. *Francis Bacon and the Style of Science*. Chicago: University of Chicago Press, 1975.

————. "Rhetorical Problems in Renaissance Science." *PR* 8 (1975): 213–29.

Vickers, Brian. *Francis Bacon and Renaissance Prose*. Cambridge: Cambridge University Press, 1968.

Wallace, Karl R. *Francis Bacon on Communication and Rhetoric or: The Art of Applying Reason to the Imagination for the Better Moving of the Will*. Chapel Hill: University of North Carolina Press, 1943.

Williamson, George. *The Senecan Amble: A Study in Prose Form from Bacon to Collier*. 1951. Reprint: Chicago: University of Chicago Press, 1966.

4

THE EIGHTEENTH CENTURY
Winifred Bryan Horner

Introduction

The eighteenth century was an important turning point in the history of intellectual thought, and that turning point is clearly evidenced in the rhetoric of the period. The eighteenth century marks the end of a long tradition of rhetoric that had its beginning in Greece in the fifth century B.C. and that for twenty centuries dominated philosophic thought and the established institutions of church and government. It also marks the start of a new tradition that branched out into the varied fields of study that we know in modern scholarship as logic, semiotics, literary criticism, oral interpretation, and linguistics, to name only a few.

Scholars speak of the "decline" of rhetoric in the eighteenth century, but actually it was a decline in name only. Rhetoric as the study of human communication survived under other names, and as the basic concepts changed focus the terminology changed as well. The actual effects of these changes were far-reaching as rhetoric spread over a number of disciplines in the nineteenth- and twentieth-century academic communities.

One of the major changes in eighteenth-century rhetoric was the shift in interest from oral to written language. In a society where business and political affairs were conducted by letter, the emphasis in education and rhetoric texts was bound to be on written language. This shift was completed in the eighteenth century with important effects on literature, some of which are

Winifred Bryan Horner teaches courses in English, linguistics, and the history of rhetoric in the Department of English at the University of Missouri–Columbia. She has written articles on historical rhetoric and composition, and her books include *Historical Rhetoric: An Annotated Bibliography of Selected Sources in English* (G. K. Hall, 1980) and *Literature and Composition: Bridging the Gap* (University of Chicago Press, 1983).

still not fully understood. A second closely allied change was the separation of poetry and rhetoric. Until the latter half of the eighteenth century, scholars still saw poetry as part of rhetoric, but after 1850 poetry was isolated. Another change in rhetorical practice was the use of English works rather than classical ones as models. Arising out of the new nationalism, primarily at the Scottish universities, this practice eventually brought about the rise of English studies. Another change that started in the Renaissance and was completed in the eighteenth century was the shift from logic as learned communication to logic as a system of inquiry. At the same time the scientific method forced the shift from deductive to inductive reasoning.

Of all the changes, the most significant was the shift from rhetoric's emphasis on speakers and the generative aspects of texts to an emphasis on readers and their interpretations of texts. Resulting in part from the epistemological and philosophical movements of the period, this shift in focus eventually led to the great critical theories of the late nineteenth and twentieth centuries.

In the eighteenth century, rhetoric was not the business of literary scholars and schoolteachers alone. It was the business of all men of learning. One cannot see the names of Joseph Priestley, Adam Smith, Robert Hartley, Thomas Sheridan, and Edmund Burke as authors of rhetorical treatises and dismiss the subject as unimportant or speak of "decline." Rhetoric was the business of the great men of the period, and in eighteenth-century rhetoric one must think in terms of basic and important change.

Certainly eighteenth-century rhetoric, particularly as it developed in Scotland, had profound effects on education, not only in Scotland but in the United States and eventually in England as well. Rhetoric within the belletristic movement, under such men as George Campbell and Hugh Blair, has shaped our study of literature and composition today.

The important changes that occurred in rhetorical theory in the eighteenth century and their long-term effects are reflected in the origin and development of the words *literature* and *psychology*. The first occurrence of the word *literature*, cited in the *Oxford English Dictionary*, in the modern sense of "writing which has claim to consideration on the ground of beauty of form or emotional effect," was 1812, and the editors note, "This sense is of very recent emergence in both France and England."

The first citation for the word *psychology* is 1693, and the second is 1748 from David Hartley's *Observations on Man*, in which he defined it as "the theory of the Human Mind."

The words were nonexistent before the eighteenth century because the concepts of literature and psychology as we know them now simply did not exist. It is the study of the mind as applied to literature—story and poetry as they developed in writing—that formed the new rhetorical theory of the eighteenth century. It was these two developing concepts, literature and psychology, that made the century so important, not only in rhetoric but in all humanistic studies.

In this essay, I shall start by considering the state of the primary works of rhetoric and continue with a description of the general secondary scholarship for the period. The next section will cover the epistemological and psychological theories as background for a consideration of the four main movements—Neo-Classicism; The Old Rhetoric, which will cover Logic and Stylistic Rhetoric; Elocution; and Belletristic Rhetoric. Each section on the main movements will include the primary figures, their works, and the secondary scholarship. In conclusion, I shall consider possibilities for future directions in scholarship.

The State of the Primary Works

Many of the minor rhetorical works of the eighteenth century survived through just one or two printings and are now available only in rare-book rooms in the larger libraries. Occasionally one can find old copies of books from the period still on library shelves. I discovered a 1773 edition of John Herries's *The Elements of Speech* in the open stacks of the University of Missouri–Columbia library. Its fairly new binding disguised the value of the edition.

Since libraries will not lend items from their rare-book collections on inter-library loan, often the only source for many of these materials is microfilm or microprint. The *Eighteenth-Century British and Continental Rhetoric and Elocution Microfilms* (hereafter abbreviated as *BCRE*), published by the University Microfilms in Ann Arbor, Michigan, in 1953, contains a large number of eighteenth-century works. Another source of microfilm materials is the *Eighteenth-Century Sources for the Study of English Literature and Culture* (hereafter abbreviated as *ECS*), a collection of works relevant to the literary, artistic, and cultural milieu of eighteenth-century England, published in 1979 by Micrographics, II, Keswick, Virginia. A third source is the micro-print series *Early American Imprints 1639–1800* (hereafter abbreviated as *EAI*), which is based on the bibliography by Charles Evans (1941–1959). It is a monumental collection of microprints that includes editions of every existent book, pamphlet, and broadside printed in the United States between 1639 and 1800.

Although these micro materials make otherwise difficult to obtain treatises more readily available to students and scholars, they can be difficult to work with. The print is faded and some manuscripts are incomplete with pages missing, and one does not know if this is a flaw in the original text or whether it occurred in the reproduction process. Finally, micro materials are a poor substitute for the original for the scholar who needs to read closely.

Consequently, scholars have welcomed the fine modern editions and facsimile reprints. Lord Kames's *Elements of Criticism* is available in a facsimile edition (1970) published by Georg Olms Verlag. But the series that finally saves eighteenth-century British rhetoric from relative obscurity is the Southern Illinois University Press Landmarks in Rhetoric and Public Address series, edited by David Potter. Students and scholars interested in eighteenth-century rhetoric would do well to start with these editions and their excellent introductions by outstanding scholars. Included are the lectures of John Lawson, Adam Smith, George Campbell, Joseph Priestley, and Hugh Blair. Unfortunately, the last three are now out of print, but the other editions are still available.

The lectures of some eighteenth-century rhetoricians are available only through manuscripts. Thus we have only Eric Skopec's "Thomas Reid's Rhetorical Theory: A Manuscript Report" (1978) for information on the unpublished manuscript of Thomas Reid's lectures on rhetoric, and for William Leechman, who lectured at the University of Glasgow from 1743 to 1766, we have only Herman Cohen's report (1968) of a student's notes of his lectures. The only record that we have of Adam Smith's lectures is also from student notes. Since prizes were awarded in the Scottish universities for the best sets of student notes, these notes are often carefully done, in clear handwriting, with title pages and tables of contents. They serve as reliable sources, but, of course, are not available to the ordinary scholar or student.

The forthcoming *Eighteenth-Century Short Title Catalogue* will include everything published in the English language in the eighteenth century in Great Britain and her possessions. With headquarters in the British Library, the catalogue has been collected from libraries all over the world. It should provide a reliable listing of books on rhetoric published during the century. The North American editor is Henry Schneider.

If more of the primary materials were readily available, the study of eighteenth-century rhetoric might well take on new excitement.

General Works

The single most important general study for eighteenth-century rhetoric is Wilbur Samuel Howell's *Eighteenth-Century British Logic and Rhetoric* (1971). Its analyses of the major works on logic and rhetoric of the eighteenth century make it indispensable for any student of the period. Howell analyzes individual works in great detail; for example, his treatment of John Ward's lectures at Gresham College covers forty-one pages. He describes Gresham College and Ward's history of the College, then examines Ward's position in the eighteenth century and the influence of his lectures, *A System of Oratory*, both within their own time and within the English rhetorical tradition as a whole. He describes in great detail Ward's treatment of *inventio*, *dispositio*, and *elocutio*, or style, and concludes with short analyses of Ward's lectures on pronunciation and memory. He ends his detailed discussion of Ward's *A System of Oratory* by documenting the work's reprintings, but he concludes, "When it first appeared in 1759, it already belonged not to its time or to the immediate future but to the past" (p. 124). Such full treatment is accorded to all of the texts Howell mentions, and he covers most of the major works of rhetoric and logic for the period.

Howell's introductory essays to each chapter can be read by themselves as an overview of eighteenth-century logic and rhetoric. The second and third chapters treat the old logic and the old rhetoric of the period. The introduction to chapter 4 is an account of the elocutionary movement, the first pages of chapter 5 outline seven dominant traits of the new logic, and chapter 6 discusses the six points of opposition to the old rhetoric held by the new rhetoricians. In chapter 7, Howell summarizes his discussion of eighteenth-century rhetoric and logic by reviewing the main trends of the time.

Two other authors who give an excellent and shorter overview of eighteenth-century rhetoric are James L. Golden and Edward P. J. Corbett in their introduction to *The Rhetoric of Blair, Campbell, and Whately* (1979). The first three pages provide a succinct but informative view of rhetoric from Corax through Francis Bacon. The authors see the eighteenth century as the beginning of the period of modern or new rhetoric and outline four responses to the classical tradition. The first held that there was no need to alter the teachings of Aristotle, Cicero, and Quintilian, the second was the development of the elocutionary movement, and the third was the rise of belletristic rhetoric. The "most revolutionary response," according to these authors, was the "emergence of the psychological-philosophical theories of public address." In discussing this response, Golden and Corbett review the epistemological theories embodied in the works of John Locke, Francis Hutcheson, David Hume, David Hartley, Thomas Reid, and Adam Smith. They review the theory of ideas developed by Locke, which led him to question the value of the syllogism. His support and that of Hume for faculty psychology and the doctrine of associationism had serious implications for the rhetorical theories of Campbell, Blair, and Whately. Locke, Hume, and Hartley concentrated on mental faculties, while Hutcheson focused on moral faculties. The philosophy of common sense advocated by the Scottish School of Philosophy, primarily by Thomas Reid, is also explained. This short overview is a succinct description of the epistemological ideas of the age that were so important for the development of the new rhetoric. Golden and Corbett conclude with the response of Campbell, Blair, and Whately to these four trends.

A short introductory article covering the latter half of the century is Douglas Ehninger's "Dominant Trends in English Rhetorical Thought, 1750–1800" (1952). Like Golden and Corbett, Ehninger identifies the dominant trends as classicism, psychological-epistemological theories of discourse, elocutionism, and belletristic rhetoric, and he discusses the primary proponents of each movement. The article is useful as an introduction to the period, but its brevity necessarily limits it.

A dissertation that covers the same period is Harold F. Harding's "English Rhetorical Theory, 1750–1800" (1937). It contains a thorough bibliography of school textbooks, essays, lectures, and other treatises on rhetoric and a section on the connections between rhetoric and literary criticism. However, Harding's thesis that eighteenth-century rhetoricians were largely unaware of the philosophical and aesthetic theories of the day is open to serious question.

A work of general importance, particularly for the student of English literature, is P. W. K. Stone's *The Art of Poetry 1750-1820* (1967). Again, this work covers the second half of the period, but it reviews the relationship, not widely recognized, between eighteenth-century poetry and rhetoric. Stone maintains that the eighteenth-century "art of poetry" was, in fact, derived from rhetorical ideas on the nature of language and the relationship between the writer and his reader. He traces the broadening of the concept of rhetoric during the period until it can no longer be distinguished from literary theory or criticism. It was this joining of classical rhetoric with empirical philosophy that resulted in rhetoric becoming a theory of criticism during the latter half of the eighteenth century.

Finally, Winifred Bryan Horner's bibliography of eighteenth-century rhetoric (1980) lists the primary works of the period and the secondary scholarship. All entries are annotated. The primary works are listed chronologically, and the annotations can be read as an overview of the period. The introduction summarizes the principal movements and classifies the primary works according to the major trends of the century.

Eighteenth-Century Epistemology and Philosophy

During the eighteenth century, there were developments in philosophic thought that had serious and enduring consequences on the rhetoric and literature of the period. These ideas, growing out of the empiricism of Locke, Berkeley, and Hume, profoundly affected English and American education, and these effects are still apparent in the second half of the twentieth century. Though Thomas Reid may be a minor figure in the current of philosophic thought, his philosophy of common sense has exerted a major influence on educational philosophy for over two hundred years.

A clear understanding of eighteenth-century rhetoric and discourse during the second half of the century must rest on an understanding of the psychological and philosophical theories of the day, for it was out of these that the theories of rhetoric and the concept of taste as the human faculty of artistic judgment developed. For this reason, the major figures and their works are included here.

John Locke's *Essay Concerning Human Understanding*, published in 1690, soon became the major influence in English education. With its emphasis on sensation and reflection, it changed the way persons viewed the world and the way rhetoricians viewed discourse. Its importance in eighteenth-century thought cannot be overestimated. Together with David Hume's *A Treatise of Human Nature* (1739–1740) and his *An Enquiry Concerning Human Understanding* (1748), it reduced the world to the limits of the human mind and its contents. Edward P. J. Corbett discusses the influence of John Locke in his "John Locke's Contribution to Rhetoric" (1982).

Out of this school came the work of David E. Hartley, *Observations on Man, His Frame, His Duty, and His Expectations* (1749), which introduced the Doctrine of the Association of Ideas first developed by David Hume in *An Enquiry*. Hartley was not an innovator; he was a compiler. He was also a doctor, and his work is a mixture of physiology and psychology. For the eighteenth century, the study of the mind was new; psychology was the new "ology" of the period. Following Hartley, Joseph Priestley was the primary exponent of associationism in the field of rhetoric.

Faculty psychology was derived from the work of Christian Wolff, a German, who wrote *Psychologia Empirica* in 1732 and *Psychologia Rationalis* in 1734. In these works, he suggested that the mind is divided into sections with separate and distinct capacities. The idea had no scientific base, but modern research on the left brain versus the right brain gives support to this view of the human mind. Faculty psychology was widely influential, especially on the work of George Campbell (1776) and Hugh Blair (1783).

Common-sense philosophy, developed in Aberdeen, is usually associated with Thomas Reid and had its fullest development in his *An Inquiry into the Human Mind, on the Principles of Common Sense* (1764). This work answered the skepticism of Locke and Hume, and in it Reid asserted that all philosophy must finally be rooted in common sense. The knowledgeable person must finally believe in his senses and know that the things he sees, hears, and touches are real. From this basis of common sense there arises a human agreement as to the nature of the world. An excellent overview of this Scottish philosophy is that of S. A. Grave (1960).

A general overall treatment of these psychological and philosophical approaches to language is Gordon McKenzie's *Critical Responsiveness: A Study of the Psychological Current in Later Eighteenth-Century Criticism* (1949). McKenzie describes the psychological approaches to literary criticism that became current in the latter half of the eighteenth century and the shift in emphasis from the external work of art to the literary experience of the reader.

This shift is represented in the eighteenth-century interest in the concept of taste, the faculty of artistic appreciation. All of the major figures in the second half of the eighteenth century devoted parts of their treatises on rhetoric to this concept. Walter Jackson Bate traces the sources of taste and its influence on romanticism in his *From Classic to Romantic: Premises of Taste in Eighteenth-Century England* (1946). An article by D. W. Jefferson, "Theories of Taste in the Eighteenth Century" (1938–1943), outlines three theories of taste that were current in the period. Herman Cohen (1958) summarizes Hugh Blair's theory of taste and compares it to those of Lord Kames, Edmund Burke, and Sir Joshua Reynolds. John Waite Bowers (1961) also compares Blair's theory of taste—unfavorably—with those of Edmund Burke and Immanuel Kant, asserting that Blair's theory is without value, because it changes with each age. Another comparative treatment is that of Phil Dolph, who in "Taste and *The Philosophy of Rhetoric*" (1968) relates Campbell's view to those of other eighteenth-century figures.

Taste is an obsolete concept and in modern speech is usually preceded with *in bad*. Nevertheless, for the eighteenth century it was useful and important in the analysis and evaluation of art of all kinds. The word is no longer in use, but the eighteenth-century concept has grown and thrived within the realm of critical theory.

Neo-Classical Rhetorics

The classical tradition was strong in the first half of the eighteenth century. There were numerous Latin editions of the works of Quintilian, Longinus, and the *Ad Herennium*, as well as Aristotle's *Rhetoric*. From the Continent, there were *L'Art de Parler* by Bernard Lamy and François Fénelon's *Dialogues sur*

Eloquence, both of which had their English translations. Fénelon was translated by William Stevenson in 1722, and there is a modern translation by Wilbur Samuel Howell with an excellent introduction (1951). The two major English neo-classical works of the century, John Lawson's *Lectures Concerning Oratory Delivered in Trinity College, Dublin* and John Ward's *A System of Oratory, Delivered in a Course of Lectures, Publicly read at Gresham College*, were published in 1758 and 1759 in London.

The first is available in an excellent facsimile edition published by Southern Illinois University Press (1972). Lawson delivered these lectures at Trinity College, Dublin, where he held the Erasmus Smith Chair for nine years. They went through four printings in the eighteenth century. In publishing his lectures, Lawson established a custom followed by other eighteenth-century rhetoricians at other colleges—a custom that makes these lectures available to us today. The lectures are clearly in the Ciceronian tradition and embrace the full canon in a reaction to rhetoric as only stylistic ornamentation. Lawson was openly hostile to some of the ideas of his day and especially to the development of the elocutionary movement.

The introduction to the facsimile edition by E. Neal Claussen and Karl R. Wallace (1972) provides a biography of Lawson and some information on the lectures themselves. In summarizing the eight characteristics of the lectures, the authors state: "The *Lectures* were firmly established upon faculty psychology, but only as it is consistent with ancient usage" (p. xlii). Ray E. Keesey's "John Lawson's Lectures Concerning Oratory" provides a good description of the *Lectures'* content, and he, like Claussen and Wallace, agrees that Lawson's work offered little that was new. The *Lectures* were, in fact, not widely influential in eighteenth-century thought. Howell, however, in *Eighteenth-Century British Logic and Rhetoric* (1971), makes a convincing case that Lawson combined elements from both the old and the new rhetorics and includes him with Hume, Priestley, Blair, and Witherspoon in a discussion of what he calls the "Discordant Consensus" (pp. 613-94).

John Ward published his two-volume *A System of Oratory, Delivered in a Course of Lectures Publicly Read at Gresham College* in London in 1759. It was a work of 879 pages that Douglas Ehninger in "John Ward and His Rhetoric" (1951) regarded as the fullest restatement of the classical canon in the English language. These fifty-four lectures were published a year after their author's death but never went into a second edition. They are available on microfilm in *ECS*, roll 1, and in *BCRE*, reel 6, item 88. Adelbert Edward Bradley, Jr., in two articles derived largely from his 1955 dissertation on John Ward, analyzes Ward's treatment of *dispositio* and *inventio* (1957, 1959).

Douglas Ehninger has maintained (1951) that John Ward's work exerted almost no influence on later rhetoricians, but in an important article on the influence of Ward on American rhetoric (1960), Ronald F. Reid argues that the statutes governing the Boylston Professor of Rhetoric and Oratory at Harvard were based on Ward's *System*. He traces the direct influence of Ward on Joseph McKean, but maintains that McKean's successor in the Boylston Chair, Edward T. Channing, "wrote in the tradition of the creative rhetorics of Campbell and Blair" (p. 344). Thus, Reid concludes that McKean stands as a transitional figure in American rhetoric in somewhat the same manner that Ward does in English rhetoric.

A final note in the neo-classical tradition should be made of John Holmes's *The Art of Rhetoric Made Easy: In Two Books*, published in 1759 before either Lawson's or Ward's works. Written primarily for youth in grammar schools, it offers nothing new and closely follows the classical tradition. In 1786 it was combined with John Stirling's *A System of Rhetoric* and was influential for many years after its first printing. Less scholarly than the works of Ward or Holmes, Holmes and Stirling's treatise was widely circulated in both England and the United States, with its last edition in 1849 in Philadelphia. It is available on microfilm in the *BCRE*, reel 5, item 45.

The Old Rhetoric: Logics and Stylistic Rhetorics

There are two threads in eighteenth-century rhetoric that are remnants of important seventeenth-century trends. The first is the stylistic rhetorics that reduced rhetoric to a single office; the second is the logics that saw rhetoric as a theory of learned communication. During the eighteenth century, logic was finally separated from rhetoric as it became a theory of inquiry rather than a theory of communication. Nevertheless, during the first half of the period there were at least three logical treatises that still viewed logic as learned communication in the seventeenth-century tradition. Although not important in the intellectual thrust of eighteenth-century rhetoric, these works were popular and widely circulated and cannot be ignored.

A treatise that held to the old view of logic and that had at least five editions in Europe in the eighteenth century was Jean Pierre de Crousaz's *La Logique*, translated into English by John Henley in 1724 as *A New Treatise of the Art of Thinking*. Isaac Watts's *Logick; Or the Right Use of Reason in the Enquiry after Truth* (1725) defines logic as "the art of using reason well in our inquiries after Truth, and the Communication of it to others" (p. 13). It went through numerous editions in England and America, and the 1789 Philadelphia sixteenth edition is available on microprint in the *EAI* series. It stands as one of the most popular textbooks of the eighteenth century.

A third important logic in the old tradition is William Duncan's *The Elements of Logick* (1748). In "The Declaration of Independence and Eighteenth-Century Logic" (1961), Wilbur Samuel Howell demonstrates the influence of this work on Thomas Jefferson and the Declaration of Independence. Like Watts's, Duncan's book went through many printings in England, Scotland, and the United States. First published anonymously in Dodsley's *The Preceptor*, it had eight London editions between 1748 and 1793.

All of these authors saw logic and rhetoric as closely related; however, by the end of the century, logic had become a theory of discovery—a method of inquiry in the new age of science—and had embarked on a life of its own separated from its rhetorical base.

The truncating of rhetoric into a system of figures of speech, so common in Renaissance rhetoric, was still evident in the eighteenth century, and books that were little more than a listing of schemes and tropes were still in circulation. Two of these are Anthony Blackwall's *An Introduction to the Classics* (1718) and Thomas Gibbons's *Rhetoric* (1767). No scholar of the eighteenth century can be unaware of the wide currency of these stylistic rhetorics, but by the end of the century they had begun to lose favor.

Elocution

General Works

When rhetoric was reduced to the fifth canon, which in the Latin doctrine was *pronuntiatio* or *actio*, it was finally reduced to voice and gesture. (Wilbur Samuel Howell discusses these terms in *Eighteenth-Century British Logic and Rhetoric*, pp. 147-51.) Developing, it is commonly assumed, as a result of criticism of public speaking, especially pulpit oratory, elocution came to hold a place of importance in lectures and handbooks both inside and outside the school curricula for well over two hundred years. As late as the 1920s, children in the United States and Great Britain took elocution. Strange as the practice may seem now, the art of delivery with emphasis on accent, pitch, voice modulation, pause, timing, and gesture became, for many people in the eighteenth century, the whole of rhetoric. The textbooks that developed out of this movement seem ridiculous to modern scholars, but they were quite serious to the eighteenth-century student.

Probably the best discussion of the books and figures associated with the elocutionary movement is that in Wilbur Samuel Howell's *Eighteenth-Century British Logic and Rhetoric* (pp. 143-203). The sources of the movement have interested a number of scholars, and Howell's "Sources of the Elocutionary Movement in England, 1700–1748" (1959) is incorporated into his book. He maintains that the movement grew out of the neoclassical rhetoric and was not consistent with the new rhetorics of the eighteenth century. Frederick W. Haberman, in "English Sources of American Elocution" (1954), acknowledges that the movement came out of the plea for improved public speaking but argues that voice and gesture were measurable physical phenomena and as such were appropriate matters for study in an age of science. G. P. Mohrmann also makes this point in his "The Language of Nature and Elocutionary Theory" (1966). Mohrmann, however, explores the roots of the elocutionary movement and discounts the idea that it arose out of criticisms of public address. Such criticisms, he maintains, had been mounted since the time of Cicero. He asserts that the method of science explains the methods of the elocutionists but not their intense interest in delivery. Mohrmann sees elocutionism as a natural outgrowth of the accepted epistemology and psychology of the period, tracing it particularly to the belief in natural language and Thomas Reid's common-sense philosophy. In another article (1965), Mohrmann argues for the influence of Kames on the elocutionary movement. In his *Elements of Criticism*, Kames either directly or indirectly, according to Mohrmann, foretold "all those postulates that were basic to elocutionary theory" (p. 203). Mohrmann further emphasizes the close personal and professional relationship between Thomas Sheridan and Kames, who had assisted in sponsoring Sheridan's lectures in Edinburgh in 1861. Finally, John Walker, Gilbert Austin, and lesser figures in the elocutionary movement openly acknowledged Kames's influence.

Warren Guthrie's "The Development of Rhetorical Theory in America, 1635-1850-V" (1951) provides, as background, an overview of the elocutionary movement in England, and his 1947 article discusses the influence of John Mason and Thomas Sheridan on rhetoric in six American colleges. Charles A. Fritz, in "From Sheridan to Rush: The Beginnings of English Elocution" (1930), also notes the influence of Joshua Steele, Thomas Sheridan, and John Walker on elocution as it was taught in American schools.

An article by Giles Wilkeson Gray, "What was Elocution?" (1960), defends eighteenth-century elocution theories and states, "The opprobrium heaped upon both theory and practice, at least as far as the originators of that theory, or those theories, may be concerned, has been undeserved" (p. 1). Gray maintains that elocution fell from grace as it became divorced from content and associated only with reading—finally degenerating into "statue-posing" and "bird calls."

Walter J. Ong, S. J., in his 1972 review of Howell's *Eighteenth-Century British Logic and Rhetoric*, connects the rise of elocutionism with the demise of orality and rhetoric and the beginning of a literate society. He maintains, "The elocutionist movement . . . shows in striking ways how the oral management of knowledge, threatened ever since the invention of writing, was by now thoroughly debilitated. . . . By the close of the eighteenth century, orality as a way of life was in effect ended, and with it the old-time world of oratory, or, to give oratory its Greek name, rhetoric" (p. 641). Ong's discussion is certainly the best conceived explanation of elocutionism.

Primary Works and Secondary Scholarship

Michel Le Faucheur's *Traitté de l'action de l'orateur*, first printed in 1657 at Paris, received its first English translation in 1702, and an anonymous pamphlet based on this translation, *Some Rules for Speaking and Action* (London, 1715), had five English editions. This publication marked the beginning of the elocutionary movement in England. Wilbur Samuel Howell discusses subsequent translations of this work in his *Eighteenth-Century British Logic and Rhetoric* (pp. 164–81), and it is clear that it came out under at least three separate titles, *An Essay upon the Action of an Orator* (1702), *The Art of Speaking in Public or an Essay on the Action of an Orator* (1727), and *An Essay upon Pronunciation and Gesture* (1750). *The Art of Speaking in Public* is available on microfilm, *BCRE*, reel 4, item 42.

John Mason's short treatise, *An Essay on Elocution or Pronunciation* (1748), only thirty-nine pages long, is one of the first English works on elocution. Now available on microfilm (*ECS*, roll 87), it went through four editions, the last in 1757.

Two other typical pamphlets of the period are *An Essay on the Action Proper for the Pulpit* (1753) and James Burgh's *The Art of Speaking* (1761). The first, often attributed to John Mason and therefore often indexed under his name, treated *actio* alone, dividing it into the soon to become familiar voice and gesture. It had only one edition and offered practical advice to preachers. James Burgh's longer treatise was written for younger students and had eighteen editions, eleven of them American. Frederick W. Haberman states that Burgh "was read by Sheridan, paraphrased by Walker, anthologized by Scott, pirated by an American publisher, quoted by Austin, and recalled in one way or another by elocutionists for over a century" ("English Sources of American Elocution," p. 114). The nature of these "recalls" is discussed below.

Probably the best known figure in the elocutionary movement of the eighteenth century was Thomas Sheridan, father of the better-known Richard Sheridan, political figure, dramatist, and author of *The Rivals* and *The School for Scandal*. Thomas Sheridan was an actor in Dublin and London, but his main role was as an educator. His three-volume *British Education*, published at London in 1756, urges the revival of the lost art of oratory. He published three works on elocution, the most important of which is *A Course of Lectures on Elocution Together With Two Dissertations on Language* (1762), now available on microfilm (*BCRE*, reel 7, item 67). Sheridan delivered his lectures, according to Wilbur Samuel Howell (*Eighteenth-Century British Logic and Rhetoric*, p. 233), at Oxford, Cambridge, London, Bath, Belfast, and Edinburgh. There were eighteen eighteenth-century editions with sections on articulation, accent, emphasis, pauses and stops, tones, and gestures. In the dissertations on language, Sheridan outlined his plan "to refine, ascertain, and reduce" the English language to a standard.

Sheridan is one of the few members of the elocutionary movement to excite much scholarly interest. He is often treated unsympathetically in biographies of his son, Richard Sheridan, but there are two accounts of his life that put him in a more favorable perspective. One is Wallace A. Bacon's "The Elocutionary Career of Thomas Sheridan (1719–1788)" (1964), and the other is W. Benzie's *The Dublin Orator: Thomas Sheridan's Influence on Eighteenth-Century Rhetoric and Belles Lettres* (1972). Bacon discusses Sheridan's early life and theater career and his *British Education*, in which Sheridan argues "with missionary zeal" for oratory as a panacea. Bacon also covers Sheridan's relations with Dr. Johnson, who dubbed him Sherry-Derry, as well as his *Lectures* and his *Dictionary*. W. Benzie's book, which analyzes the major works mentioned above, demonstrates the farsightedness of Sheridan's views on education and emphasizes his influence on modern lexicography.

Benzie establishes Sheridan as a member of the Natural School of elocution, as opposed to James Burgh, who is classified as the first member of the Mechanical School to issue instructions on how to express various states of emotion. Burgh treats pity in the following manner: "Pity, a mixed passion of love and grief, looks down upon distress with lifted hands; eyebrows drawn down; mouth open; and features drawn together" (*The Art of Speaking*, p. 24).

Joshua Steele, whose *An Essay Towards Establishing the Melody and Measure of Speech to be Expressed and Perpetuated by Peculiar Symbols* appeared in 1775, and John Walker, whose *Elements of Elocution* was published in 1781, were also members of the Mechanical School. Both works are available on microfilm (*BCRE*). Walker's widely circulated text gives careful instructions for expressing certain passions by placement of hands and feet as well as by eye, nose, head, and eyebrow movements. Steele presents a complicated notation system for recording intonation and rhythm patterns somewhat similar to musical notations. In his 1953 article, John Newman argues for the influence of Steele in the development of the Walker-Rush elocutionary movement in America. Certainly this school found its culmination in the work of Gilbert Austin in the nineteenth century.

One of the few disputes in eighteenth-century rhetorical scholarship involves what came to be called "the burglarizing of James Burgh." The dispute was initiated in a 1952 article by Wayland M. Parrish in which he maintained that John Walker only reprinted with very slight revisions most of James Burgh's descriptions of the passions. In a 1965 article, Jack Hall Lamb defended Walker against additional charges of plagiarizing from Steele, and in 1969 David H. Grover defended Walker on all counts, maintaining that he acted as a synthesizer and compiler. In 1976, Mary C. Murphy refuted Parrish's accusation against Walker and maintained that Thomas Sheridan's essay on elocution, included in the introduction to *A Rhetorical Grammar* (1781), is a direct copy of James Burgh's *The Art of Speaking*. Murphy further maintained that Thomas Sheridan, unlike Walker, who acknowledges Burgh, "took credit for the essay by referring to himself in the Preface as 'I' and 'the author'" (p. 141).

A work that should be noted as influential in the United States is Noah Webster's *An American Selection of Lessons in Reading and Speaking*, first published in 1785. It contained a section on elocution and had a wide circulation in the United States as a textbook. Charles Evans's bibliography lists forty editions.

Belletristic Rhetoric

In the second half of the eighteenth century rhetorical theory was dominated by six men: Edmund Burke; Joseph Priestley; Henry Home, Lord Kames; Adam Smith; George Campbell; and Hugh Blair. These men introduced a new rhetoric and were influential in shifting the emphasis from the creative act to the interpretive act and in opening the way for the study of English literature in the nineteenth century. This rhetoric marked the beginning of the theories of literary criticism that developed so richly in the nineteenth and twentieth centuries. Literary criticism would not have been possible without the new rhetoric, which, in turn, would never have come about without the philosophical and psychological theories of the day. The eighteenth century opened up new realms in humanistic thought.

The works of these six men are all preserved and appear in modern editions. Kames, Priestley, and Blair are published in facsimile editions, and the Southern Illinois University Press edition of Campbell's *Philosophy of Rhetoric* is the first modern one of that important work. The lectures of Adam Smith (1762–1763) come down to us only through a set of student notes, which do not cover the full year. In his introduction to the Southern Illinois University Press edition, John Lothian explains that from the handwriting, the lectures appear to be notes taken by a student, "written at speed in the lecture room, and not a fair copy" (p. 195). The editors' introductions to these several editions of eighteenth-century belletristic rhetoric vary widely and will be discussed later.

Four of these six sets are lectures first delivered in the city of Edinburgh, and their authors, Kames, Smith, Campbell, and Blair, were leaders in the Scottish Enlightenment. Edmund Burke was a Londoner, and Priestley was a lecturer at Warrington Academy in northwest England. Finally, many of them are better known for activities other than rhetoric, as I indicate below. It was an age in which the study of rhetoric was the concern of everyone, and these men made important contributions to that study.

Edmund Burke

Edmund Burke, noted statesman and conservative, was a figure of consequence in English political circles of the eighteenth century. He protested the restraint of trade and urged British reconciliation with the American colonies. Born in Ireland, he supported Irish interests as well. His treatise, *A Philosophical Enquiry into the Origin of our Ideas of the Sublime and the Beautiful*, which he started writing before he was nineteen, was published in 1756 when he was only twenty-seven. A second edition appeared in 1757 to which was added "An Essay on Taste." The work had forty-five editions, the last in 1958, edited with an introduction by James T. Boulton.

Burke defines taste as "that faculty or faculties of the mind, which are affected with, or which form a judgment of, the works of imagination and the elegant arts" (1757, p. 5). Burke represents his contemporaries in this view, but Herman Cohen points out that Burke does not specifically view taste as applied only to rhetoric (1958). It is for him a faculty for the appreciation of all the arts. Since Burke's career as a rhetor and a diplomat overshadows his career as a rhetorician, the secondary scholarship tends to concern itself with those aspects of his life. Consequently, his "Essay on Taste" is often treated only peripherally in its relationship to his other major works.

Joseph Priestley

Joseph Priestley, best known as the discoverer of oxygen, is important in the history of rhetorical theory for his *A Course of*

Lectures on Oratory and Criticism (1777). Priestley delivered these lectures in 1762 at the age of twenty-nine at Warrington Academy, one of the important English dissenting academies. In his preface, Priestley supports the Doctrine of the Association of Ideas and applies it to criticism. He acknowledges his debt to Lord Kames and John Ward but argues against the Scottish philosophy of common sense. Although Priestley included a section on elocution in his classroom lectures, it is not part of the published work. The lectures have had only five printings.

These lectures are described by Wilbur Samuel Howell (*Eighteenth-Century British Logic and Rhetoric*, pp. 632–47) and discussed in a lengthy introduction to the Southern Illinois University Press facsimile edition by Vincent M. Bevilacqua and Richard Murphy (1965). The introduction covers Priestley's life and works and the background of the *Lectures*. Called upon to teach at Warrington Academy, according to his biographers, Priestley had no great fondness for his subject of language and belles lettres. He composed his lectures by drawing on a number of materials current at the time, including the lectures of John Ward, John Lawson, and Lord Kames. Therefore, the lectures are eclectic with additions from Priestley's own ideas, particularly on associationism, which he readily applied to his subject.

In "Campbell, Priestley, and the Controversy Concerning Common Sense" (1964), Bevilacqua delineated the common sense/associationism controversy and the effect of that controversy on the rhetorical system of Priestley. There is a dissertation on Priestley by Ross Stafford North (1957), which examines Priestley's views on language and rhetoric in relation to eighteenth-century philosophic thought. Unfortunately, North does not appear to have done any additional work on Priestley.

Henry Home, Lord Kames

Henry Home, Lord Kames, was described by one critic as "having a finger in every bowl of porridge in Scotland" (Bushnell, "Lord Kames and Eighteenth Century Scotland," p. 252). His influence has already been noted in connection with Thomas Sheridan and Adam Smith. Certainly he was important in the age of enlightenment in Scottish thought and in the shift to literary criticism and belles lettres in rhetorical history.

Vincent Bevilacqua's dissertation (1961) presents a full account of Kames's rhetorical theory. He asserts that Kames saw human nature as the unifying principle for his rhetoric. Much of the dissertation appears in other articles by Bevilacqua listed in this bibliography.

A more readily available source of information is Helen Whitcomb Randall's "The Critical Theory of Lord Kames" (1940-1941). Written prior to the discovery of Adam Smith's lecture notes, Randall's work cannot take into account the influence of Kames on Smith, but it provides a biography of Kames, a thirty-five-page analysis of *Elements of Criticism*, and a useful outline of the book's history with quotes from current reviews and letters. Appendixes contain an index of books and authors cited in Kames's work and a list of editions.

Arthur E. McGuinness's *Henry Home, Lord Kames* (1970) is a good summary of the man's life and work. Chapter 3 covers the *Elements*, and chapter 4 considers the alterations that Kames made in traditional rhetorical theory. Howell (1971) does not give much attention to the *Elements of Criticism*, and Robert Voitle's introduction to the facsimile edition (1970) is brief. Randall's discussion (1940–1941) is still the most thorough of this man who is known as the father of literary criticism.

Adam Smith

Adam Smith is best known to the world as an economist and only secondarily as a rhetorician. Smith lectured on rhetoric and belles lettres in the city of Edinburgh from 1748 to 1751. He then moved to the University of Glasgow where he was professor of logic for one year and professor of moral philosophy until 1763. He appears to have delivered the same set of lectures in both professorships. His lectures on rhetoric are not available to us in their full form since Adam Smith ordered that they be destroyed before his death. Fortunately, in 1961, an edition of a student's notes was published with an introduction by John Lothian. The edition was hailed as one of the most valued discoveries of our time, but its impact, whether from imperfect copy or lack of interest, has been disappointing. The edition is incomplete (see discussion under The State of the Primary Works above) and difficult to work with since the individual lectures are only numbered with no titles to indicate their content.

Wilbur Samuel Howell (1971) gives us additional insight into Smith's lectures as seen through the eyes of three of his contemporaries, John Millar, James Woodrow, and Hugh Blair, and further demonstrates their importance in the Scottish enlightenment (pp. 537–75). Lord Kames urged Smith to deliver these lectures in Edinburgh, and Smith was followed in that lectureship by Robert Watson, who left to continue the lectures at the University of St. Andrews, and by Hugh Blair, who was subsequently appointed first Regius Professor of Rhetoric and Belles Lettres at the University of Edinburgh. Thus Adam Smith's lectures set the pattern. Howell concludes, "Smith's rhetorical theory is remarkable for its originality, its validity, and its timeliness" (p. 575).

Among Smith's biographers, there was speculation that he burned his lectures because they had been largely taken over by Hugh Blair. In his introduction to Blair's *Lectures*, Harold F. Harding asserts that plagiarism was not an issue but acknowledges that Blair was influenced by Smith in combining the study of belles lettres with rhetoric.

Two articles by Vincent Bevilacqua furnish excellent material both on the origins of Smith's lectures in eighteenth-century thought and on their influence on Lord Kames and Hugh Blair. "Adam Smith's Lectures on Rhetoric and Belles Lettres" (1965) is a careful analysis of the lectures and makes the point, now generally accepted, that "young Smith appears to have been the teacher and Blair and Kames the students" (p. 59). The other article is "Adam Smith and Some Philosophical Origins in Eighteenth-Century Rhetorical Theory" (1968). In both articles Bevilacqua stresses that Smith reflected eighteenth-century thought more than classical theory and gave impetus to the Scottish belles lettres movement. Smith adapted a stylistic-belletristic view of rhetoric based on eighteenth-century views of ethics, aesthetics, and criticism.

There is one dissertation on "Adam Smith and Belles Lettres" (The University of Mississippi, 1966) by Frank Morgan, Jr.

George Campbell

George Campbell's *The Philosophy of Rhetoric* (1776) is one of the most important rhetorical treatises in the eighteenth century. It was reprinted numerous times and used as a textbook in American colleges well into the nineteenth century. Its direct influence was impressive, but its indirect influence on theories of composition and rhetoric is immeasurable. Its "ends of discourse" still shape twentieth-century composition readers. A 1981 article by John Hagaman outlines the influence of *The Phi-

losophy of Rhetoric on contemporary invention. The *Philosophy* is available in a modern edition in the Southern Illinois University Press Landmark series with an introduction by Lloyd F. Bitzer (1963).

Bitzer points out the importance of Campbell's concept of rhetoric as a "general art of discourse" (p. xiv). He discusses the features of common-sense philosophy, taking in turn Campbell's views on phenomenalism, empiricism, skepticism, sensationalism, and naturalism as well as his theory of human nature.

Campbell is well covered in rhetorical scholarship, although, with the exception of Wilbur Samuel Howell's excellent account in *Eighteenth-Century British Logic and Rhetoric* (pp. 577–612) and Hagaman's work cited above, much of the secondary scholarship is from the sixties. An excellent perspective on Campbell is in the introduction by James Golden and Edward P. J. Corbett to *The Rhetoric of Blair, Campbell, and Whately* (1968), mentioned earlier under the discussion of general works.

Lloyd Bitzer has written one article on the influence of David Hume's philosophy on Campbell and another on Campbell's Doctrine of Evidence as depending on common-sense philosophy (1960, 1969). Clarence W. Edney has also written a number of articles on Campbell, and his "George Campbell's Theory of Logical Truth" (1948) discusses Campbell's logic. Howell takes up the same subject in his discussion of Campbell's view of the syllogism (1971, pp. 401-8).

George Campbell has probably aroused more scholarly interest than any other figure in eighteenth-century rhetoric besides Hugh Blair, and a lively dispute about whether he was a true innovator or only another rhetorician in the classical tradition took place in scholarship in the late 1960s. Douglas Ehninger initiated the discussion with his dissertation (Ohio State, 1949) and two articles from that work (1955, 1963) in which he asserts that Campbell, as well as Blair and Whately, was an anti-classicist and actually reversed that trend in eighteenth-century theory by placing the emphasis on the hearer rather than on the speaker or text. In "George Campbell and the Classical Tradition" (1963), Douglas McDermott supports Ehninger's 1963 position by saying, "In linking rhetoric with the psychological principles of the human mind Campbell may indeed, be said to bring us into new country" (p. 409).

The spring 1968 *Journal of the Western Speech Association* was devoted to a symposium on "The Rhetorical Theory of George Campbell." This issue includes four papers written by Dominic La Russo, Herman Cohen, G. P. Mohrmann, and Phil Dolph, edited with an introduction by Ernest Ettlich. La Russo takes issue with Ehninger and McDermott by asserting that *The Philosophy of Rhetoric* "might well be characterized as an eclectic work which is a product not of a great and original mind, but rather the shadow of a *zeitgeist* that reflects a social and intellectual transition" (p. 86). Ehninger answered La Russo in the fall 1968 issue by reasserting his 1963 position that Campbell is revolutionary as the first influential rhetorician to point the science in a new direction, taking as his starting point the mental processes of the listener. The other two papers in the symposium treat the psychological and philosophical bases of Campbell's rhetoric.

Hugh Blair

In his "Editor's Introduction" to the Southern Illinois University Press facsimile edition of Hugh Blair's *Lectures on Rhetoric and Belles Lettres* (1965), Harold F. Harding remarks that there were "scores of thousands of copies" of these lectures "printed over scores of years" (p. v). Certainly Hugh Blair was by far the most influential of the eighteenth-century Scottish rhetoricians and his work the most widely disseminated, not only in Scotland but in England and the United States as well. The lectures were published in 1783 and reprinted, abstracted, condensed, edited, adapted, and reissued in textbooks for over one hundred years on both sides of the Atlantic. More than any other person, Blair turned the compass of rhetoric in new directions; more than any other name, his is associated with those new directions.

The best introduction to Blair is Harold F. Harding's introduction to the facsimile edition. He discusses the relationship between Blair and Adam Smith and investigates the suggestion by John Rae, Smith's biographer, that Blair's lectures are only a reproduction of Smith's. In this introduction, Harding puts to rest the presumption that Smith burned his lectures to save the reputation of his friend. He points out the similarities in the two sets of lectures, but concentrates on the notable differences. He gives Smith credit for combining the study of rhetoric and belles lettres, an idea followed by all of Smith's successors that had important educational repercussions. Harding asserts that it is natural that Blair's lectures gained fame for him since he "spent a lifetime teaching his subject, practicing it, and, indeed, trying to save souls by it" (p. xxv). Smith's lecture notes, however, "come down to us two centuries later as a literary curiosity." Harding concludes his essay with the statement that Blair was neither "original, comprehensive, nor profound," but that his popularity continued unabated in American classrooms until 1828 (p. xxv).

Warren Guthrie (1948) and Clarence W. Edney (1954) trace the influence of Blair on American rhetoric, and both maintain that American rhetoric was dominated by Blair and Campbell until the middle of the nineteenth century. Robert M. Schmitz has provided us with a book-length study of Hugh Blair, valuable for its list of editions, adaptations, and anthologies of Blair's works, but its date, 1948, precedes John Lothian's discovery of the Adam Smith notes, and therefore Schmitz's study is of limited value.

James Golden is the most authoritative voice on Hugh Blair, and his introduction with Edward P. J. Corbett to *The Rhetoric of Blair, Campbell, and Whately* (1968) furnishes an excellent picture of Hugh Blair in the context of the eighteenth century. Golden, together with Ehninger, has written two articles, one on the extrinsic sources, the other on the intrinsic sources of Blair's popularity (1955, 1956). Blair's lectures were delivered for twenty-four years in Edinburgh, went through more than seventy editions, and were translated into French, Italian, Spanish, and German. These two articles seek a rationale for this popularity.

Future Directions

With the notable exception of Wilbur Samuel Howell's *Eighteenth-Century British Logic and Rhetoric*, most of the scholarship on eighteenth-century rhetoric is outdated. At least 90 percent of the works cited in my bibliography were written before 1970. The material that postdates 1970 is often not central to rhetoric but is concerned with peripheral subjects such as psychology, philosophy, or the Scottish Enlightenment. The fact is that after 1970, the secondary scholarship almost ceases to exist. Few of the insights of modern critics, literary or language scholars, or linguists have been applied to eighteenth-century rhetorical writings, and what scholarship there is is too often patently descriptive. Few questions have been posed; few issues have been raised.

In addition, the scholarship lacks the breadth that comes from different perspectives. Almost all of the work in eighteenth-century rhetoric was done in speech departments in the late 1960s, and, as a result, the scholarship lacks the multidisciplinary variety and richness that one finds in the other periods. Classical rhetoric, for example, includes scholarship from classical studies, philosophy, and intellectual history, and the field of Renaissance rhetoric is greatly enriched by scholarship from English literary scholars. Such is not the case with eighteenth-century rhetorical scholarship. The *Publications of the Modern Language Association* and *Eighteenth-Century Studies in Literature* contain not a single article on rhetoric for this period. The subject of historical rhetoric has been virtually ignored by literary scholars and by recent researchers in speech and communications. As a result, the field is truly barren of fresh perspectives and new insights.

One wonders why a period so important in the study of English literature and the development of critical theory and so crucial to nineteenth- and twentieth-century education has been so abandoned by scholars in other fields, particularly English. The fact is that rhetoric, and especially its development in the elocutionary movement and in freshman composition, is still a bad word in academic circles. Freshman composition, with its emphasis on surface matters of punctuation and spelling, is too close to the tradition of elocution and stylistic rhetoric for English scholars to be comfortable with it. Unaware of the larger philosophic rhetoric, they are still uneasy about being associated with the empty rhetorics of surface form and correctness. As a result, scholarship in rhetoric, of any kind, has not only not been encouraged in English departments, it has been actively discouraged. Of late, a new generation of literary scholars has been spawned who do not disown their rhetorical roots; rather they are unaware of them. To them rhetoric is freshman composition. Prejudices disappear slowly, but those scholars who are interested in the study of language must, in their research quest, sooner or later acknowledge the centrality of historical rhetoric to that study.

The field of research is there for any scholar who is interested in language and its place in humanistic studies and the history of ideas. Certainly the shift in the eighteenth century from a study of the speaker and the text to a study of the reader and the interpretation of the text deserves close scrutiny. This shift occurred also in the study of music. How did the invention of print, the dissemination of books, and the rise of the universities affect this shift? Certainly, the inquiring literary scholar needs to investigate the development of "literature" as a new concept in the eighteenth century. Could the literary scholar find reasons in eighteenth-century rhetoric for the rise of fiction and the development of the novel in this period? Any student interested in human communication cannot help but be intrigued by the shift from oral to written language in rhetorical theory in the eighteenth century. Finally, what effect did the development of psychology in the eighteenth century, the new study of the mind, have on these other changes, and, in turn, what effect did these other changes have on the development of psychology?

All of these are large and important questions and all are interrelated. Possibly no single one can be answered within the scholarly confines of any single discipline, but answers may best come from a number of scholars in a number of disciplines. Answers to one might well help us in answering others. Eighteenth-century rhetoric might well furnish the thread that will connect the past to the present and weave together the rich tapestry of modern language scholarship.

Bibliography

Primary Works

Anon. *The Art of Speaking in Public or an Essay on the Action of an Orator*. London, 1727.

——. *An Essay on the Action Proper for the Pulpit*. London, 1753.

——. *An Essay upon Pronunciation and Gesture, Founded upon the Best Rules and Authorities of the Ancients*. London, 1750.

——. *An Essay upon the Action of an Orator; As to his Pronunciation and Gesture, Useful both for Divines and Lawyers, and necessary for all Young Gentlemen, that study how to Speak well in Publick*. London, 1702.

Blackwall, Anthony. *An Introduction to the Classics*. London, 1718. Reprinted with revisions and additions in Robert Dodsley, *The Preceptor*. London, 1748.

Blair, Hugh. *Lectures on Rhetoric and Belles Lettres*. 2 vols. London and Edinburgh, 1783. Reprinted in facsimile: Harold F. Harding, ed. 2 vols. Southern Illinois University Press Series, Landmarks in Rhetoric and Public Address, edited by David Potter. Carbondale: Southern Illinois University Press, 1965.

Burgh, James. *The Art of Speaking*. London, 1761.

Burke, Edmund. *A Philosophical Enquiry into the Origin of our Ideas of the Sublime and the Beautiful*, 1757. Edited with an introduction and notes by James T. Boulton. Notre Dame: University of Notre Dame Press, 1958.

Campbell, George. *The Philosophy of Rhetoric*. London, 1776. Reprinted: New Edition, London, 1850. New Edition reprinted in facsimile: Lloyd F. Bitzer, ed. Southern Illinois University Press Series, Landmarks in Rhetoric and Public Address, edited by David Potter. Carbondale: Southern Illinois University Press, 1963.

Crousaz, Jean Pierre de. *A New Treatise of the Art of Thinking; Or, a Compleat System of Reflections, Concerning the Conduct and Improvement of the Mind*. 2 vols. London, 1724.

Duncan, William. "The Elements of Logick." In Robert Dodsley, *The Preceptor*. London, 1748.

Gibbons, Thomas. *Rhetoric*. London, 1767.

Hartley, David E. *Observations on Man, His Frame, His Duty, and His Expectations*. London, 1749.

Holmes, John. *The Art of Rhetoric Made Easy: In Two Books*. London, 1739.

Home, Henry, Lord Kames. *Elements of Criticism*. 3 vols. Edinburgh, 1762. Reprinted in facsimile: 3 vols. Anglistica and Americana, A Series of Reprints Selected by Bernhard Fabian et al. Hildesheim and New York: Georg Olms Verlag, 1970.

Hume, David. *A Treatise of Human Nature*. 3 vols. London, 1739–1740.

————. *An Enquiry Concerning the Human Understanding*. London, 1748.

Lawson, John. *Lectures Concerning Oratory Delivered in Trinity College, Dublin*. London, 1758. Reprinted in facsimile: E. Neal Claussen and Karl R. Wallace, eds. Southern Illinois University Press Series, Landmarks in Rhetoric and Public Address, edited by David Potter. Carbondale: Southern Illinois University Press, 1972.

Locke, John. *Essay Concerning Human Understanding*. London, 1690.

Mason, John. *An Essay on Elocution or Pronunciation*. London, 1748.

Priestley, Joseph. *A Course of Lectures on Oratory and Criticism*. London, 1777. Reprinted in facsimile: Vincent M. Bevilacqua and Richard Murphy, eds. Southern Illinois University Press Series, Landmarks in Rhetoric and Public Address, edited by David Potter. Carbondale: Southern Illinois University Press, 1965.

Reid, Thomas. *An Inquiry into the Human Mind, on the Principles of Common Sense*. London and Edinburgh, 1764.

Sheridan, Thomas. *A Course of Lectures on Elocution Together With Two Dissertations on Language*. London, 1762.

Smith, Adam. *Lectures on Rhetoric and Belles Lettres Delivered in the University of Glasgow by Adam Smith Reported by a Student in 1762-63*. Edited by John M. Lothian. Southern Illinois University Press Series, Landmarks in Rhetoric and Public Address, edited by David Potter. Carbondale: Southern Illinois University Press, 1971.

Steele, Joshua. *An Essay Towards Establishing the Melody and Measure of Speech to be Expressed and Perpetuated by Peculiar Symbols*. Piccadilly, 1775.

Walker, John. *Elements of Elocution. Being the Substance of a Course of Lectures on the Art of Reading: Delivered at several Colleges in the University of Oxford*. London, 1781.

Ward, John. *A System of Oratory, Delivered in a Course of Lectures Publicly Read at Gresham College*. 2 vols. London, 1759.

Watts, Isaac. *Logick; Or the Right Use of Reason in the Enquiry after Truth*. London, 1725.

Webster, Noah. *An American Selection of Lessons in Reading and Speaking*. Philadelphia, 1785. Reprinted: 3d ed., Greatly Enlarged. Philadelphia, 1787.

Secondary Works

Bacon, Wallace A. "The Elocutionary Career of Thomas Sheridan (1719-1788)." *SM* 31 (March 1964): 1–53.

Bate, Walter Jackson. *From Classic to Romantic: Premises of Taste in Eighteenth-Century England*. Cambridge: Harvard University Press, 1946.

Benzie, W. *The Dublin Orator: Thomas Sheridan's Influence on Eighteenth-Century Rhetoric and Belles Lettres*. Leeds Texts and Monographs, n.s., edited by A. C. Cawley and R. C. Alston. The University of Leeds School of English, 1972.

Bevilacqua, Vincent M. "Adam Smith and Some Philosophical Origins of Eighteenth-Century Rhetorical Theory." *MLR* 63 (1968): 559-68.

———. "Adam Smith's Lectures on Rhetoric and Belles Lettres." *Studies in Scottish Literature* 3 (July 1965): 41–60.

———. "Campbell, Priestley, and the Controversy Concerning Common Sense." *SSJ* 30 (Winter 1964): 79–98.

———. "Philosophical Assumptions Underlying Hugh Blair's *Lectures on Rhetoric and Belles Lettres*." *WS* 31 (Summer 1967): 150–64.

———. "Philosophical Influences in the Development of English Rhetorical Theory: 1748 to 1783." *Proceedings of the Leeds Philosophical and Literary Society, Literary and Historical Section* 12 (April 1968): 191–215.

———. "Philosophical Origins of George Campbell's *Philosophy of Rhetoric*." *SM* 32 (March 1965): 1–12.

———. "The Rhetorical Theory of Henry Home, Lord Kames." Ph.D. diss., University of Illinois at Urbana-Champaign, 1961.

———. "Two Newtonian Arguments Concerning 'Taste.'" *PQ* 47 (October 1968): 585–90.

Bevilacqua, Vincent, and Richard Murphy. "Editors' Introduction." In *A Course of Lectures on Oratory and Criticism*, by Joseph Priestley, pp. lix–lxix. Carbondale: Southern Illinois University Press, 1965.

Bitzer, Lloyd F. "Editor's Introduction." In *The Philosophy of Rhetoric*, by George Campbell, pp. ix–xxxvii. Carbondale: Southern Illinois University Press, 1963.

———. "Hume's Philosophy in George Campbell's *Philosophy of Rhetoric*." *PR* 2 (Summer 1969): 139–66.

———. "A Re-Evaluation of Campbell's Doctrine of Evidence." *QJS* 46 (April 1960): 135–40.

Boulton, James T. "Editor's Introduction." In *A Philosophical Enquiry into the Origin of our Ideas of the Sublime and the Beautiful*, by Edmund Burke, pp. xv–cxxvii. Notre Dame: University of Notre Dame Press, 1968.

Bowers, John Waite. "A Comparative Criticism of Hugh Blair's Essay on Taste." *QJS* 47 (December 1961): 384–89.

Bradley, Adelbert Edward, Jr. "John Ward's Theory of Rhetoric." Ph.D. diss., Florida State University, 1955.

Bradley, Bert E., Jr. "The *Inventio* of John Ward." *SM* 26 (March 1959): 56–63.

———. "John Ward's Concept of *Dispositio*." *SM* 24 (November 1957): 258–63.

Bushnell, Nelson S. "Lord Kames and Eighteenth Century Scotland." *Studies in Scottish Literature* 10 (April 1973): 241–54.

Claussen, E. Neal, and Karl R. Wallace. "Editors' Introduction." In *Lectures Concerning Oratory*, by John Lawson, pp. ix–liii. Carbondale: Southern Illinois University Press, 1965.

Cohen, Herman. "Hugh Blair's Theory of Taste." *QJS* 44 (October 1958): 265–74. Reprinted in *Readings in Rhetoric*, edited by Lionel Crocker and Paul A. Carmack, pp. 333–49. Springfield, Ill.: Charles C. Thomas, 1965.

———. "The Mirror Image: Eighteenth Century Elocutio and the New Philosophy." *WS* 26 (Winter 1962): 22–27.

———. "William Leechman's Anticipation of Campbell." *WS* 32 (Spring 1968): 92–99.

Corbett, Edward P. J. "John Locke's Contribution to Rhetoric." In *The Rhetorical Tradition and Modern Writing*, edited by James J. Murphy, pp. 73–84. New York: Modern Language Association, 1982.

Dolph, Phil. "Taste and *The Philosophy of Rhetoric*." *WS* 32 (Spring 1968): 104–13.

Edney, Clarence W. "English Sources of Rhetorical Theory in Nineteenth-Century America." In *History of Speech Education in America*, edited by Karl R. Wallace, pp. 80–104. New York: Appleton-Century-Crofts, 1954.

———. "George Campbell's Theory of Logical Truth." *SM* 15 (1948): 19–32.

———. "Hugh Blair's Theory of *Dispositio*." *SM* 23 (March 1956): 38–45.

Ehninger, Douglas. "Campbell, Blair, and Whately: Old Friends in a New Light." *WS* 19 (October 1955): 263–69.

———. "Campbell, Blair, and Whately Revisited." *SSJ* 28 (Spring 1963): 169–82. Reprinted in *Readings in Rhetoric*, edited by Lionel Crocker and Paul A. Carmack, pp. 359–73. Springfield, Ill.: Charles C. Thomas, 1965.

———. "Dominant Trends in English Rhetorical Thought, 1750–1800." *SSJ* 18 (September 1952): 3–12. Reprinted in *Readings in Rhetoric*, edited by Lionel Crocker and Paul A. Carmack, pp. 297–307. Springfield, Ill.: Charles C. Thomas, 1965.

———. "George Campbell and the Revolution in Inventional Theory." *SSJ* 15 (May 1950): 270–76.

———. "George Campbell and the Rhetorical Tradition: A Reply to La Russo." *WS* 32 (Fall 1968): 276–79.

———. "John Ward and His Rhetoric." *SM* 18 (March 1951): 1–16.

Ehninger, Douglas, and James Golden. "The Intrinsic Sources of Blair's Popularity." *SSJ* 21 (Fall 1955): 12–30.

Ettlich, Ernest [Earl], Dominic La Russo, Herman Cohen, G. P. Mohrmann, and Phil Dolph. "Symposium: The Rhetorical Theory of George Campbell." *WS* 32 (Spring 1968): 84–113.

Fritz, Charles A. "From Sheridan to Rush: The Beginnings of English Elocution." *QJS* 16 (February–November 1930): 75–88. Reprinted in *Readings in Rhetoric*, edited by Lionel Crocker and Paul A. Carmack, pp. 319–32. Springfield, Ill.: Charles C. Thomas, 1965.

Golden, James L. "Hugh Blair: Minister of St. Giles." *QJS* 38 (April 1952): 155–60.

Golden, James, and Douglas Ehninger. "The Extrinsic Sources of Blair's Popularity." *SSJ* 22 (Fall 1956): 16–32.

Golden, James L., and Edward P. J. Corbett. *The Rhetoric of Blair, Campbell, and Whately*. New York: Holt, Rinehart and Winston, 1968, 1979.

Grave, S. A. *The Scottish Philosophy of Common Sense*. Oxford: Clarendon Press, 1960.

Gray, Giles Wilkeson. "What was Elocution?" *QJS* 46 (February 1960): 1–7.

Grover, David H. "John Walker: The 'Mechanical' Man Revisited." *SSJ* 34 (Summer 1969): 288–97.

Guthrie, Warren. "The Development of Rhetorical Theory in America, 1635–1850: Domination of the English Rhetorics." *SM* 15 (1948): 61–71.

———. "The Development of Rhetorical Theory in America 1635–1850 –V: The Elocution Movement—England." *SM* 18 (March 1951): 17–30. Reprinted in *The Province of Rhetoric*, edited by Joseph Schwartz and John A. Rycenga, pp. 255–74. New York: The Ronald Press Co., 1965.

———. "The Development of Rhetorical Theory in America, 1635–1850: The Growth of the Classical Tradition, 1730–1785." *SM* 14 (1947): 38–54.

Haberman, Frederick W. "English Sources of American Elocution." In *History of Speech Education in America, *, edited by Karl R. Wallace, pp. 105–26. New York: Appleton-Century-Crofts, 1954.

Hagaman, John. "On Campbell's *Philosophy of Rhetoric* and Its Relevance to Contemporary Invention." *RSQ* 21 (Summer 1981): 145–55.

Harding, Harold F. "Editor's Introduction." In *Lectures on Rhetoric and Belles Lettres*, by Hugh Blair, pp. viii-xl. Carbondale: Southern Illinois University Press, 1963.

———. "English Rhetorical Theory, 1750–1800." Ph.D. diss., Cornell University, 1937.

Hargis, Donald E. "James Burgh and *The Art of Speaking*." *SM* 24 (November 1957): 275–84.

Hooker, Edward Niles. "The Discussion of Taste, from 1750 to 1770." *PMLA* 49 (1934): 577–92.

Horner, Winifred Bryan. "The Eighteenth Century." In *Historical Rhetoric: An Annotated Bibliography of Sources in English*, edited by Winifred Bryan Horner, pp. 187–226. Boston: G. K. Hall, 1980.

Howell, Wilbur Samuel. "Adam Smith's Lectures on Rhetoric: An Historical Assessment." *SM* 36 (November 1969): 393–418. Reprinted with revisions in *Essays on Adam Smith*, edited by Andrew S. Skinner and Thomas Wilson, pp. 11–43. Oxford: Clarendon Press, 1975.

———. "The Declaration of Independence and Eighteenth-Century Logic." *WMQ*, 3d ser., 18 (October 1961): 463–84. Reprinted in *A Casebook on the Declaration of Independence*, edited by Robert Ginsberg, pp. 194–215. New York, 1967. Also reprinted in Wilbur Samuel Howell, *Poetics, Rhetoric, and Logic: Studies in the Basic Disciplines of*

132 / Rhetoric

Criticism, pp. 163–90. Ithaca and London: Cornell University Press, 1975.

———. *Eighteenth-Century British Logic and Rhetoric*. Princeton: Princeton University Press, 1971.

———. *Fénelon's Dialogues on Eloquence: A Translation with an Introduction and Notes*. Princeton: Princeton University Press, 1951.

———. "John Locke and the New Rhetoric." *QJS* 53 (December 1967): 319–33.

———. "Sources of the Elocutionary Movement in England: 1700–1748." *QJS* 45 (February 1959): 1–18. Reprinted with considerable expansion in his *Eighteenth-Century British Logic and Rhetoric*, pp. 143–203.

Jefferson, D. W. "Theories of Taste in the Eighteenth Century." *Proceedings of the Leeds Philosophical and Literary Society, Literary and Historical Section* 5 (1938–1943): 1–9.

Keesey, Ray E. "John Lawson's Lectures Concerning Oratory." *SM* 20 (March 1953): 49–57. Reprinted in *Readings in Rhetoric*, edited by Lionel Crocker and Paul A. Carmack, pp. 283–96. Springfield, Ill.: Charles C. Thomas, 1965.

Lamb, Jack Hall. "John Walker and Joshua Steele." *SM* 32 (November 1965): 411–19.

La Russo, Dominic. "Root or Branch? A Re-examination of Campbell's 'Rhetoric.'" *WS* 32 (Spring 1968): 85–91.

Lehmann, William C. *Henry Home, Lord Kames, and the Scottish Enlightenment: A Study in National Character and in the History of Ideas*. The Hague: Martinus Nijhoff, 1971.

Lothian, John M. "Introduction." In *Lectures on Rhetoric and Belles Lettres Delivered in the University of Glasgow by Adam Smith Reported by a Student in 1762-63*, by Adam Smith, pp. xi-xl. Carbondale: Southern Illinois University Press, 1971.

McDermott, Douglas. "George Campbell and the Classical Tradition." *QJS* 49 (December 1963): 403–9. Reprinted in *Readings in Rhetoric*, edited by Lionel Crocker and Paul A. Carmack, pp. 349–58. Springfield, Ill.: Charles C. Thomas, 1965.

McGuinness, Arthur E. *Henry Home, Lord Kames*. New York: Twayne Publishers, 1970.

McKenzie, Gordon. *Critical Responsiveness: A Study of the Psychological Current in Later Eighteenth-Century Criticism*. University of California Publications in English, 20 (1949).

———. "Lord Kames and the Mechanist Tradition." *Essays and Studies*. University of California Publications in English, 14 (1943): 93–121.

Mohrmann, G. P. "George Campbell: The Psychological Background." *WS* 32 (Spring 1968): 99–104.

———. "Kames and Elocution." *SM* 32 (June 1965): 198–206.

———. "The Language of Nature and Elocutionary Theory." *QJS* 52 (April 1966): 116–24.

Murphy, Mary C. "Detection of the Burglarizing of Burgh: A Sequel." *CM* 43 (June 1976): 140–41.

Newman, John B. "The Role of Joshua Steele in the Development of Speech Education in America." *SM* 20 (March 1953): 65–73.

North, Ross Stafford. "Joseph Priestley on Language, Oratory, and Criticism." Ph.D. diss., University of Florida, 1957.

Ong, Walter J., S. J. "Review of *Eighteenth-Century British Logic and Rhetoric*." *William and Mary Quarterly* 29 (October 1972): 637–43.

Parrish, W[ayland] M. "The Burglarizing of Burgh, or the Case of the Purloined Passions." *QJS* 38 (December 1952): 431–34.

Perrin, Porter Gale. "The Teaching of Rhetoric in the American Colleges before 1750." Ph.D. diss., University of Chicago, 1936.

Randall, Helen Whitcomb. "The Critical Theory of Lord Kames." *Smith College Studies in Modern Languages* 22 (1940–1941).

Reid, Ronald F. "John Ward's Influence in America: Joseph McKean and the Boylston Lectures on Rhetoric and Oratory." *SM* 27 (November 1960): 340–44.

Sandford, William P. *English Theories of Public Address, 1530-1828*. Columbus, Ohio: H. L. Hedrick, 1931.

Schmitz, Robert M. *Hugh Blair*. New York: King's Crown Press, 1948.

Skopec, Eric Wm. "The Theory of Expression in Selected Eighteenth-Century Rhetorics." In *Explorations in Rhetoric*, edited by Ray E. McKerron, pp. 119–36. Glenview, Ill.: Scott, Foresman and Co., 1982.

———. "Thomas Reid's Fundamental Rules of Eloquence." *QJS* 64 (October 1978): 400–408.

———. "Thomas Reid's Rhetorical Theory: A Manuscript Report." *CM* 45 (August 1978): 258–64.

Stone, P. W. K. *The Art of Poetry 1750-1820*. New York: Barnes and Noble, 1967.

Voitle, Robert. "Introduction." In *Elements of Criticism*, by Henry Home, Lord Kames, l:i–xiv. Hildesheim and New York: Georg Olms Verlag, 1970.

5

THE NINETEENTH CENTURY
Donald C. Stewart

Until very recently, scholarship in nineteenth-century rhetoric had no status—in departments of English. Departments of speech, on the other hand, have, for several decades, been producing a steady stream of scholarship in all the historical periods of rhetoric. It is not surprising, therefore, that more than 90 percent of the secondary scholarship in nineteenth-century rhetoric has come out of speech departments. Albert Kitzhaber's doctoral dissertation, "Rhetoric in American Colleges: 1850–1900" (1953), is a case in point. Colleagues in a department of speech would have regarded it as an original contribution to knowledge and an indication that the writer had a promising future in the profession. To his colleagues in English departments, however, it signified nothing more than the author's completion of the terminal degree. Kitzhaber had to discover other ways of establishing himself in the profession of English.

There are discoverable reasons for this phenomenon. In the late nineteenth century the profession of English established itself, first, by overcoming the opposition of entrenched classicists and securing a place alongside modern languages in the college curriculum; second, by separating itself from what it regarded as peripheral to its real interests: oratory and linguistics. By 1947 Wayland Parrish could say, in "The Tradition of Rhetoric," "English teachers . . . have abandoned the very name of rhetoric, and the classical tradition is now completely in our hands" (p. 467). The irony of the situation has been that

Donald C. Stewart is Professor of English at Kansas State University, Manhattan. The author of *The Authentic Voice* (William C. Brown, 1972); "The Nineteenth Century," in *Historical Rhetoric: An Annotated Bibliography of Selected Sources in English,* edited by Winifred Bryan Horner (G. K. Hall, 1980); and "Two Model Teachers and the Harvardization of English Departments," in *The Rhetorical Tradition and Modern Writing,* edited by James J. Murphy (Modern Language Association of America, 1982), he is also the 1983 Chair (President) of the Conference on College Composition and Communication.

the department entrusted with teaching millions of students to write has also been the department which lost touch with the historical tradition that could have informed its work in this area. Very recently, however, it has come to the attention of more and more English departments that those who teach the writing courses are not prepared professionally to do so, and one of the significant gaps in the professional preparation of these instructors is this lack of knowledge of rhetoric's history and its relationship to modern composition programs.

Nineteenth-century rhetoric poses some special problems, the greatest of which is that it has apparently had no intellectual, philosophical, or theoretical center. The problem, in part, has been described by John Elliott Braun in a doctoral dissertation entitled "The Philosophical Roots of the Nineteenth-Century 'Repose' of Rhetoric, with Emphasis on the Idea of Communication in the Thought of Josiah Royce" (1977). He begins his abstract with the following observation: "Historians of rhetorical theory seem to be in implicit agreement that little of philosophical significance to rhetoric developed during much of the nineteenth century. Most analyses of modern theories of rhetoric either ignore the period completely, or assign it to slumbering 'repose.'"

Those who take this position, he says, argue that rhetoric in the nineteenth century didn't adapt itself to two predominant philosophical themes: Kantian subjectivity and Hegelian historicism. But he suggests that the "repose" may not have been what it seems and turns to the work of Franz Theremin, Sören Kierkegaard, Charles Sanders Peirce, and Josiah Royce as correctives.

Interesting as Braun's approach is, it is not a complete description of what happened to rhetoric in the century. The historian of rhetoric in this period has to confront the fact that rhetoric in the nineteenth century splintered into a number of strands, some of which underwent mutations and survived, others of which simply disappeared. I propose to identify these strands, to discuss briefly major representatives of each, to take up significant scholarship dealing with both trends and figures in the century, and, finally, to suggest the direction that future scholarship in this field might take.

At the outset, however, I must point out one significant problem for scholars working in this field. With the exception of J. Jeffery Auer and Jerald L. Banninga's edition of John Quincy

Adams's *Lectures on Rhetoric and Oratory* (1962), and the Southern Illinois University Press's Landmark editions of Gilbert Austin's *Chironomia* (1966), Edward T. Channing's *Lectures Read to the Seniors in Harvard College* (1968), Thomas De Quincey's *Essays on Rhetoric* (1967), Richard Whately's *Elements of Rhetoric* (1963), and Chauncey Allen Goodrich's *Essays from Select British Eloquence* (1963), primary materials are scattered and in generally poor shape. Many are consigned to the rare-book rooms of the libraries which have them, and scholars are dependent on the services of interlibrary loans to acquire these books, even for a short period of time. Availability of materials thus becomes a problem, but not an insurmountable one.

The Primary Works

Turning to the field itself, then, one can detect the following strands of rhetorical theory and practice at various stages in the nineteenth century: (1) classical, (2) elocutionary, (3) psychological-epistemological, (4) belletristic, and (5) practical. I will examine the primary works for each in turn.

Classical Rhetoric

Classical rhetoric as a force in the everyday lives and vocations of people had, of course, been dead since the collapse of the Roman Empire, but the tradition established primarily by Plato, Aristotle, Cicero, and Quintilian had lived on, modified by succeeding ages through the eighteenth century. By the end of the eighteenth century, however, it was nearly defunct, and it survived in a highly visible manner only for about twenty years in the nineteenth century, primarily in the work of the first two holders of the Boylston Chair of Rhetoric at Harvard: John Quincy Adams and Joseph McKean. McKean did not leave any published lectures, but Adams did, in two volumes that never went into a second printing in his lifetime. They reflect Adams's knowledge of the classical tradition and his desire, despite the conflicting pull of political duties, to fulfill his responsibilities as specified in the articles establishing the Boylston Chair. Auer and Banninga, in their edition of Adams's *Lectures on Rhetoric and Oratory*, describe them "as the first attempt by an American to reunite rhetorical theory with classical doctrines" (p. 1). Among the works Adams studied in preparing his lectures were Aristotle's *Rhetoric*; the anonymous *Rhet-*

orica ad Herennium; Quintilian's *Institutes of Oratory;* Cicero's *De Oratore, Orator,* and *Orations;* Plato's *Gorgias, Phaedrus,* and *Protagoras;* Hugh Blair's *Lectures on Rhetoric and Belles Lettres;* George Campbell's *Philosophy of Rhetoric;* John Walker's *Elements of Elocution;* Thomas Sheridan's *Lectures on Elocution;* John Lawson's *Lectures Concerning Oratory;* and Lord Kames's *Elements of Criticism.*

The sequence of lectures indicates clearly the nature of his topics. After an inaugural lecture, he took up an overview of the history of rhetoric and oratory, gave two lectures to objections against eloquence and the origin of oratory, then discussed the Roman rhetoricians, specifically Cicero and Quintilian. The history of rhetoric behind him, he concentrated, in the remainder of his lectures, on specific rhetorical topics: the concept of status, topoi, demonstrative, judicial, deliberative, and pulpit oratory, the qualities of an orator, the parts of a discourse (introduction, narration of facts, argument, refutation, and conclusion), and finally matters of style, primarily figurative language. On the whole, the lectures are a restatement of classical doctrines, but two aspects of them are noteworthy. First, as already noted, they represent an attempt by an American who, although familiar with the British rhetorics, attempted to break away from them. Second, Adams's emphasis on deliberative and judicial oratory reflects the preoccupations and needed competencies of those in an emerging democracy. The lectures were not much noted, however, because of the increasing popularity of the elocutionary movement, which reached its zenith in America in the first half of the nineteenth century.

Elocutionary Rhetoric

The most significant nineteenth-century works on elocution were Gilbert Austin's *Chironomia* (1806) and James Rush's *The Philosophy of the Human Voice* (1827). Austin, an Irish clergyman who conducted a school for the sons of Irish nobility, was a fine scholar with an educational mission: to elevate the study of delivery, particularly physical gesture, to a position equal to that shared by invention, arrangement, style, and memory. "Although the ancient writers have left various and complete systems of rhetoric, as far as relates to the four first divisions, viz. invention, disposition, elocution (that is, choice of language), and memory" he says in his preface to the work, "and although modern writers have expounded, and detailed, and added to all these precepts, insomuch that in every language abundant instructions can be obtained in all that relates to these *four* divisions by every man who studies public speaking; and although within the British islands, in all these divisions, the public speakers have arrived at distinguished excellence; yet it is a fact, that we do not possess from the ancients, nor yet from the labours of our own countrymen, any sufficiently detailed and precise precepts for the *fifth* division of the art of rhetoric, namely, *rhetorical delivery*, called by the ancients *actio* and *pronunciatio.* . . . My object in this work is therefore to contribute my share of labour towards the completion of the rules for the better study and acquisition of rhetorical delivery, the *fifth* and least cultivated, but if we are to believe ancient authorities, not the least important division of the art" (pp. ix–x).

Austin's book is distinguished in two respects. First, he dissected the physical actions of delivery in a way not previously done by developing an elaborate notational scheme for indicating, within an imaginary sphere, a speaker or actor's body, hand, and foot positions (his book contains 122 meticulously drawn sketches), and he gives specific directions for lawyers, preachers, politicians, and actors functioning in their respective spheres. Second, he intended his notational scheme to be a guide for subsequent readers as to the ways certain speeches, both in real life and onstage, were given. In his way, he was attempting to provide a historical record of public speaking similar to what is accomplished today with sophisticated video and audio equipment.

All in all, Austin was a model teacher in that he combined knowledge of his subject, a historical sense of educational methods and purposes, and a willingness to experiment with new modes.

Rush is unique in that he was a medical doctor who wrote his book in the odd bits of time he was able to eke out of his medical practice over the course of three years. The book is characterized by clarity of purpose, attention to the minute details of voice use, and an ironic wit that expresses Rush's skepticism that teachers of elocution will pay any attention to, much less make use of, the insights in his book. General scholarly opinion is that his book was heeded, but only superficially by too many of those it was written to serve.

Rush states his purpose early and fully: "In the following essay, the reader will find an analysis of the human voice, which will enable an Elocutionist of any nation, to reduce to established form, the best modes of speech in his language. He will also find the outline of a system of principles that I have ventured to propose, upon a survey of those excellencies of utterance, which are accommodated to the temper and habits of the English ear; and which, in analogy with the above named arts, may be called the Ideal Beauty of speech" (pp. xxiii–xxiv). He is quite clearly annoyed with those for whom "the high accomplishments in Elocution are supposed to be, universally, the unacquired gifts of genius, and to consist of powers and graces 'beyond the reach of art.' So seem the plainest services of arithmetic to a savage" (p. xxvi). In general, common sense, a passion for scientific accuracy, and scorn of romantic and imprecise language characterize Rush's introduction.

The body of the text contains very precise descriptions of the pitch, timbre, glides, and other sounds of the human voice with frequent use of musical terms and analogies to explain the concepts. Rush believed he had given elocution a scientific basis if its practitioners and teachers would only be willing to study his system and apply it, although he indicated frequently that he did not think they would. However, both Austin and Rush were far more influential than they thought they would be, and their works are still regarded as the finest treatises on elocution in the nineteenth century.

Psychological-Epistemological Rhetoric

A third strand of nineteenth-century rhetoric, the psychological-epistemological, is exemplifed in Richard Whately's *Elements of Rhetoric* (1828). Whately is often linked with Blair and Campbell, the three of them generally being regarded as the most influential rhetoricians of the period between 1780 and 1880. There are three times as many published scholarly articles on Whately as there are on any other nineteenth-century rhetorical figure, and despite the fact that only three individuals are responsible for eleven different pieces on Whately, he is the only figure of the period about whom one can say that a body of scholarship is developing.

In the Southern Illinois University Press Landmarks edition of Whately's *Rhetoric*, Douglas Ehninger identified six significant characteristics of the book: (1) it is an ecclesiastical rhetoric with service of the Cross, not Caesar, in view; (2) it focuses persistently upon the "problems and methods of oral argumentation" (xii); (3) unlike Campbell's *Philosophy of Rhetoric,* its predecessor, it is a practical textbook, not a theoretical inquiry into the nature of communication; (4) it underwent continuous revision, its seven editions spanning a third of a century; (5) it is uneven, the sections on the nature of rhetoric, logic, and delivery being the strongest, those on persuasion and style the weakest; and (6) it rejects the elocutionary and belletristic traditions in rhetoric but endorses and carries to its logical completion the psychological-epistemological tradition.

> For while in denying rhetoric an investigatory method of its own Campbell and Priestley had made it exclusively a managerial science, these writers had left unformulated the principles and methods of 'management' as they apply in the crucial area of invention.
>
> Accepting the challenge thus posed, Whately developed an inventional system aimed at systematizing the selection and application of cogent 'reasons,' just as the ancients had systematized the process of choosing an appropriate argumentative position and discerning the proofs inherent in it. (xxviii)

Whately's book, while not dominating the field of rhetorical instruction throughout the rest of the nineteenth century, was a consistent force in the period. James Berlin in 1980 argued that Whately's ideas on rhetoric were among those shaping the composition course that developed in the late nineteenth century and persists today.

Belletristic Rhetoric

Belletristic rhetoric, that which focused primarily on style and the criticism of literature, is a fourth discernible strand in nineteenth-century rhetoric. It is significant because it contributed strongly to the movement that eventually established departments of English. I divide major works in this strand into two categories: those that are primarily theoretical; and those that are essentially textbooks with a belletristic emphasis.

The figure of greatest stature in this area is clearly the English essayist Thomas De Quincey, whose five essays on rhetoric were first gathered together in 1889–1890 in David Masson's *The Collected Writings of Thomas De Quincey.* Fred Newton Scott in *De Quincey's Essays on Style, Rhetoric, and Language* (1893) and Helen Darbishire in *De Quincey's Literary Criticism* (1909) are the only other individuals to collect these essays before Frederick Burwick edited them for the Landmarks edition.

The essays are entitled "Rhetoric," "Style," "Language," "Conversation," and "A Brief Appraisal of the Greek Literature in Its Foremost Pretensions." Burwick notes several important features of the essays as a collected body of material on rhetoric. First, their emphasis is belletristic, not oratorical. Second, De Quincey developed the essays from his own idea of the nature of the informal essay, which, he said, began in a paradox and was developed with polemical skill. A paradox De Quincey defined as some truth which ran counter to general opinion. "Thus in *Rhetoric* (1828), we find De Quincey correcting the popular misconceptions of rhetoric and basing his own definition on an interpretation of Aristotle that counters much scholarly opinion. The essay on *Style* (1840–41) opens with an argument against the British notion that manner and matter are separate entities in composition. The same argument is continued in *Language* (n.d.), where he also discusses misconceptions concerning the national attributes of languages. In *Conversation* (1847), the paradox is that conversation as a fine art depends not upon brilliant speech, but upon a rhetoric of sympathy and association. And in *A Brief Appraisal of the Greek Literature* (1838–39), he examines the negative aspects of Greek poetry, prose, and oratory often ignored in the general veneration of Grecian culture" (*Essays on Rhetoric*, p. xii). Burwick makes one other observation of considerable significance about these essays, that there is a common philosophical and intellectual thread running through them. "De Quincey's signal contribution to the history of rhetoric is that he brought together for the first time the principal elements of Scottish associationism and German aesthetics" (p. xiii).

One should also note that De Quincey's essays are full of factual errors—his prodigious memory occasionally betrayed him—and genuinely entertaining writing. His account of German rhetoric (he likens it to the phenomenon of snakes in Iceland—there are none) and of the German sentence is a breath of fresh air to one accustomed to reading the more ponderous prose of solemn rhetoricians: "Every German regards a sentence in the light of a package, and a package not for the mailcoach but for the waggon, into which his privilege is to crowd as much as he possibly can. Having framed a sentence, therefore, he next proceeds to *pack* it, which is effected partly by unwieldly tails and codicils, but chiefly by enormous parenthetic involutions. All qualifications, limitations, exceptions, illustrations, are stuffed and violently rammed into the bowels of the principal proposition. That all this equipage of accessaries is not so arranged as to assist its own orderly development no more occurs to a German as any fault than that in a package of shawls or carpets the colours and patterns are not fully displayed. To him it is sufficient that they are *there*" (*Essays on Rhetoric*, p. 122).

A small but controversial and influential theoretical work on rhetoric was Herbert Spencer's "The Philosophy of Style," which appeared unsigned in the *Westminster Review* in October 1852. In it he amplified his principle of the economy of style. The ultimate criterion of a good style, he said, is that it presents ideas so that they can be understood by the reader with the least possible mental effort. A style that calls attention to itself and is difficult causes the reader to expend mental energy better applied to assimilating the idea the words are expressing.

It is an intriguing hypothesis but one which occasionally led Spencer into chauvinistic remarks on a topic like the proper collocation of a substantive and its adjective. He argued, for example, that English's "the black horse" is superior to its French equivalent, "un cheval noir," because "cheval," coming first, generates certain pictures (perhaps brown, gray, or spotted horses) that have to be checked by the following "noir," whereas "black," preceding "horse," inclines the mind to be receptive to what black object follows. The naiveté of this kind of psychology is apparent and amusing to the sophisticated linguist today who is not so certain about the structure of the mind and of language acquisition and use as Spencer was more than a century ago.

Spencer, assuming the superiority of his principle of economy, however, went on to illustrate its validity and usefulness through the examples of inverted sentence forms, figures, and the brevity of poetry, which is what makes poetry superior to prose. He also put forth a principle of organic unity in composition, a unity derived from a great writer's intuitive perception of how often and in what circumstances to employ principles of economy. On this matter, Fred Newton Scott was to link Spencer with Plato (otherwise very strange bedfellows), who stated the principle of organic unity in the *Phaedrus* when he said that a composition should have a body and appropriate head and feet (see "Rhetoric Rediviva").

A third belletristic work, highly theoretical and little known but of far greater significance than has generally been recognized, was Gertrude Buck's doctoral dissertation under Fred N. Scott, published as *The Metaphor—A Study in the Psychology of Rhetoric* (1899). Albert R. Kitzhaber, the only one who appears to have studied Buck's paper, calls it the only serious attempt in that era to solve "the essential problem of the nature and function of figurative language" ("Rhetoric in American Colleges: 1850–1900," p. 282). Drawing on the data of the experimental psychology of her time, Buck first attacked the assumption that metaphor was a response to the essential poverty of language, that it expressed a need for ornamentation in language. Her most provocative, and perhaps most profound, insight was that metaphor was not mechanical but organic, that it developed out of undifferentiated language into a clearly differentiated structure. She questioned traditional assumptions about the aesthetics of the metaphor, and she rejected the notion of mixed metaphors, which she said were never mixed in the mind of the person who produced them. Recognizing the shortcomings of the study, especially from a modern point of view, Kitzhaber concluded by observing, "Buck deserves much credit for her courage in brushing away the accumulated dust of well over two thousand years and for making an earnest attempt to attack the subject of metaphor from a wholly new point of view, bringing to bear on it the most recent and most pertinent information she could find, even though that knowledge was drawn from another discipline. In a period when rhetorical theory was becoming steadily more isolated from other fields of knowledge, Buck's attitude was unusually and commendably independent" (p. 291). That "unusual and commendable independence," it is likely, was in no small measure attributable to the two individuals Buck acknowledges as having directed her work and given her the fundamental philosophic considerations in it: Scott and John Dewey.

Edward T. Channing's *Lectures Read to the Seniors in Harvard College* (1856) revealed how far the third Boylston Professor of Rhetoric had departed from the charge originally accepted by John Quincy Adams. Channing seems to have rejected much of classical rhetoric, in particular the topics for invention (because he believed that no great thinker needed artificial aids to develop his subjects) and the essential function of rhetoric in an oral society. His first lecture clearly revealed his perceptions of the ancient orator as one who employed a variety of stratagems to accomplish his will with an undisciplined mob. The modern writer he perceived as one laboring in the quiet of his study writing for an unseen audience and moving them with sweet reason.

In Channing's defense it can be said that he sought to adapt rhetoric to the needs of his time which meant, specifically, observing and experiencing human nature and adjusting rhetoric accordingly. His perceptions about human nature seem to have been strongly influenced by the Scottish philosopher Thomas Reid, who was also an influence in the work of Blair, Campbell, and Whately. Channing viewed rhetoric as a comprehensive art affecting all communication in language, and this conception determined the nature of his teaching. He was evidently a believer in faculty psychology, the notion that the mind was strengthened by exercise of its primary faculties, and he apparently thought that students would profit most from writing on provocative subjects of interest to them. In this respect he would be a thoroughly modern teacher of composition.

Despite the fact that Channing kept literary criticism as an after-class activity, a number of his lectures were of this kind, and it is noteworthy that his successor, Fancis Child, gravitated immediately to literary scholarship and never looked back. The belletristic interests of the third Boylston professor had prepared the way for the fourth's eventually becoming Harvard's first professor of English.

Two belletristically oriented textbooks widely used in the nineteenth century deserve mention here. The first, Alexander Jamieson's *A Grammar of Rhetoric and Polite Literature* (1820), was divided into seven books: Of Language and Style and the Foundation of Eloquence; Of the Structure of Language, or the Principles of General Grammar; Of the Nature and Structure of Sentences, the General Principles of Perspicuity, and the Harmony of Periods; Of Figures; On the Nature of Taste and the Sources of Its Pleasures; General Characters of Style; and Poetry. Book 1 contains a very romantic and unscientific account of the differences between primitive and modern language (an account essentially based on the doctrine of the perfectability of man), and it even becomes somewhat humorous in its use of examples from the poems of Ossian to illustrate the highly metaphorical aspect of primitive languages. Book 2 is a predictable treatment of Latin-based grammar, a discussion of national, reputable, and present usage, which seems heavily indebted to Campbell, and of the virtues and faults of style, which comes straight from Blair. The discussion of sentence grammar in book 3 is unoriginal and Latinate, and the author's exposition of such topics as strength, harmony, and unity in sentences; figures of writing; taste; kinds of styles (dry, plain, neat, elegant, and flowery); and the directions for forming a good style reflect even more clearly his indebtedness to Blair, Campbell, and Lord Kames. Jamieson concentrates primarily on arrangement, style, and delivery, particularly on style, and ignores invention and memory. All in all, Jamieson's work does not have any fresh ideas about rhetoric, but the presentation must have been appealing to those who used it as a text. It went through nearly sixty editions in the nineteenth century.

Samuel Newman's *A Practical System of Rhetoric* (1827) was the first American text for written composition. Its emphasis is practical, and its subject is, primarily, style. Newman implies that previous books on rhetoric did not balance theory with practice, hence his decision to explain the rules for forming a good style, then to illustrate them with examples, and finally to ask students to apply the theory and practice they had supposedly learned.

The introduction of the book does take a modern view toward the priorities of good writing. First comes substance, then arrangement, then style. And Newman clearly implies that a major fault of bad writing is a lack of knowledge. But his book concentrates primarily on forming a good style from prose models, a time-honored practice, and his recommendations that students should be familiar with the best models of style and compose frequently and with care were not particularly original even at that time.

Practical Rhetoric

Of the last set of primary works to be discussed here, one can only say that while some or all are touched by the kinds of rhetorical theory already cited—classical, psychological-epistemological, or belletristic (since they are textbooks for written composition they would, by necessity, not be touched by the work of the elocutionists)—they come down to us today as the ancestors of our modern composition textbooks. They are the originators and carriers of a tradition in composition called "current-traditional" rhetoric by Daniel Fogarty, a tradition that, according to Richard Young, is under fire for its failure to adequately describe the composing process or deal effectively with invention (see "Paradigms and Problems: Needed Research in Rhetorical Invention").

A major work in this category is, of course, Alexander Bain's *English Composition and Rhetoric*, which went through several editions from the time of its first publication in 1866 into the 1890s. Bain, who was primarily a psychologist and logician but who occupied the chair of rhetoric at Aberdeen, saw his book as being more closely allied to the works of Blair, Campbell, and Whately than to recent books in the field. This is a curious observation because one might have a much more difficult time establishing a common link between these three than is superficially apparent. Blair is the spokesman for belletristic rhetoric and Campbell the godfather of psychological-epistemological rhetoric. Although Whately follows in that line, he differs from Campbell on a number of important issues. Perhaps Bain sought association with his three predecessors because of their prestige. If he wanted to exert influence equal to theirs on the teaching of written composition, he certainly succeeded. More than any of his contemporaries, he established two features of composition teaching which have persisted with remarkable tenacity: the concept of the organic paragraph and separating discourse into the so-called forms of discourse: narration, description, exposition, and argument. Bain adds a fifth category, poetry, which was employed only sometimes. Only in very recent years have the modes of discourse been challenged—by James Britton, Kitzhaber, and most recently Robert Connors, who catalogs their rise and fall—but they continue to persist, on the surface, at least, in many modern textbooks.

Bain's rules for paragraph construction are still being presented, particularly the concept of the topic sentence indicating the subject of a paragraph, his insistence that paragraphs should be formed around a single idea, and the notion that sentences within a paragraph should bear on this single idea. He rejects invention as part of rhetoric—the burden of finding subject matter belongs to other disciplines (perhaps those that are to provide the information dealt with in expository paragraphs: mathematics, natural philosophy, chemistry, physiology, natural history, and the human mind)—and even says that the English teacher cannot provide the student with a fund of expression.

Rhetoric he defines as the means whereby spoken or written language is made effective. Its ends are to inform, to persuade, and to please, and they correspond to the three departments of the mind: the understanding, the will, and the feelings. Clearly, this early and influential text was dominated by faculty psychology, but while that emphasis may have disappeared, Bain's forms of discourse and rules for paragraphing are with us yet. The most serious challenge to the latter was provided by Richard Braddock in 1974 (see "The Frequency and Placement of Topic Sentences in Expository Prose"), but many recent textbooks have still not responded to Braddock's challenge.

David J. Hill's *The Science of Rhetoric* (1877), published slightly over a decade after the first edition of Bain's *Rhetoric,* differs from other composition texts of the era in that it is identified by its author as "a systematic presentation of laws of discourse for advanced classes," not as a beginning text.

Hill rejected several contemporary notions of the nature and function of rhetoric. For example, he argued that Whately limited rhetoric by treating it as a branch of logic, Blair by making it a department of applied aesthetics, and Theremin by linking it to ethics. These are incomplete perceptions of rhetoric, according to Hill. "The specific province of the rhetorician is to render given ideas effective in producing mental changes in others. Rhetoric treats of thought militant. Logic furnishes conceptions which are formally *true*; aesthetics, conceptions which are *beautiful*; ethics, conceptions which are *just.* Rhetoric takes these conceptions and establishes them in the mind of another" (p. 3).

Hill then rejected the traditional categories of rhetoric. No useful rules for invention can be given, he believed; disposition (arrangement or organization) depends on the nature of the subject (the traditional five-part structure of the classical oration—introduction, narration of facts, argument, refutation, and conclusion—he found too mechanical to be useful and not adaptable to a variety of composing situations, a point with which I would agree); taste, beauty, and sublimity belong to aesthetics, not rhetoric; elocution is too important in itself to be taken up as a part of rhetoric; study of the history and origin of language is of little use to the person who must employ it for rhetorical purposes; the study of genres is not too productive; and terms such as *purity, propriety, precision, clearness,* and *vivacity* are too vague for his purposes.

At this point, one might well wonder just what Hill thought rhetoric was. In his text, although it appears to be dominated by the forms of discourse codified by Bain, Hill gave this answer: "The rhetorical process extends farther than the mere *presentation* of ideas; it is complete only when those ideas *are referred to the preexisting ideas* of the person addressed in such a manner that they will effect the desired change. All mental laws take place in accordance with certain laws. As an *art,* Rhetoric communicates ideas according to these laws; as a *science,* it discovers and establishes these laws. Rhetoric is, therefore, the science of the laws of effective discourse" (p. 37). His book is, then, organized around laws of mind, of idea, and of form. Under laws of mind he discussed *reason, imagination,* and *memory.* The laws of idea he separated into ideas of individual objects and general notions. His law of form was essentially derived from Herbert Spencer's principle of economy, which Hill translated thus: "That form of language is most excellent which yields its contained idea with the least expenditure of mental energy" (p. 147).

On the whole the book is an attempt to establish rhetoric on a primitive psychological basis. In that sense, although the psychology Hill accepted has long been rejected, the book anticipates modern work, particularly the linking of cognitive psychology and the composing process.

Adams Sherman Hill, the fifth Boylston Professor of Rhetoric and no relation to David Hill, exerted more influence on late nineteenth-century rhetorical theory and practice than he should have. He had taken two degrees from Harvard and was a practicing journalist when Charles William Eliot called him to return to his old school as an assistant to Francis Child. When Child was offered Harvard's first chair of English literature in 1876, Hill was elevated into the Boylston Chair. His *The Principles of Rhetoric and Their Application,* first published in 1878 and modified in the second edition of 1895, was the principal freshman rhetoric text at Harvard for more than thirty years. The book focused on principles of style, particularly word choice, and Hill's dogmatic judgments about usage and editorial correctness. In the 1895 edition he added sections on the forms of discourse because practically every textbook of that period was including them. Hill's book is well written, but it does not contain a single fresh idea about rhetoric, even for that era, and it severely limited the conception of what rhetoric should be. But it became one of a few books whose influence shaped early twentieth-century perceptions of what the study of rhetoric should be (he excluded invention and did very little that was significant with arrangement), essentially a study of style and editing, and thus contributed to the movement which, consciously or unconsciously, separated rhetoric as taught in the schools from meaningful acts of communication in real life.

John Genung of Amherst, not so dogmatic as Hill, produced a small rhetoric in 1885 whose success prompted him to amplify it into *The Practical Elements of Rhetoric* of 1886, another of the late nineteenth-century texts that greatly influenced the teaching of composition in American schools in the early twentieth century. A point should be made at this time. I began talking about works that were influential in the history of nineteenth-century rhetoric. The term *rhetoric* is shifting to *composition* in this discussion of late nineteenth-century works, however, because rhetoric, as discussed in the treatises of Blair, Campbell, and Whately, for example, was ceasing to exist. What was left of the rhetorical tradition was carried on by the elocutionists— who were in the process of forming their own national professional organization in speech—and through the composition texts written by those in English departments who were much involved in this work.

Genung split rhetoric into the study of style and invention. Style he defined as follows: "Under this heading are discussed the various rhetorical principles that are developed from grammars: how to use words and figures, and how to build them together so as to impart to the whole a desired power and quality. The sphere of the work of style is the construction of sentences and paragraphs" (p. 7).

Genung tied invention to logic and to what I would call principles of arrangement: thesis statements, introductions, development, and conclusions; and to the forms of discourse he labeled narration, description, exposition, argument, and persuasion. He distinguished argument developed through rigorous logic from practical persuasion, which one uses when the force of logic fails. In this work he acknowledged the influence of Bain.

Genung rejected invention as a process of generating material on a subject: "The first stage, the finding of material by thought or observation, is the fundamental and inclusive office of invention, the distinctive power that we designate in the popular use of the term. Herein lies obviously, the heart and centre of literary production; it is what the writer finds, in his subject or in the world of thought, that gauges his distinction as an author. *Yet this is of all processes, the one least to be invaded by the rules of the text-book.* It is a work so individual, so dependent on the peculiar aptitude and direction of the writer's mind, that each one must be left for the most part to find his way alone, according to the impulse that is in him. . . . Such invention is incommunicable by teaching" (p. 217; italics mine).

Genung's book is a congenial one, well written and devoid of the dogmatic tone that characterizes Hill's book, but it, too, does not contain a really fresh approach to the study of rhetoric. Yet it was a significant force in composition teaching for decades.

A. S. Hill's contemporary at Harvard, Barrett Wendell, made his contribution to the teaching of writing in *English Composition,* a series of lectures given at the Lowell Institute in November and December 1890. The book has had an enduring influence on subsequent composition textbooks, both because of its organization and because of three concepts that emerged from it. Wendell defined style as "the expression of thought and feeling in the written word" and expressed his belief that modern style was the result of a struggle between good use and principles of composition. In discussing style he took up, in order, the word, the sentence, the paragraph, and the whole composition, a still popular pattern. "Each of these elements," he says, "I shall examine in detail, inquiring first how far it is affected by the paramount authority of good use and then how within the limits of good use it may be made, by means of the principle of composition or otherwise, to assume various forms and to perform various offices" (pp. 39, 40).

He developed another set of concepts, Unity, Coherence, and Mass (later converted to Emphasis by his contemporaries), the acquisition of which he felt contributed to clearness, force, and elegance in writing. It is quite clear that Wendell gives no thought to invention as the technique of generating ideas for writing, and his discussion of arrangement, particularly in the paragraph and the whole composition, is heavily indebted to Bain, whom he acknowledges.

Like Hill, Wendell exerted a tremendous influence on twentieth-century composition practice, and, indirectly, he influenced another trend that has had considerable vogue in later years. One of his students, Henry Pearson, was thoroughly taken with Wendell's method of teaching writing, but he wanted to make one significant change: to invert the order in which the topics were taken up. Pearson's *The Principles of Composition* (1897) has the basic Wendellian concepts, but he began with the whole composition and worked down, through the paragraph, to the sentence, to the word. Pearson thought this was more sound psychologically than the other method. So did Sheridan Baker of Michigan, who, in his *Practical Stylist* (1966), later amplified into *The Complete Stylist*, worked from the big end of the composition triangle to the small. Judging from the number of schools that have adopted Baker's book, one would have to say that this approach is still popular.

Two other works in the composition/rhetoric strand at the end of the nineteenth century deserve attention. The first, Edwin Lewis's *The History of the English Paragraph* (1874), was the only scholarly study of this unit of discourse in the nineteenth century. Lewis studied seventy-three prose writers and came away with the following conclusions: (1) the paragraph emerged and gained popularity because it was more economical than the long periodic sentence; (2) writers have recognized, from the beginning, a unit of discourse longer than the sentence; (3) loose paragraphs (those in which the subject is stated first and then developed) have been more popular than those constructed differently; (4) Tyndal was the first English writer to have any sense of the paragraph; (5) the average number of words per paragraph had not changed significantly at the time of his study; (6) the modern paragraph had been influenced by a medieval tradition that a paragraph distinguishes a stadium of thought.

The significance of the study was that it attempted to define the paragraph in a scientific and scholarly way. Unfortunately, the paragraph theory of the textbooks became classroom gospel, and paragraph theory atrophied at the turn of the century. Only recently have scholars attempted some systematic and descriptive accounts of what the paragraph as a unit of discourse really is.

A second important work in this strand, Fred Scott and Joseph Denney's *Paragraph-Writing* (1893), grew out of classroom exercises developed by the two when they were beginning their teaching careers at Michigan. Scott stayed in Ann Arbor for the rest of his life, but Denney went to Ohio State where he had a distinguished career as professor of English, head of the department, and eventually dean of the College of Arts and Sciences. The first edition of *Paragraph-Writing* (1891) came out in response to the demand from teachers in preparatory schools and colleges. However, according to the authors, the book "goes farther. Its aim is to make the paragraph the basis of a method of composition, to present all the important facts of rhetoric in their application to the paragraph" (p. iii).

Scott and Denney promoted the idea of teaching the paragraph as a theme in miniature. There were two distinct advantages in this method, one for students, one for teachers. Scott's sister Harriet, principal of the Detroit Training School for Teachers, had reported that children learning to read comprehended a paragraph-group or sequence of sentences better than single sentences. Both single sentences out of context and longer units of discourse were more difficult for them to comprehend than a paragraph. Scott and Denney also argued that students had far less trouble producing a paragraph than a longer piece of discourse, but that in producing a paragraph they would be required to do all that the longer unit required. Thus, the paragraph, both for student comprehension and for production, seemed the ideal unit of discourse to work with. There was a practical benefit for teachers, also. They were caught in the middle of the back-to-basics movement of the era, and paper grading had become impossible. The paragraph proved to be a much more manageable assignment for teachers to grade, and many more could be assigned than themes.

In all of this, Scott and Denney were doing nothing particularly new to the modern composition teacher, and they acknowledged the influences of Bain, D. J. Hill, A. S. Hill, and Barrett Wendell, but they provided one chapter not found in discussions of paragraphs at that time: a section which tried to discover some psychological bases for paragraphing. They defined an essay as "the result of sustained movement of a writer's thought toward a definite goal" (p. 96) but noted intermediate stages in this movement. These are the paragraph divisions, and they can occur in a variety of patterns, which Scott and Denney diagram. While not as sophisticated as some contemporary models (the Pitkin paragraph, for example) they show these authors thinking along lines congenial to modern composition theorists but almost unique in their own time.

Secondary Works

Turning from the primary to the secondary work, we can say that the most notable feature of scholarship in nineteenth-century rhetoric is its relative absence. There are those, of course, who would argue that this absence is justified; there is very little in nineteenth-century rhetoric that merits serious scholarly inquiry. I do not share that point of view. As we have seen, some rather significant events in the history of rhetoric occurred in the nineteenth century. The classical tradition nearly vanished and was supplanted by a variety of emphases already cited: the psychological-epistemological emphasis that George Campbell originated and Richard Whately carried on in his own way; the belletristic emphasis coming from Hugh Blair, which was reinforced by, and, in my judgment, may have prepared the way for, the increased interest in literary criticism that has been the preoccupation of English departments in the twentieth century; the elocutionary movement that prepared the way for modern speech departments; and finally the emergence of practical composition which, because of the direction it took and the lack of prestige it came to have, reduced rhetoric almost to copyreading and correcting of usage. The latter event is most significant because it represented a break with a significant intellectual tradition. As I have pointed out already, those in speech departments were keeping their contact with the tradition of rhetoric, but those in English departments, charged with teaching students to write, lost sight of the tradition and the major documents in it. More than anything else, that loss of contact with the tradition among those who taught composition was the cause of the sterility of composition instruction noted by Kitzhaber and the phenomenon cited by many but expressed best by Paul Bryant who, in an article called "A Brand New World Every Morning," likened many contemporary composition instructors who keep reinventing the wheel to farmyard geese.

Joseph Duffey, chairman of the National Endowment for the Humanities, recently told a Presidential Task Force on the Arts and the Humanities, "The humanities have to do with memory, with the sense of history and heritage, a sense of civilization itself. The importance of the areas of learning which make these qualities possible must not be underestimated. A loss of memory is as much of a handicap to a nation, as to an individual.

Amnesia is a debilitating affliction for a nation as well as an individual" ("Some Remarks," pp. 1–2). The point I have been trying to make is that a profession cannot afford a loss of memory either; unfortunately, teachers of English composition have suffered a bad case of amnesia when it comes to any knowledge of nineteenth-century rhetoric and composition. They simply do not know the roots from which the course they teach grew and thus are unprepared to evaluate what they now do in terms of the long tradition of rhetoric or even as a modification of what developed a century ago.

The scholarship that does exist can be divided into studies that attempt to generalize about specific periods or topics, and studies that examine individual authors.

Between 1949 and 1974 there were eight studies that attempted to generalize broadly about rhetoric in the nineteenth century. The fourth section of Warren Guthrie's "The Development of Rhetorical Theory in America, 1635–1850" deals with the emergence of an indigenous American rhetoric in the early nineteenth century as Americans were breaking away from the British. In 1954 John Hoshor amplified the thesis of the Guthrie study in "American Contributions to Rhetorical Theory and Homiletics." Ronald Reid and Paul Ried completed studies on Harvard's Boylston Chair of Rhetoric in the same year, 1959, each of them concerned with the way changes in the holders of the chair reflected changing perceptions of rhetoric in the nineteenth century. Hal Weidner's doctoral dissertation, "Three Models of Rhetoric" (1975), traces the evolution of eighteenth- and nineteenth-century rhetorical theory from what he calls traditional (Aristotelian) to mechanical (Campbellian) to vitalistic (essentially an attitude favoring inspiration and rejecting the notion of one's developing conscious control of invention) and eventually to the practical rhetoric of the late nineteenth century. John Faulkinberry ("An Examination of Trends in Rhetorical Theory," 1972) examined selected nineteenth-century textbooks in order to trace changing concepts of rhetoric in the century, and Albert Kitzhaber ("Rhetoric in American Colleges," 1953) and Harold Jordan ("Rhetorical Education in American Colleges and Universities," 1952) look specifically at individuals, events, and trends that occurred in the latter half of the century.

Interesting as all these studies are, and I must point out that five of them are doctoral dissertations, my judgment is that

Kitzhaber provides the best overall picture of what happened in the nineteenth century. He traces the influence of the major British rhetoricians, particularly Blair, Campbell, and Whately, looks at developments early in the century, identifies those who did most to shape theory and practice in the latter half of the century—Bain, A. S. Hill, Wendell, Genung, and Scott (who is the only one identified by Kitzhaber as an original thinker)—and discusses significant rhetorical topics: the emergence and atrophying of paragraph theory, the four forms of discourse, and matters of style.

A few studies have dealt with specific topics over a period of time in this era. Fred Haberman (1954) and Marie Hochmuth and Richard Murphy (1954) studied elocution in the century; Elbert Harrington (1948) and Ernest Ettlich (1966) have examined invention; and Virgil Baker (1953), Kitzhaber, and, most recently, Robert Connors (1981) have taken turns at examining the forms of discourse.

Scholarship on major figures in the period is not much more advanced. A body of scholarship has developed around only one significant figure in the entire century: Richard Whately. I must point out, by the way, that my discussion of secondary materials includes, out of necessity, reviews, dissertations and even some master's theses, published articles in journals, and prefaces to editions of various authors' works. Editions of the work of nineteenth-century rhetoricians are not abundant. The Southern Illinois University Press Landmarks series offers editions only of Gilbert Austin, Edward Channing, Thomas De Quincey, Chauncey Allen Goodrich, and Richard Whately. Auer and Banninga's edition of John Adams's *Lectures* is the only other work of this kind on nineteenth-century figures of which I am aware.

Whately is the subject for slightly over two dozen pieces of scholarship, and a number of aspects of his work have been examined: his discussions of invention, arrangement (dispositio), argument, logic, presumption and burden of proof, his relationship to the rhetorical tradition, his relationship to Blair and Campbell, and his influence on current traditional rhetoric. Clearly, the existing work has not exhausted what might be said about Whately, but enough scholarship exists that one can examine it and begin to generalize about it.

The same cannot be said for other nineteenth-century figures, even those whose work has received some examination.

There are about eight pieces on De Quincey, each taking a different tack. His bringing together of Scottish associationism and German aesthetics has been discussed, as have his relationship to Richard Whately and his attitudes on science, rhetoric, and poetry, on rhetoric and the national character, and on public speaking. One scholar has even noted some inconsistencies between De Quincey's "Rhetoric" and his later positions. The difficulty with such a study, of course, is that it is limited by the assumption that a writer is obliged to be consistent, even over the course of years when his ideas on a subject may and probably should change.

Studies of John Quincy Adams, E. T. Channing, and James Rush have been done. And a few articles, the best being those by Paul Rodgers (1965) and Ned Shearer (1972, 1973), have honed in on Alexander Bain's contribution to paragraph theory and to the forms of discourse he is given credit for codifying. In no sense, however, could one say that a developed body of scholarship has come into being around any of these figures or any other of their contemporaries.

Primarily between 1927 and 1934, *The Quarterly Journal of Speech* attempted to fill some gaps in this period by running a series of reviews of rhetorical works by lesser known nineteenth-century rhetoricians: Samuel Kirkham, Henry Mandeville, William Russell, William Shedd, Ebenezer Porter, and John Witherspoon. But these were pretty much discontinued, and gaps remain.

Summing up the present state of scholarship in nineteenth-century rhetoric, we may say first that while a few useful and valuable studies that attempt to generalize about the period or movements within it do exist, they are but starting points for further work. The body of scholarship that exists around only one figure, Richard Whately, is a model for what must be done for other prominent figures during the period, particularly Austin, Rush, De Quincey, Coleridge, Hazlitt, Newman, Witherspoon, Bain, Theremin, A. S. Hill, Genung, Wendell, and Scott. In addition, we need more thorough scholarly pieces on many significant minor rhetoricians who have either been overlooked or were briefly noticed in the *Quarterly Journal of Speech*'s series of reviews nearly fifty years ago. As I have pointed out, most of this work has been done by people in speech departments, but in the last five to ten years a new surge of interest in rhetoric in all periods, and even in the nineteenth century, has begun to develop in departments of English. Recent studies in the period by Edward P. J. Corbett, Andrea Lunsford, Hal Weidner, Robert Connors, Leo Rockas, James Berlin, Winifred Horner, Nan Johnson, Gerald Mulderig, Stephen Judy, and myself are beginning to supplement work done by Kitzhaber and Wallace Douglas, the only two of their generation in English departments who have contributed significantly to our knowledge of nineteenth-century rhetoric.

The irony in this situation is that English departments still do not care a great deal about rhetorical theory or history. But a depressed job market for literary specialists coupled with a public outcry for better teaching of writing has made the composition/rhetoric specialist respectable for the time being. A second irony is that the general public has a rather superficial notion of what good writing instruction is. Too many still perceive it as correcting of mechanical errors, spelling, and usage. The gap between a work like James Kinneavy's *A Theory of Discourse* and the public's perception of what good writing is is equal to the gap between the technology of the space shuttle and that of a ball-point pen. While the opportunity lasts, however, composition/rhetoric specialists are making the most of it and attempting to bring new rigor and depth to their discipline.

Future Directions

What remains to be done? The first step has already been partially taken by this work and by my chapter on the nineteenth century in a previous one, *Historical Rhetoric: An Annotated Bibliography of Selected Sources in English,* edited by Winifred Bryan Horner (1980). This work contains bibliographies of both primary and secondary materials on the period. These, added to the extensive bibliography in Kitzhaber's "Rhetoric in American Colleges" and those of other long studies of the period, have begun to map the territory to be covered.

Clearly, we still need more general studies duplicating and bringing up to date work done by those already cited. Before that can be accomplished fruitfully, however, I believe we will need both editions and a number of studies of both major and minor figures. For example, we have no definitive edition of Alexander Bain's work. Considering Bain's influence, that would appear to be a significant gap. We need a sufficient number of studies of De Quincey's essays on rhetoric of the quality of Frederick Burwick's introduction to the Landmarks editions, to use an obvious example, to establish some sort of critical dialectic that will eventually define De Quincey's contribution to rhetorical theory so that it can be fitted into a longer, general work about the period. One has only to compare the quantity of literary criticism developed around comparable nineteenth-century writers to realize the shallowness of the intellectual soil in which we now work. Editions would serve two purposes. First, they would give us reliable texts from which to work in producing a body of scholarship about the various figures. Second, they would make accessible a number of books that are extremely difficult to get now. I personally would welcome a revival of the Southern Illinois University Press Landmarks editions of works in rhetoric. Whether or not the market justifies such an effort remains to be seen.

Once sufficient time has elapsed for the bibliographies to sort out what we should study and scholarship has sufficiently accumulated around a number of figures and trends in the period—the sifting and winnowing always necessary before clear judgments can be made about any person's contribution to the work in a field—we will be prepared for books generalizing about nineteenth-century rhetoric.

Definitive studies of nineteenth-century rhetoric, equivalent to the works by W. S. Howell on Renaissance and eighteenth-century rhetoric, can then be written by persons who have a solid knowledge of the primary and secondary work (which will have developed by then) on the period, a depth of knowledge in the nineteenth century's intellectual and educational milieu, and a depth of knowledge in the history of rhetoric from classical times to the present. For these reasons, my best guess is that a truly definitive work on this period cannot be written before 1990.

Bibliography

Primary Sources

Adams, John Quincy. *Lectures on Rhetoric and Oratory, Delivered to the Classes of Senior and Junior Sophisters in Harvard University.* 2 vols. Cambridge: Hilliard and Metcalf, 1810. Reprinted: J. Jeffrey Auer and Jerald L. Banninga, eds. New York: Russell and Russell, 1962.

Austin, Gilbert. *Chironomia, or a Treatise on Rhetorical Delivery.* London: T. Cadell and W. Davies, 1806. Reprinted in fascimile: Mary Margaret Robb and Lester Thonssen, eds. Southern Illinois University Press Series, Landmarks in Rhetoric and Public Address, edited by David Potter. Carbondale: Southern Illinois University Press, 1966.

Bain, Alexander. *English Composition and Rhetoric.* New York: D. Appelton and Co., 1866.

Baker, Sheridan. *The Complete Stylist.* New York: Thomas Crowell, 1966.

Buck, Gertrude. *The Metaphor—A Study in the Psychology of Rhetoric.* Contributions to Rhetorical Theory, no. 5. Edited by Fred Newton Scott. Ann Arbor: Inland Press, 1899.

Channing, Edward T. *Lectures Read to the Seniors at Harvard College.* Boston: Ticknor and Fields, 1856. Reprinted: Dorothy Anderson and Waldo Braden, eds. Southern Illinois University Press Series, Landmarks in Rhetoric and Public Address, edited by David Potter. Carbondale: Southern Illinois University Press, 1968.

Day, Henry N. *The Art of Discourse.* New York: Charles Scribner and Co., 1867.

De Quincey, Thomas. *De Quincey's Literary Criticism.* Edited by Helen Darbishire. London: Henry Frowde, 1909.

———. *De Quincey's Essays on Style, Rhetoric, and Language.* Edited by Fred Newton Scott. Boston: Allyn and Bacon, 1893.

———. *Essays on Rhetoric.* Edited by Frederick Burwick. Southern Illinois University Press Series, Landmarks in Rhetoric and Public Address, edited by David Potter. Carbondale: Southern Illinois University Press, 1967.

Genung, John Franklin. *The Practical Elements of Rhetoric.* 2d ed. Boston: Ginn and Co., 1886.

Goodrich, Chauncey Allen. *Select British Eloquence.* New York: Harper and Brothers, 1852.

Hill, Adams Sherman. *The Principles of Rhetoric and Their Application.* 2d ed. New York: American Book Co., 1895.

Hill, David J. *The Science of Rhetoric.* New York: Sheldon and Co., 1877.

Hope, M. B. *The Princeton Text-Book in Rhetoric.* Princeton, N.J.: John T. Robinson, 1859.

Jamieson, Alexander. *A Grammar of Rhetoric and Polite Literature.* First American from last London edition. New Haven: A. H. Maltby, 1820.

Lewis, Edwin H. *The History of the English Paragraph*. Chicago: University of Chicago Press, 1894.

Newman, Samuel P. *A Practical System of Rhetoric*. Portland: Shirley and Hyde, 1827.

Pearson, Henry G. *The Principles of Composition, with an Introduction by Arlo Bates*. Boston: D. C. Heath and Co., 1897.

Peirce, Charles Sanders. "Ideas, Stray or Stolen, About Scientific Writing, No. 1." Edited by John Michael Krois. *PR* 11 (Summer 1978): 147–55.

Rush, James. *The Philosophy of the Human Voice*. Philadelphia: J. Maxwell, 1827.

Scott, Fred Newton. "Rhetoric Rediviva." Edited by Donald C. Stewart. *CCC* 31 (December 1980): 413–19.

Scott, Fred Newton, and Joseph Villiers Denney. *Composition-Rhetoric, Designed for Use in Secondary Schools*. Boston: Allyn & Bacon, 1897.

———. *Paragraph-Writing*. Boston: Allyn and Bacon, 1893.

[Spencer, Herbert]. "The Philosophy of Style." *Westminster Review* 114 (October 1852): 234–47.

Wendell, Barrett. *English Composition: Eight Lectures Given at the Lowell Institute*. New York: Charles Scribner's Sons, 1891.

Whately, Richard. *Elements of Rhetoric*. London, Oxford: John Murry and J. F. Parker, 1828. Reprinted: Douglas Ehninger, ed. Southern Illinois University Press Series, Landmarks in Rhetoric and Public Address, edited by David Potter. Carbondale: Southern Illinois University Press, 1963.

Secondary Sources

Anderson, Dorothy I. "Edward T. Channing's Definitions of Rhetoric." *SM* 14 (1947): 81–93.

Anderson, Robert. "James Rush—His Legacy to Interpretation." *SSJ* 33 (Fall 1967): 20–28.

Auer, J. Jeffrey, and Jerald L. Banninga. "The Genesis of John Quincy Adams's Lectures on Rhetoric and Oratory." *QJS* 49 (April 1963): 119–32.

Baker, Virgil L. "Development of Forms of Discourse in American Rhetorical Theory." *SSJ* 18 (May 1953): 207–15.

Berlin, James. "Richard Whately and Current-Traditional Rhetoric." *CE* 42 (September 1980): 10–17.

Braddock, Richard. "The Frequency and Placement of Topic Sentences in Expository Prose." *Research in the Teaching of English* 8 (1974): 287–302.

Braun, John Elliott. "The Philosophical Roots of the Nineteenth-Century 'Repose' in Rhetoric, with Emphasis on the Idea of Communication in the Thought of Josiah Royce." Ph.D. diss., University of Michigan, 1977.

———. "The 'Speculative Rhetoric' of Charles Sanders Peirce." *PR* 14 (Winter 1981): 1–15.

Brockriede, Wayne E. "Bentham's Philosophy of Rhetoric." *SM* 23 (November 1956): 235–47.

Bryant, Paul. "A Brand New World Every Morning." *CCC* 25 (February 1974): 30–33.

Burke, Rebecca J. "Gertrude Buck's Rhetorical Theory." Occasional Papers in the History and Theory of Composition, no. 1. Edited by Donald C. Stewart. Manhattan: Kansas State University, 1978.

Burwick, Frederick. "Introduction." In *Essays on Rhetoric,* by Thomas De Quincey, pp. xi–xlviii. Southern Illinois University Press Series, Landmarks in Rhetoric and Public Address, edited by David Potter. Carbondale: Southern Illinois University Press, 1967.

Cherwitz, Richard A., and James W. Hikins. "John Stuart Mill's *On Liberty:* Implications for the Epistemology of the New Rhetoric." *QJS* 65 (February 1979): 12–25.

Cockerhan, Louis W. "Alexander Bain's Philosophy of Rhetoric." Ph.D. diss., Univeristy of Illinois, 1968.

Connors, Robert J. "The Rise and Fall of the Modes of Discourse." *CCC* 32 (December 1981): 444–55.

Corbett, Edward P. J. "Some Rhetorical Lessons from John Henry Newman." *CCC* 31 (December 1980): 402–12.

———. "What Is Being Revived?" *CCC* 18 (October 1967): 166–72.

Crocker, Lionel. "The Rhetorical Influence of Henry Ward Beecher." *QJS* 18 (February 1932): 82–87.

———. "Robert Green Ingersoll's Influence on American Oratory." *QJS* 24 (April 1938): 299–312.

Davis, Richard Beale. "James Ogilvie, an Early American Teacher of Rhetoric." *QJS* 28 (October 1942): 289–97.

Denton, George B. "Herbert Spencer and the Rhetoricians." *PMLA* 34 (March 1919): 89–111.

———. "Origin and Development of Herbert Spencer's Principle of Economy." In *The Fred Newton Scott Anniversary Papers,* pp. 55–92. Chicago: University of Chicago Press, 1929.

Douglas, Wallace. "Rhetoric for the Meritocracy." In *English in America,* edited by Richard Ohmann, pp. 97–132. New York: Oxford University Press, 1976.

Duffey, Joseph. "Remarks Prepared for a Meeting of the Presidential Task Force on the Arts and the Humanities." *American Council of Learned Societies Newsletter* 32 (Summer–Fall 1981): 1–5.

Durham, Weldon B. "The Elements of Thomas De Quincey's Rhetoric." *SM* 37 (November 1970): 240–48.

Edney, C. W. "George Campbell's Theory of Public Address." Ph.D. diss., University of Iowa, 1946.

———. "Richard Whately on Dispositio." *SM* 21 (August 1954): 227–34.

Ehninger, Douglas. "Campbell, Blair, and Whately: Old Friends in a New Light." *WS* 19 (October 1955): 263–69.

———. "Campbell, Blair, and Whately Revisited." *SSJ* 28 (Spring 1963): 169–82.

———. "Introduction." In *Elements of Rhetoric,* by Richard Whately, pp. ix–xxx. Southern Illinois University Press Series, Landmarks in Rhetoric and Public Address, edited by David Potter. Carbondale: Southern Illinois University Press, 1963.

———. "Whately on *Dispositio.*" *QJS* 40 (December 1954): 439–41.

Einhorn, Lois J. "Consistency in Richard Whately: The Scope of His Rhetoric." *PR* 14 (Spring 1981): 89–99.

Ettlich, Ernest Earl. "John Franklin Genung and the Nineteenth Century Definition of Rhetoric." *CSSJ* 17 (November 1966): 283–88.

———. "Theories of Invention in Late Nineteenth Century American Rhetorics." *WS* 30 (Fall 1966): 233–41.

Faulkinberry, John L. "An Examination of Trends in Rhetorical Theory as Delineated in Certain American Rhetoric Textbooks Written by American Authors from 1800 to 1900." Ph.D. diss., University of Southern Mississippi, 1972.

Fritz, Charles A. "From Sheridan to Rush: The Beginnings of English Elocution." *QJS* 16 (February 1930): 75–88.

Goodfellow, Donald M. "The First Boylston Professor of Rhetoric and Oratory." *NEQ* 19 (September 1946): 372–89.

Gray, Giles W., and Lester Hale. "James Rush, Dramatist." *QJS* 29 (February 1943): 55–61.

Grover, David H. "Elocution at Harvard: The Saga of Jonathan Barber." *QJS* 51 (February 1965): 62–67.

Guthrie, Warren. "The Development of Rhetorical Theory in America, 1635–1850." *SM* 13 (1946): 14–22; 14 (1947): 38–54; 15 (1948): 61–71; 16 (August 1949): 98–113; 18 (March 1951): 17–30.

Haberman, Frederick. "De Quincey's Theory of Rhetoric." *Eastern Public Speaking Conference, 1940, Papers and Addresses,* pp. 191–203. New York: The H. W. Wilson Co., 1940.

———. "English Sources of American Elocution." In *A History of Speech Education in America,* edited by Karl Wallace, pp. 105–26. New York: Appleton-Century-Crofts, 1954.

———. "John Thelwall: His Life, His School and His Theory of Elocution." *QJS* 33 (October 1947): 292–98.

Hale, Lester L. "Dr. James Rush." In *A History of Speech Education in America,* edited by Karl Wallace, pp. 219–37. New York: Appleton-Century-Crofts, 1954. Reprinted in *Readings in Rhetoric,* edited by Lionel Crocker and Paul A. Carmack, pp. 529–41. Springfield, Ill.: Charles C. Thomas, 1965.

———. "Dr. James Rush—Psychologist and Voice Scientist." *QJS* 35 (December 1949): 448–55.

———. "Principles of James Rush as Applied to Interpretation." *SSB* 7 (November 1941): 43–45.

Hance, Kenneth G. "The Elements of the Rhetorical Theory of Phillips Brooks." *SM* 5 (December 1938): 16–39.

Harrington, Elbert. "Rhetoric and the Scientific Method of Inquiry." *University of Colorado Studies, Series in Language and Literature* 1 (December 1948): 1–64.

Hochmuth, Marie, and Richard Murphy. "Rhetorical and Elocutionary Training in Nineteenth-Century Colleges." In *A History of Speech Education in America,* edited by Karl Wallace, pp. 153–77. New York: Appleton-Century-Crofts, 1954.

Horner, Winifred. "Scottish Roots for the Rhetorical Tradition." In *The Rhetorical Tradition and Modern Writing,* edited by James J. Murphy, pp. 85–95. New York: Modern Language Association, 1982.

Hoshor, John P. "American Contributions to Rhetorical Theory and Homiletics." In *A History of Speech Education in America,* edited by Karl Wallace, pp. 129–52. New York: Appleton-Century-Crofts, 1954.

———. "Lectures on Rhetoric and Public Speaking, by Chauncey Allen Goodrich." *SM* 14 (1947): 1–38. Reprinted in *Readings in Rhetoric,* edited by Lionel Crocker and Paul A. Carmack, pp. 474–528. Springfield, Ill.: Charles C. Thomas, 1965.

Hostettler, Gordon F. "George Saintsbury's View of Rhetoric." *WJSC* 41 (Fall 1977): 210–20.

Howell, Wilbur S. "De Quincey on Science, Rhetoric, and Poetry." *SM* 13 (1946): 1–13.

Howes, Raymond F. "Coleridge and Rhetoric." *QJS* 12 (June 1926): 145–56.

Hudson, Hoyt. "De Quincey on Rhetoric and Public Speaking." In *Historical Studies of Rhetoric and Rhetoricians,* edited by Raymond F. Howes, pp. 198–214. Ithaca: Cornell University Press, 1961. Reprinted in *Studies in Rhetoric and Public Speaking in Honor of James A. Winans,* pp. 132–51. New York: Russell and Russell, 1962.

Johnson, Nan. "Innovations in Nineteenth-Century Pedagogy: The Rhetorics of Henry Day, M. B. Hope, and Franz Theremin." In *The Rhetorical Tradition and Modern Writing,* edited by James J. Murphy, pp. 105–18. New York: Modern Language Association, 1982.

Jordan, Harold M. "Rhetorical Education in American Colleges and Universities, 1850–1915." Ph.D. diss., Northwestern University, 1952.

Judy, Stephen. "Composition and Rhetoric in American Secondary Schools, 1840–1900." *EJ* 68 (April 1979): 34–39.

King, Andrew A. "Thomas De Quincey on Rhetoric and National Character." *CSSJ* 24 (Summer 1974): 128–34.

Kitzhaber, Albert R. "Rhetoric in American Colleges: 1850–1900." Ph.D. diss., University of Washington, 1953.

Leathers, Dale G. "Whately's Logically Derived Rhetoric: A Stranger in Its Time." *WS* 33 (Winter 1969): 48–58.

Lunsford, Andrea. "Essay Writing and Teachers' Responses in Nine-teenth-Century Scottish Universities." *CCC* 32 (December 1981): 434–43.

McKerrow, Ray E. "Campbell and Whately on the Utility of Syllogistic Logic." *WJSC* 40 (Winter 1976): 3–13.

———. "'Method of Composition': Whately's Earliest 'Rhetoric.'" *PR* 11 (Winter 1978): 43–58.

———. "Probable Argument and Proof in Whately's Theory of Rhetoric." *CSSJ* 36 (Winter 1975): 259–66.

Mohrmann, G. P. "The Real Chironomia." *SSJ* 34 (Fall 1968): 17–27.

Mulderig, Gerald. "Nineteenth-Century Psychology and the Shaping of Alexander Bain's *English Composition and Rhetoric.*" In *The Rhetorical Tradition and Modern Writing,* edited by James J. Murphy, pp. 95–104. New York: Modern Language Association, 1982.

Parrish, Wayland Maxfield. "The Tradition of Rhetoric." *QJS* 33 (December 1947): 464–67.

———. "Whately and His Rhetoric." *QJS* 15 (February 1929): 58–79. Reprinted in *Readings in Rhetoric,* edited by Lionel Crocker and Paul A. Carmack, pp. 374–96. Springfield, Ill.: Charles C. Thomas, 1965.

———. "Whately on Elocution." In *The Rhetorical Idiom: Essays in Rhetoric, Oratory, Language, and Drama, Presented to Herbert A. Wichelns,* edited by Donald C. Bryant, pp. 43–52. Ithaca: Cornell University Press, 1958.

Pence, Orville. "The Concept and Function of Logical Proof in the Rhetorical System of Richard Whately." *SM* 20 (March 1953): 23–39.

Pomeroy, Ralph S. "Whately's *Historic Doubts:* Argument and Origin." *QJS* 49 (February 1963): 62–74.

Rahskopf, Horace G. "John Quincy Adams: Speaker and Rhetorician." *QJS* 32 (December 1946): 435–41. Reprinted in *Readings in Rhetoric,* edited by Lionel Crocker and Paul A. Carmack, pp. 463–73. Springfield, Ill.: Charles C. Thomas, 1965.

Ray, John W. "The Moral Rhetoric of Franz Theremin." *SSJ* 40 (Fall 1974): 33–49.

Reid, Ronald F. "The Boylston Professorship of Rhetoric and Oratory, 1806–1904: A Case Study of Changing Concepts of Rhetoric and Pedagogy." *QJS* 45 (October 1959): 239–57.

Ried, Paul E. "The Boylston Chair of Rhetoric and Oratory." *WS* 24 (Spring, 1960): 83–88. Reprinted in *Readings in Rhetoric,* edited by Lionel Crocker and Paul A. Carmack, pp. 456–62. Springfield, Ill.: Charles C. Thomas, 1965.

———. "Francis Child: The Fourth Boylston Professor of Rhetoric and Oratory." *QJS* 55 (October 1969): 268–75.

———. "Joseph McKean: The Second Boylston Professor of Rhetoric and Oratory." *QJS* 46 (April 1960): 419–24.

Robb, Mary Margaret, and Lester Thonssen. "Introduction." In *Chironomia*, by Gilbert Austin, pp. ix–xxi. Southern Illinois University Press Series, Landmarks in Rhetoric and Public Address, edited by David Potter. Carbondale: Southern Illinois University Press, 1966.

Rockas, Leo. "The Quintilian of Amherst: John Franklin Genung." *NEQ* 54 (March 1981): 54–73.

Rodgers, Paul C. "Alexander Bain and the Rise of the Organic Paragraph." *QJS* 51 (December 1965): 399–408.

Scott, Fred Newton. "Introduction" and "Notes." In *Essays on Style, Rhetoric, and Language*, by Thomas De Quincey, pp. iii–v, ix–xxiv. Boston: Allyn & Bacon, 1893.

Self, Robert T. *Barrett Wendell*. Twayne United States Authors Series, no. 261. Boston: G. K. Hall, 1975.

Shearer, Ned. "Alexander Bain and the Genesis of Paragraph Theory." *QJS* 58 (December 1972): 408–17.

———. "Alexander Bain and the Teaching of Rhetoric." *CSSJ* 23 (Spring 1973): 36–43.

Sproule, J. Michael. "The Psychological Burden of Proof: On the Development of Richard Whately's Theory of Presumption." *CM* 43 (June 1976): 115–29.

Stewart, Donald C. "The Barnyard Goose, History, and Fred Newton Scott." *EJ* 67 (November 1978): 14–17.

———. "The Nineteenth Century." In *Historical Rhetoric: An Annotated Bibliography of Selected Sources in English*, edited by Winifred Bryan Horner, pp. 229–69. Boston: G. K. Hall, 1980.

———. "Rediscovering Fred Newton Scott." *CE* 40 (January 1979): 539–47.

———. "Two Model Teachers and the Harvardization of English Departments." In *The Rhetorical Tradition and Modern Writing*, edited by James J. Murphy, pp. 118–30. New York: Modern Language Association, 1982.

Talley, Paul M. "De Quincey on Persuasion, Invention, and Style." *CSSJ* 16 (November 1965): 243–54.

Tyler, John M. "John Franklin Genung." *Amherst Graduates' Quarterly* 9 (February 1920): 67–68.

Vancil, David Lee. "The Disappearance of *Topoi* in English Rhetoric: 1550–1830." Ph.D. diss., University of Illinois, 1974.

Weidner, Hal Rivers. "Three Models of Rhetoric: Traditional, Mechanical, and Vital." Ph.D. diss., University of Michigan, 1975.

Wellek, Rene. "De Quincey's Status in the History of Ideas." *PQ* 23 (July 1944): 248–72.

Winans, James A. "Whately on Elocution." *QJS* 31 (February 1945): 1–8. Reprinted in *Readings in Rhetoric,* edited by Lionel Crocker and Paul A. Carmack, pp. 397–408. Springfield, Ill.: Charles C. Thomas, 1965.

Young, Richard. "Paradigms and Problems: Needed Research in Rhetorical Invention." In *Research on Composing: Points of Departure,* edited by Charles Cooper and Lee Odell, pp. 29–47. Urbana: National Council of Teachers of English, 1978.

CONTEMPORARY RHETORIC

James L. Kinneavy

Introduction, Definition, and Boundaries

The concept of a "present state of scholarship" mandates a chapter on contemporary rhetoric: if the rest of the work is more than antiquarianism, there ought to be a lively present state of the art in our century. And indeed there is. But sketching the picture for this century is not as easy as it might seem. Rhetoric, for various reasons, has been systematically exiled from entire disciplines in many countries until quite recently. Yet, in several critical areas of daily existence, rhetoric has at no time in history been so pervasive. This paradox of scholarly contempt and practical fealty has created, on the one hand, serious chasms in scholastic investigations and, on the other, unmanageable mountains of partially mapped information.[1]

This concurrent poverty and richness almost condemns the present attempt to failure at the outset. In addition, the very meaning of the term *rhetoric* in this century further complicates the issue. Yet the attempt must be made. There are so many important investigations going on by large groups of scholars exploring common and overlapping concerns yet often not communicating with one another that some endeavor must be made to bring them together, even at the risk of forgetting,

James L. Kinneavy teaches in the department of English at the University of Texas at Austin. He is the author of *A Theory of Discourse,* an influential book in contemporary rhetoric, and he has written a number of other books on the subject as well.

1. I would like to acknowledge a debt of gratitude to many of my colleagues who have advised me of works in their field of specialty. It is impossible for any one person to keep up with the entire field of rhetoric. Consequently, I have consulted with the following scholars in compiling this chapter: Richard A. Cherwitz, Wayne A. Danielson, John A. Daly, Lester L. Faigley, Nancy R. Harrison, James W. Hay, Robert C. Jeffrey, Horace M. Newcomb, Robert M. Shelton, Gayatri Chakravorti Spivak, James W. Tankard, Jr., and John A. Walter.

neglecting, or underestimating the importance of some and overemphasizing others.

A brief outline of the position of rhetoric at the beginning of this century might help the beginning student understand the current situation. On the Continent, rhetoric was almost totally in academic eclipse. The decline of rhetoric in France has been examined in some detail by Paul Ricoeur in *The Rule of Metaphor* (1977) and Gérard Genette in *Figures III* (1972). The ambivalent attitude in nineteenth-century Germany toward rhetoric and its eventual disfavor have been chronicled by Joachim Goth in *Nietzsche und die Rhetorik* (1970). At Oxford and Cambridge, despite the continuation of the weekly or fortnightly written essays presented to the tutor, rhetoric as a subject for reading and examinations was no longer required by the end of the nineteenth century. In Belgium, rhetoric as a required reading topic in universities was discontinued in the middle of the 1920s, as Chaim Perelman tells us in *The Realm of Rhetoric* (1982).

In the United States, the academic transfers of rhetoric were both more perceptible and more dramatic than in much of Europe. With the establishment of departments of English in American universities in the latter part of the nineteenth century, the allocation of the various components of the liberal arts tradition of the trivium was an early and overriding concern. Writing in the first issue of *PMLA* in 1886, James Morgan Hart, J.U.D., in an article entitled "The College Course in English Literature, How It May Be Improved," illustrated the issue with disarming candor: "What does *not* rightfully pertain to English literature? Settling this preliminary question will help us greatly. The main question resolves itself into three: What are we to do with logic, with rhetoric and with English philology (Anglo-Saxon and Early English)?" (p. 84). Hart was here speaking of the disposition of the basic components of education in Western civilization for over two thousand years. He would have relegated logic and rhetoric to philosophy and retained some philology in literature departments.

The response to his suggestions was not long in coming. In 1914, speech teachers in English departments, dissatisfied with their inferior status, dramatically walked out of the convention of the National Council of Teachers of English and set about establishing their own departments. In effect, they took rhetoric and dialectic and elocution with them. And the systematic study of rhetoric in America until quite recently has remained the province of scholars in departments of speech communications. The same decade also saw logic disposed of. The appearance in 1910 of Whitehead and Russell's *Principia Mathematica* sent a clear signal to every liberal arts teacher that he was no longer an expert in logic. Logic quickly found its new scholarly home in departments of philosophy and mathematics. Since neither speech nor philosophy has been often required for undergraduates, the demise of the core training in the liberal arts can be dated from this decade in American education.

English departments, however, were still saddled with the job of training the incoming student to write logically and persuasively, although English teachers were given no training in either logic or rhetoric as a discipline. Nor were English teachers expected to engage in rhetorical scholarship. It might be added, nevertheless, that this did not prevent English teachers from writing most of the textbooks used in composition classes for the next fifty years in America. Generally they adopted without question the modified approach to the modes of discourse (narration, description, argumentation, and exposition) derived from Alexander Bain and the paragraph approach of Barrett Wendell and others outlined by Donald Stewart in the preceding chapter. Important exceptions to these tendencies in the first half of the century were the work of I. A. Richards, *The Philosophy of Rhetoric* (1936) and his collaboration with C. K. Ogden in *The Meaning of Meaning* (1923), and the work of Richard M. Weaver, probably best seen in an anthology of his materials, *Language Is Sermonic: Richard M. Weaver on the Nature of Rhetoric* (1970).

Teachers in English departments awoke from their dogmatic slumbers in this regard only in the sixties. Massive increases in college registrations brought hordes of students to composition classes, many of whom were only marginally literate. With the appearance of Edward P. J. Corbett's *Classical Rhetoric for the Modern Student* (1965) and Wayne C. Booth's *The Rhetoric of Fiction* (1961), English departments can be said to have revived their scholarly concerns with rhetoric. Today, one of the brightest features of English departments is their concern with the many varied scholarly and practical regions of rhetoric. It is precisely these regions that I hope to outline in the following pages.

One of these regions that has only recently elicited some systematic scholarship in English departments is the general history of rhetoric—with the major exceptions of Wilbur Samuel Howell and Sister Miriam Joseph, whose work on the Renaissance, the eighteenth century, and Shakespeare is covered in earlier chapters of this book. This renewed historical interest is evidenced by the present book itself, and also by Winifred Bryan Horner's companion volume, *Historical Rhetoric: An Annotated Bibliography of Selected Sources in English* (1980). On a larger scale, there has been the formation of the International Society for the History of Rhetoric, which promises a biannual journal, *Rhetorica*, the first issue of which is to appear in the spring of 1983; it will be published at the University of California at Davis.

The structure of English departments and the curriculum of the usual college composition courses have also been subjected to some scrutiny. Arthur N. Applebee's *Tradition and Reform in the Teaching of English* (1974) is a start in this direction. This interest has been carried forward by a group of writers interested in studying the way in which what they call the current paradigm in composition instruction evolved: Richard E. Young (1980), James A. Berlin and Robert P. Inkster (1980), and Maxine Hairston (1982). In a somewhat similar vein, twelve authors attempt to relate the rhetorical tradition to current writing techniques in *The Rhetorical Tradition and Modern Writing* (1982), edited by James J. Murphy.

History, however, is not as prominent an area as some of the other contemporary interests of rhetoricians. A survey of some of these fields is an exciting odyssey, although limitations must be placed upon the endeavor. In the first place, the projected audience of this book is the body of potential scholars drawn mainly from instructors and graduate students in English and related areas. Consequently, some facets of the discipline fundamental to particular areas of rhetoric removed from the immediate concerns of such departments are not considered in this chapter. Within the English department's province, further, some areas are arbitrarily being excluded. Thus literature and literary criticism and theory, except as they overlap overtly with rhetoric, are excluded. So also are folklore, linguistics, drama, and the philosophy of language—with similar reservations. Thus, I will not consider some of the following very legitimate areas of rhetoric: marketing, managerial rhetoric, discussion and debating techniques, interviewing, oral interpretation, film and radio and television production (as such), literary theory and criticism, linguistics, general semantics and modern linguistic semantics, narrative theory, theory of description, axiology, logic, and the philosophy of science. Finally, entire areas of modern psychology, such as learning theory and cognitive science, are also excluded.

The list of topics included will, by implication, define the areas of rhetoric that I consider promising for scholarship at the current time.

The rationale for the sequence, after some initial reference materials, is based upon the semiotic model that I have elaborated in *A Theory of Discourse* (1980). First are considered a number of works emphasizing the relation of the situational context to the rhetorical text. Then material relevant to general theories of discourse or interpretation or pragmatics is considered. Then follow nine sections having to do with particular functions of discourse. The first three, informal logic, dialectic and exploration, and information theory (with short notices on journalism and technical writing), all relate to expository writing. The next four, political rhetoric and propaganda, religious oratory, rhetorical criticism (with a short notice on advertising), and women's voices, all concern persuasive discourse. The eighth section is devoted to self-expression as a rhetorical issue, and a final section is devoted to media of discourse (mass media and small group media).

These nine sections all have to do with pragmatics. Two sections are then devoted to semantic issues. The first explores semiotics and semiology, a major field of investigation at the present time. In the second, rhetoric as metaphor is considered; this is possibly the dominant view of rhetoric on the Continent at the present time and raises a critical issue both in Europe and America in this century, the epistemological basis or bases of rhetoric.

Syntactic issues currently being investigated are not considered in isolation but are examined in the final section of the book having to do with teaching composition and rhetoric.

Reference Works

There are, unfortunately, few general reference works devoted specifically to rhetoric. This is partly due to the sprawling nature of the discipline; it has no major departmental base, nor is there a unifying national or international group or conference. Nevertheless, some bibliographic works do exist as well as some indexes and some dictionaries and glosses.

The closest thing to an annual bibliography is the coverage in the *Rhetoric Society Quarterly*. This periodical (a bargain at four dollars a year) draws its material from the *Weekly Record* listings. It is quite complete since the compilers have a very comprehensive view of rhetoric, but it is limited to American publications, an increasingly important drawback, although its frequent bibliographic surveys compensate, in part, for this deficiency. A new journal, *Rhetorik: Ein internationales Jahrbuch*, published in Stuttgart, promises an annual bibliography, which will complement *Rhetoric Society Quarterly*. Most of the periodicals mentioned in connection with the various areas covered below do publish annual indexes.

A few surveys of rhetorical materials exist. *Rhetoric Society Quarterly*, in 1977 and 1978, published two articles by Joachim Dyck covering rhetorical studies in West Germany from 1971 to 1976. They are excellent and cover the educational spectrum from the high school through the university. A less comprehensive survey for France was made by Michèle Lacoste in *Communications* (1970). The entire issue was devoted to rhetoric and contains, in addition, Roland Barthes's excellent summary of classical rhetoric for French readers, Gérard Genette's study of the decline of rhetoric in France (later incorporated into *Figures III*), and Franz Gunther's three-page bibliography of rhetorical research in the United States. Finally, the *Rhetoric Society Quarterly* in fall 1981 listed all of its excellent bibliographic surveys over the past eleven years (sixty-nine in all, ranging from thorough surveys on most of the important figures in classical rhetoric to lengthy bibliographies on public address in Great Britain and a fine bibliography of rhetorical movements of the nineteenth and twentieth centuries, such as slavery, women's rights, civil rights, and so on).

Indexes relating to rhetoric are also limited. However, the superb *Index to Journals in Communication Studies Through 1979*, edited by Ronald J. Matlon, covers fourteen major American journals: *Quarterly Journal of Speech, Speech Monographs, The Speech Teacher, Southern Speech Communication Journal, Western Speech, Central States Speech Journal, Today's Speech, Bulletin of the Association of Departments & Administrators in Speech Communication, Philosophy and Rhetoric, Journal of Communication, Journalism Quarterly, Journal of Broadcasting, Journal of the Ameri-*

can Forensic Association, and *Human Communication Research.* There is no doubt that this index is the single most valuable bibliographic tool for twentieth-century rhetoric available. Its strength, the American rhetorical scene for sixty-six years, is also its limitation: its coverage of the Continent is very spotty. All of the tables of contents are reproduced, a 150-page indexing of twelve major subjects with detailed subtopics is given, and there is an index of contributors. Two editions have appeared, the latest being 1979. Both editions cover all of the periodicals since the founding of the periodical (thus *Quarterly Journal of Speech* goes back to 1915).

The second most useful index, particularly to the researcher interested in teaching composition, is the monthly *Current Index to Journals in Education,* which indexes about three hundred journals across the entire field of education. By supplementing this with the monthly index of *Resources in Education,* a more practical and less research-oriented publication, one gets a fairly thorough survey of this area of rhetoric. The latter publication includes books, practicum papers, instructional materials, speeches, legal materials, audiovisual references, tests, and so on. Many of the descriptors of the thesaurus, which is periodically enlarged, relate to areas of rhetoric. Both of these publications are part of the Educational Retrieval Information Centers (ERIC).

Several of the more general citation indexes have made rhetoric and allied areas a part of their more comprehensive coverage. Thus the *Arts and Humanities Citation Index* covers 1,100 periodicals fully and an additional 5,000 selectively. As a result, for example, the May–August 1981 entries under *rhetoric, rhetorical, rhetoricity,* and so on run to 269 items. The *Social Sciences Citation Index* also covers many journals that include materials related to rhetoric; it indexes 1,500 journals fully and 2,800 selectively. Finally, the *Education Index,* the *Religion Index,* and the *Catholic Periodical Index,* more traditional vehicles, also cover rhetorical materials.

Four dictionaries and glossaries ought to be mentioned also. Three are more historical than contemporary, but all are useful. Henri Morier, *Dictionnaire de poétique et de rhétorique* (1961), and Heinrich Lausberg, *Handbuch der literarischen Rhetorik: Eine Grundlegung der Literaturwissenschaft* (1960), are both interested in the overlap of rhetoric and literature. Both are excellent in their chosen province, the history of rhetoric. Much smaller, but handy, is Richard A. Lanham's *A Handlist of Rhetorical Terms* (1969); as in the larger works of Morier and Lausberg, Lanham's emphasis is on literary concerns. Linda Woodson, in *A Handbook of Modern Rhetorical Terms* (1979), attempts to consider more contemporary material particularly germane to the teaching of composition. In this sense her work supplements the other three. Nevertheless, it is clear that there is no work that attempts a comprehensive coverage of the rich concepts of the many areas of contemporary rhetoric.

Some Promising Areas of Study in Contemporary Rhetoric

Situational Context

Certainly one of the most overpowering concepts in contemporary rhetoric, obvious in many different disciplines, is the notion that a piece of discourse must be judged against the situational and cultural contexts in which it was produced and in which it is being interpreted. Rhetoricians in different disciplines, students of classical rhetoric, some philosophers, some theologians, speech act theorists, and literary critics join together in affirming this tenet of contemporary rhetoric.

Among writers in the field of speech communication, Lloyd F. Bitzer, in "The Rhetorical Situation" (1968), almost made this notion a manifesto of the journal *Philosophy and Rhetoric* in its first issue. Bitzer's work has been supported by many others in the discipline since and it has also been attacked on occasion. Richard Vatz, in "The Myth of the Rhetorical Situation" (1972), one of the more notable retorts, precipitated a controversy on the issue. At its extreme, the obsequiousness of text to situational context can reduce rhetoric to history and dismiss language as an insignificant echo of political or economic action.

Kenneth Burke, however, whose pentad structure of act, agent, agency, purpose, and scene is a continual assertion of the importance of the various elements of the dramatic context of discourse, maintains the central importance of man as a symbolic animal. His *Grammar of Motives* (1969) may be his most extended statement on situational context, but his whole corpus is a commentary on the issue. In English departments, tagmemicists have applied to the rhetorical process of composing Kenneth L. Pike's theory of interpreting a culture by the internal (emic) norms of the members of the culture itself (1960). Richard Young, Alton L. Becker, and Kenneth L. Pike's *Rhetoric: Discovery and Change* (1970) may be the best rhetorical application of this tagmemic principle.

The classical parallel to this notion, the concept of timeliness or *kairos*, was the core of Plato's rhetorical theory (see *Phaedrus* 272a), but it was only given prominence in this century by Augusto Rostagni in "Un Nuovo capitolo nella storia della retorica e della sofistica" (1922) and by Mario Untersteiner's sympathetic treatment in *The Sophists* (1954). Its application to composition can be seen in James Kinneavy's "The Relation of the Whole to the Part in Composition and in Interpretation Theory" (1979). He also shows the importance of the idea in Freud and the speech act theorists, particularly in Mary Louise Pratt's *Toward a Speech Act Theory of Literary Discourse* (1977).

A strong movement in modern anthropology reflects the same concern. Ethnomethodology, the idea that the methodology of analysis of a given culture ought to be conditioned by the norms of that culture, has been a major movement in the same direction of increasing emphasis on situational and cultural context. Two summary treatments of this movement are Roy Turner, ed., *Ethnomethodology: Selected Readings* (1974), and Houston Wood and Hugh Mehan, *The Reality of Ethnomethodology* (1975).

Finally, the new critical reaction against the near autonomy of the text in literary criticism has resulted in different emphases on situational context by various movements in philosophical and literary criticism. Jacques Derrida in *Dissemination* (1981), Edward W. Said in *Beginnings* (1975), the group anthologized by Josué Harari in *Textual Strategies* (1979), Stanley Fish in *Is There a Text in This Class?* (1980), and others all underscore the same motif from different perspectives.

Communication Theory, Hermeneutics, and Pragmatics

Most communication theories, theories of interpretation, and theories of general discourse also stress the critical relation of the language product to the cultures that produced and interpret it. In this sense they reinforce the emphasis of the works in the previous section; this is particularly true of theories of general interpretation and the latest theories of pragmatics.

General communication theories in this century have been derived from two major sources, in my opinion. First there are the many theories using the information theory structure of Claude E. Shannon and Warren Weaver, presented in *The Mathematical Theory of Communication* (1964). An influential example of such a theory can be seen in Colin Cherry, ed., *Pragmatic Aspects of Human Communication* (1974). A more psychological view of the process can be seen in George A. Miller, *Communication, Language and Meaning* (1973). A view incorporating the influence of modern mass media can be seen in Wilbur Schramm, *Men, Messages, and Media: A Look at Human Communication* (1973).

The second major source for general communication theories in this century has been the semiotic structure elaborated by Charles W. Morris in *Signs, Language, and Behavior* (1946). It has been used by semioticians, linguists, literary theorists, logicians, information theorists, composition theorists, and so on. We will return to this model in some detail in the section on semiotics below.

In addition to general communication theory considered under that nomenclature, a second important comprehensive view of the entire language process is that of hermeneutics. Beginning with biblical and legal theories of interpretation, the hermeneutic process was generalized to all of the humanities by Friedrich Schleiermacher and Wilhelm Dilthey in the nineteenth century. Martin Heidegger then enlarged this notion to that of philosophical hermeneutics, a view that considers all understanding at any level to be an interpretation of the world. His position is presented in *Being and Time* (1962, pp. 182–210), in which he also considers the forestructure that anyone brings to a process of interpretation (pp. 275–77, 358–364, 370, 424, especially). This forestructure and the resulting structures of interpretation are carefully analyzed by Hans-Georg Gadamer in *Truth and Method* (1975). Rudolf Bultmann applied these notions to biblical interpretation in Hans Werner Bartsch's collection called *Kerygma and Myth: A Theological Debate* (1953) and in other works. Heidegger's interpretation theories also strongly influenced such French thinkers as Paul Ricoeur, Jacques Derrida, and Jacques Lacan; the first two of these consider rhetoric at great length (see below, the section "Rhetoric as Metaphor").

The relation of the Heideggerian forestructure to rhetoric was already implicit in the remark of Schleiermacher that rhetoric was the obverse side of the coin from hermeneutics. And, since in Heidegger, every act of intelligence is an act of interpretation, it is easy to view rhetoric as the interpretation of the world to someone who, in turn, interprets the writer's interpretation. Consequently, Heidegger's forestructure (and Gadamer's "prejudices" and Bultmann's "myths") become immediately relevant to the *process* of writing.

A strikingly similar position can be seen in three current theories in pragmatics. Daniel Bobrow and Donald Norman's "Some Principles of Memory Schemata" (1975), Roger Schank and Robert Abelson's "Scripts, Plans, and Knowledge" (1977), and Marvin Minsky's "A Framework for Representing Knowledge" (1975) are all quite parallel, in reading theory, to the work of the hermeneuticists in interpretation theory. All of the theories posit a background of information and prejudgments brought to the business of interpreting anything.

The pragmatic position was not arrived at immediately. There were earlier syntactic emphases by two Prague school linguists, Vilém Mathesius (in Josef Vachek, 1964, though the work was done in the 1930s), and Frantisek Daneŝ, "One Instance of Prague School Methodology: Functional Analysis of Utterance of Text" (1970). These were followed by semantic emphases in analyzing whole discourses. The work of Walter Kintsch (1974) and of Teun van Dijk and Kintsch (1978) is possibly some of the best in that area.[2]

Informal Logic

Certainly one of the success stories of the twentieth century has been the formalization of logic, which has permitted the creation of mathematical logic and the application of logic to computers. But the very precision and rigidity of the categories of formal logic have also made quite clear that much of the logic of ordinary discourse and of some technical discourse in areas like value theory, law, ethics, and politics is not amenable to the inflexible axioms and obstinate inference patterns of formal logic. Consequently, there has been a chorus of voices in several areas speaking for an informal logic.

Possibly the most conspicuous of these voices are those of Belgian rhetoricians Chaim Perelman and L. Olbrechts-Tyteca in *The New Rhetoric: A Treatise on Argumentation* (1969), in which they argue for a reconsideration of the topics of Aristotle in a

2. For this material in pragmatics I am heavily indebted to a 1982 speech, "Discourse Topic," by Lester Faigley, of the University of Texas at Austin.

modern way and apply this new logic to law, political reasoning, and other areas. Stephen E. Toulmin, also interested in legal reasoning, has elaborated an interesting combination of deductive and inductive reasoning in *The Uses of Argument* (1958) and later works. His model has been heavily adopted in speech communication departments, especially because of the work of Douglas Ehninger (1974). Kurt Baier's *The Moral Point of View: A Rational Basis of Ethics* (1958) has launched in ethics and value theory the movement often called the logic of *good reasons*. He argues that in these areas we are often willing to settle for less than the ultimate and perfect axiom or reason and operate with only good reasons.

Ethnomethodologists, referred to above in the section on situational context, object to the rigid imposition of an outside norm on a subculture: to understand the practical reasoning of a subculture, it is unfair to assess it by the standards of scientific reasoning. Two-thirds of Roy Turner's anthology *Ethnomethodology: Selected Readings* (1974) are devoted to this issue.

Some influential Marxists, for different reasons, question the validity of the quantification of some political and sociological concepts. Friedrich Pollock, Theodor W. Adorno, and Max Horkheimer in essays in Paul Connerton, ed., *Critical Sociology* (1976), raise these issues. Other thinkers, arguing for a *praxis,* rather than a *theoria,* approach the subject somewhat differently. Jürgen Habermas, in *Theory and Practice* (1973), analyzes the kind of thinking that eventuated in action and revolution in Hegel and Marx; and Richard J. Bernstein, in *Praxis and Action* (1971), attempts a more contemporary analysis of this kind of thought.

Finally, a group of cognitive psychologists have also differentiated the logic of informal discourse from that of the formal logicians. Typical of such investigations is that of Richard Nisbett and Lee Ross, *Human Inference: Strategies and Shortcomings of Social Judgment* (1980).

Dialectic, Exploration, and Epistemology

Questioning the validity of the rules of formal logic as they apply to some types of human situations is really an epistemological inquiry. So also are the major concerns of this section. Chaim Perelman has done much of his work in the periodical *Dialectica,* dedicated to the provisional and changing nature of knowledge. As Frédéric Gonseth said in the first issue of this periodical, "Real scientific progress is not a step from certitude to certitude, from reality to reality, it is a step from provisional and cumulative evidence to further provisional and cumulative evidence" ("L'Idée de dialectique aux entretiens de Zurich," p. 32). The tentative, sometimes even questionable, nature of scientific knowledge is a major motif in modern thought generally. Its application to rhetoric has been made by men such as Jacques Derrida in his essay "White Mythology" (1974), which I will mention again in relation to rhetoric as metaphor. Other frontal attacks on the security of scientific thought, such as those made by Karl Popper in *The Logic of Scientific Discovery* (1959) and Paul Feyerabend in *Against Method: Outline of an Anarchistic Theory of Knowledge* (1978), are applied to rhetoric by disciples and practitioners. Both emphasize the negative and even mythical nature of science. An attempt to apply Feyerabend's theories to rhetoric has been made in the first volume of a new periodical devoted to rhetoric, *Pre/ Text* (1980). The application of Popper's and Feyerabend's work to rhetoric will conceivably cleanse the stables of much accumulated filth. Some of our rhetorical theories are eminently falsifiable, though they are not verifiable at all.

Popper and Feyerabend have drawn many of their conclusions from examining scientists in the process of exploring. The concept of exploration as such has proved a rich field for modern rhetoric and composition theory. Richard H. Young, Alton L. Becker, and Kenneth L. Pike, in *Rhetoric: Discovery and Change* (1970), apply their own exploratory principles (their heuristic) to the process of writing a theme. Their heuristic is derived from scientific roots; it is not surprising, therefore, that for these three rhetoricians, rhetoric is almost reduced to a pursuit for truth, or to a dialectic.

Another heuristic, that of Thomas A. Kuhn, outlined in *The Structure of Scientific Revolutions* (1970), has also been given several adaptations to rhetoric, particularly by Kinneavy, *A Theory of Discourse* (1980), and by several freshman textbook writers, such as John J. Ruszkiewicz, *Well-Bound Words: A Rhetoric* (1981).

Kenneth Burke's work, referred to in the section on situational context, is also a clear illustration of the application to rhetoric of a dialectic that is at least partially Hegelian in origin. Large sections of the *Grammar of Motives* are devoted explicitly to dialectic.

Finally, some works explicitly devoted to the epistemology of rhetoric must be considered. Ernesto Grassi, in *Rhetoric as Philosophy: The Humanist Tradition* (1980), argues against the separation of rhetoric from philosophy and attempts to show historically how the influence of Cicero has been more important for the philosophical tradition than we now concede. Samuel Ijselling, in *Rhetoric and Philosophy in Conflict: An Historic Survey* (1976), takes a similar approach to the epistemological issue. These historic procedures can be profitably juxtaposed to the rather synchronic techniques of a fair number of writers in speech communication journals. Henry W. Johnstone (1969), Robert L. Scott (1976), Richard A. Cherwitz (1977, 1982), and others have all attempted to move rhetoric from its traditional position as an after-the-fact deliverer of truth to a truth having a creative (they call it epistemic) function in certain kinds of discourse.

Three other avenues of research in epistemology—highly promising for rhetorical implications, in my opinion—are the three approaches to the subject–object problem proposed by Martin Heidegger, Georg Lukács, and Theodor W. Adorno. Heidegger's solution to the subject–object dichotomy, presented in *Being and Time* (1962, pp. 244–56, especially), establishes a primordiality of hermeneutic thought over scientific thought; if rhetoric is included in hermeneutic thought (as poetry is), then another important epistemology of rhetoric must be examined, an epistemology that will obviously be related to the Heideggerian concept of forestructure examined above in the section on hermeneutics.

In addition, the Marxist theory of subject–object convergence in society as presented in Lukács, *History and Class Consciousness* (1974), and the curious primacy of object in Adorno's analysis (1978) both have major rhetorical ramifications. Both Lukacs and Adorno insisted that society, especially economic and industrial society, so severely conditions the "reality" of any given individual and the way in which such a "reality" is perceived that talk about simple subject and simple object is impossible. In effect, the rhetoric of capitalism must be considered in talking about knower and known, or subject and object.

Information Theory, Journalism, and Technical Writing

A final group of scholars operating in the area of expository writing or referential discourse whose views have rhetorical implications includes information theorists, journalists, and teachers of technical writing. Their conjunction is made possible because at least the news function of journalism is ordinarily conceived of as being that of conveying information. Technical writing is included here because one of the major functions of nearly all technical writing is the transmission of information. Information theory, news writing, and technical writing all share the common informative concern.

Like the work in pragmatic theory discussed above, the movement in information theory in rhetoric has moved from the syntactic to the semantic to the pragmatic. Claude Shannon and Warren Weaver's *The Mathematical Theory of Communication* (1964) inaugurated the syntactic phase in this country and, as we have seen, influenced theories of communication. With the important application of this theory to the semantic level by Yehoshua Bar-Hillel and Rudolf Carnap in *Language and Information: Selected Essays on Their Theory and Application* (1964), it became possible to make rhetorical applications at particular discourse levels. Rulon S. Wells made the move to pragmatics in "A Measure of Subjective Information" (1961). A much more extensive application to informative discourse as such was made by James L. Kinneavy in *A Theory of Discourse* (1980).

A short notice must also be given to journalism. An influential book outlining different views of the functions of journalism is Frederick S. Siebert, Wilbur Schramm, et al., *Four Theories of the Press: The Authoritarian, Libertarian, Social Responsibility, and Soviet Communist Concepts of What the Press Should Be and Do* (1956). Two journeyman introductions to the business of reporting are Curtis MacDougall, *Interpretive Reporting* (1977), and Mitchell V. and Blair Charnley, *Reporting* (1979). A more technical book is Philip Meyer, *Precision Journalism: A Reporter's Introduction to Social Science Methods* (1979). A book questioning the capitalistic and totalitarian control of news channels is Herbert I. Schiller, *Communication and Cultural Domination* (1976).

Much of the work of technical writers in our society has affinities with journalism and the communication of information. It must, however, be said that not much interesting work has gone on in the rhetoric of technical communication. No major theoretical work has yet influenced writers of texts or teachers in this area or practitioners. Some general work in the philosophy of science will eventually make an impression in this area, but it has not to date. And some of the theories implied by works such as Gordon H. Mills and John A. Walter, *Technical Writing* (1978), will be examined more fully. Joseph Racker, in *Technical Writing: Techniques for Engineers* (1960), likewise makes some interesting distinctions among audiences and writers that could develop into a theory.

Probably the most promising research in this area is being done by scholars examining the ways in which information can be more effectively packaged. J. C. Redish, of the Document Design Project in Washington, D.C., has, for instance, looked more carefully at legal and government documents in *The Language of Bureaucracy* (1981). More theoretically interesting, perhaps, are the issues raised by Veda R. Charrow, in *Linguistic Theory and the Study of Legal and Bureaucratic Language* (1981), a study from the same research center.

There are two recent book-length surveys of technical writing, one edited by Sarojini Balachandran (1977) and one by Gerald J. Alred, Diana C. Reep, and Mohan R. Limaye (1981). The first is restricted in time to books and articles since 1965 and in scope to material about engineers and scientists. It is an excellent annotated bibliography about such topics as encouraging engineers to write, training engineers and scientists to write, manual writing, the impact of computers and word processors on writing, and so on. The second is a larger historical view and a larger conceptual definition of technical writing, particularly because it incompasses business writing.

Propaganda, Political Rhetoric, and Commercial Advertising

The next four sections generically relate to what I have called *persuasive* discourse. Sometimes, particularly in "Rhetorical Criticism" and "Women's Voices," items mentioned relate to more than one area (for example, some items are certainly relevant to scientific or literary discourse also). Because of the increasing importance of mass media in our society, persuasive discourse has penetrated almost every aspect of our lives. Indeed, it may be that the twentieth century is the most persuasive of all centuries. It is indeed possible that human beings have been manipulated by verbal techniques more in our era than at any other time in history. Yet this aspect of language is often almost totally ignored by entire language departments of English, French, Spanish, Russian, and so on.

One person who for decades has studied political propaganda is Harold D. Lasswell. Possibly his best theoretical book on the subject is *Language of Politics* (1965), written in conjunction with several of his associates. His *Propaganda and Promotional Activities: An Annotated Bibliography,* reprinted in 1969, is still a major work. Another important voice has been that of Leonard Doob, *Public Opinion and Propaganda* (1966). A European analysis of Nazi propaganda is Eugen Hadsmovsky's *Propaganda and National Power: The Organization of Public Opinion for National Politics* (1972). Most of the works mentioned so far in this section are earlier studies of propaganda in World Wars I and II. A more recent study of Russian propaganda is that of Frederick C. Barghoorn, *Soviet Union Propaganda* (1964).

Some of the best analyses of American domestic and foreign political rhetoric have been made by writers in departments of speech communication. *The Index to Journals in Communication Studies Through 1979,* cited above, for instance, lists thirty-four entries under Nixon, twenty-seven under Roosevelt, thirty-two under Southern oratory. It also includes analyses of British and European political rhetoric. Some of the better practical analysts are also good theorists. A few of these, for whom both a theoretical and an analytical entry are listed in the bibliography, are L. W. Rosenfield (1968, 1976), Bruce E. Gronbeck (1975, 1978), David L. Swanson (1977, 1978), and Walter R. Fisher (1973, 1980).

Political rhetoric is a concern of the Frankfurt Marxist critics, but they also examine the influence of the political propaganda on the economic scene in a more careful way than do any of the studies hitherto presented. Consequently, their works are an excellent bridge between politics and advertising. Theodor W. Adorno's *Introduction to the Sociology of Music* (1976), Jürgen Habermas's *Communication and the Evolution of Society* (1979), Max Horkheimer's *Critical Theory* (1972), and Herbert Marcuse's *One-Dimensional Man* are a few of the important works in this area.

In advertising, which has been looked at more constructively than critically, a few major works present a good background to the subject. A recent poll indicates that the most widely read work in advertising is not a scholarly work at all, but a biographical report by David Ogilvie, *Confessions of an Advertising Man* (1980). Two excellent textbooks that have dominated the field for decades are Otto Kleppner and Norman Govoni, *Advertising Procedures* (1979), and Charles Sandage et al., *Advertising: Theory and Practice* (1979). Two analytical works on advertising, influential in several university departments, are Erving Goffman, *Gender Advertisements* (1979), and the earlier study of Marshall McLuhan, *The Gutenberg Galaxy* (1962).

Religious Oratory

The scholarship in religious oratory is not nearly as interesting, in my opinion, as that in political or commercial rhetoric. However, at least two interesting intersections—those of preaching with mass media and of preaching with modern theology—show some rhetorical potential.

Probably the most thorough coverage of the history of preaching written in this century is Yngve Brilioth, *A Brief History of Preaching* (1965). This work covers, however, only the first part of this century, since it first appeared in 1945. Bibliographically, there is an exhaustive collection of American materials by William Thompson and William Toohey, *Recent Homiletical Thought: A Bibliography, 1935–65* (1967). Thompson, a Baptist, and Toohey, a Catholic, coedit the book-review section of *Preaching,* a periodical that attempts to cover the current scene. Harry Caplan and Henry H. King, in a series of monographs between 1949 and 1956, have compiled bibliographies on preaching for Italian, Spanish, Scandinavian, Dutch, English, German, and French. Karl Rahner, S.J., has edited *The Renewal of Preaching: Theory and Practice* (1968), an attempt at a coverage of preaching in ten different countries, which has much bibliographic material (nearly all Catholic).

Three important influences can be seen in American preaching in this century. First there is the overpowering influence of the nineteenth-century masterpiece by John A. Broadus, *On the Preparation and Delivery of Sermons,* a book in its twenty-ninth edition in 1944 since its appearance in 1870. This text's audience was not at all limited to Baptist ministers, possibly because of its deep roots in classical rhetorical theory. Broadus says, quite candidly, "The author's chief indebtedness for help has been to Aristotle, Cicero, and Quintilian, and to Whately and Vinet. The two last (together with Ripley) had been his textbooks" (p. xiii). These rhetorical, rather than doctrinal, sources are evident in the organization of the text—a quite basic arrangement of argument, style, and delivery—and in the virtues of style—clarity, energy, elegance.

The second overpowering influence in American preaching has been that of Harry Emerson Fosdick. Fosdick's famous statement on preaching, "What Is the Matter with Preaching?" in 1928, became a manifesto for much of the pulpit practice in America for the next fifty years. His charge to ministers to address a problem of his listeners that they could see as relevant to their lives has moved sermons away from the exegesis of Scripture to the exploratory and topical. He has been held responsible even for some of the current tendencies in television oratory by such figures as Jerry Falwell and for the techniques of such mass media performers as Billy Graham. In this general area, Bruce Rosenberg's *The Art of the American Folk Preacher* (1970) should also be mentioned.

Theology has made some impressive marks on preaching in this century, mostly in the latter half of the century. Rudolf Bultmann, arguably the single most dominant theologian of the last fifty years, by emphasizing the message of the Gospel, the proclamation function of the minister, and the necessity of presenting the biblical message in modern terms (demythologized from the biblical presentations) heavily influenced Christian preaching theory and practice in both Protestant and Catholic circles. In particular his premise that the biblical message must be separated from the myths of the first century A.D. and translated into the language of modern times necessitated a new view of pulpit practice. Dietrich Ritschl's *A Theology of Proclamation* (1960), Otto Semmelroth's *The Preaching Word: On the Theology of Proclamation* (1965), and the work of Rahner mentioned above, *The Renewal of Preaching*, clearly show this legacy. Rahner's influence (with others) has almost totally changed the Catholic posture on the importance of preaching in the church.

Rhetorical Criticism

In a generic sense, of course, most of the critical essays referred to in this entire essay constitute rhetorical criticism. However, the term has taken on a particular meaning for a large group of writers, mostly in departments of speech communication, in the past half-century. That meaning was wrestled with in a seminal book edited by Lloyd F. Bitzer and Edwin Black, *The Prospect of Rhetoric. Report of the National Developmental Project* (1971). Many of the major names in the field are included in this collection, and it represents some of the major motifs of the movement, such as criticism of the rhetorical tradition, the movement to science, and the incorporation of models from the social sciences.

The attack on traditional, but especially neo-Aristotelian, rhetoric came, however, in a full blast from Edwin Black's *Rhetorical Criticism: A Study in Method* (1965), a very influential text. Other important names in the field must be mentioned as well. Herbert W. Simons, *Persuasion: Understanding, Practice and Analysis* (1976), has given new directions to the study of persuasion. Donald Bryant's "Rhetoric: Its Function and Its Scope" and A. Craig Baird's *Rhetoric: A Philosophical Inquiry* (1965) were both influential in asking questions, the answers to which constitute rhetorical criticism today. They inquired about the scope of rhetoric, the epistemology of rhetoric, its relation to philosophy, and so on.

Some of the important names in the field have already been mentioned in other contexts and are included in the bibliography under the sections indicated: Lloyd Bitzer in considering situational context (section III); L. W. Rosenfield, Bruce E. Gronbeck, David L. Swanson, and Walter R. Fisher under political rhetoric (section VIII); Henry W. Johnstone, Robert I. Scott, and Richard A. Cherwitz under epistemological problems (section VI); Lionel Crocker and Harry Caplan and Henry H. King under religious rhetoric (section IX).

One severe qualification must be made about putting some of these writers under *persuasion* as a concept distinguished from referential discourse. Particularly the writers connected with the epistemic nature of rhetoric would not want their work to exclude what I have called exploratory or scientific discourse—and I do not intend such an exclusion here.

Women's Voices

While there is little feminist work that labels itself "rhetorical," the interdisciplinary character of "women's studies" has led to developments that can be said to find their motivation precisely in an attempt to explain women's responses to what is—in Lloyd Bitzer's definition of the term—women's "rhetorical situation."[3]

In 1971, the National Council of Teachers of English published an attempt to face this issue, *A Case for Equity,* a collection of essays that explored, as the editor Susan McAllester put it, the "puzzling . . . dilemma of American women in 1971 as encoun-

---

3. This section was written by Nancy Harrison.

tered by college teachers and students," especially in departments of English. This publication was followed by an issue of *College English* edited by Elaine Hedges and entitled "Women Writing and Teaching," which again addressed the status of women in universities. Two of the essays in that issue have become classic: "When We Dead Awaken: Writing as Re-Vision," by Adrienne Rich; and Tillie Olsen's "Women Who Are Writers in Our Century: One Out of Twelve."

It is not surprising that originally much of the feminist work in discourse analysis was done in English departments by women who sought to isolate "female" qualities in women's writings and to distinguish feminine rhetorical and discursive practices from their masculine counterparts. The most recent notable example of the theory and analysis of discourse within the framework of literary analysis is Sandra M. Gilbert and Susan Gubar's *The Madwoman in the Attic: The Woman Writer and the Nineteenth-Century Literary Imagination* (1979). Their references in this work, coupled with the bibliographic material in their *Shakespeare's Sisters: Feminist Essays on Women Poets* (1979), cover useful earlier material.

Noteworthy are three anthologies that fill a previously "empty" space in our literature both of analysis and of imagination, a deficiency that has hampered attempts at an inclusive, systematic study that could call itself, with authority, "women's studies." *But Some of Us Are Brave: Black Women's Studies* (1982), edited by Gloria T. Hull, Patricia Bell Scott, and Barbara Smith, contains a thorough interdisciplinary overview of black women's studies, including a good bibliography. *Sturdy Black Bridges: Visions of Black Women in Literature* (1979), edited by Roseann P. Bell, Bettye J. Parker, and Beverly Guy-Sheftall, contains analytical articles, interviews, and a sampling of the imaginative literature of black woman writers. *The Third Woman: Minority Women Writers of the United States* (1980), edited by Dexter Fisher, is primarily an anthology of writing by minority women. However, the introductory material to each section as well as the bibliographic appendix are useful additions to a comprehensive view of women's discourse. The book is also an excellent introductory textbook.

The holistic or synthesizing tendency of feminist analysis has been sustained and encouraged by two interdisciplinary publications that remain central to ongoing study: *Feminist Studies*, founded by Ann Howard Calderwood in 1969 and first published in 1972, and *Signs: Journal of Women in Culture and Society,* established in 1975 under the editorship of Catherine R. Stimpson.

One practitioner who has consistently advanced and reviewed feminist theory in order to define and articulate it and to establish a truly representative pluralistic approach is Annette Kolodny. Some of her early essays include "Some Notes on Defining a 'Feminist Criticism'" (1975) and "The Feminist as Literary Critic" (1976). Two more recent essays, "A Map for Rereading: Or, Gender and the Interpretation of Literary Texts" (1980) and "Dancing Through the Minefield: Some Observations on the Theory, Practice, and Politics of a Feminist Literary Criticism" (1980), are especially useful in their attempt to explore and describe the situation in which women interact and "read" one another in the larger "texts" of their lives as well as in the textual discourse they produce.

Special issues of journals that concern themselves with theory and analysis of textual interpretation have been devoted to feminist theory, highlighting current concerns and strategies. Of note here is an issue of *Critical Inquiry* on "Writing and Sexual Difference" (1981). In this issue Elaine Showalter's "Feminist Criticism in the Wilderness" deserves special attention. Showalter categorizes, reviews, and evaluates the state of current feminist theoretical concerns, schools of thought, and methodologies. The bibliographical information in the article's footnotes is a good starting point for a comprehensive view of feminist discourse analysis.

Another area of current interest is the American interpretation and use of European discourse theory, especially French feminist theory, which is often psychoanalytically and ideologically oriented to a degree that "home-grown" theory is not. *New French Feminisms* (1980), edited by Elaine Marks and Isabelle de Courtivron, offers the American reader a sampling of French feminist theory along with an informative introduction and a thorough bibliography. Current interest in French feminist theory is further demonstrated by special issues of *Signs* (1981) and of *Yale French Studies* (1981). The latter also reflects a tendency in feminist theoretical enterprises to collective and collaborative work. Another collection that attempts to bring together American and Continental concerns is *The Future of Difference,* edited by Hester Eisenstein and Alice Jardine (1980).

Finally, an excellent example of the synthesizing approach that typifies feminist analysis at this point is *Women and Language in Literature and Society* (1980), edited by Sally McConnell-Ginet, Ruth Borker, and Nelly Furman. In addition, many of the essays collected here demonstrate how feminist theory can be especially helpful in reader- or audience-oriented analysis. Again, the bibliographical offerings throughout the book furnish material for a thorough examination of the disciplines interacting in this text—linguistics, anthropology, and textual criticism. As an indicator of current concerns and practices in women's textual criticism and interpretation, *Women and Language in Literature and Society* is exemplary, a collection that cannot help but inform the general reader as well as the reader "cutting across" disciplines.

Self-Expression

A last type of rhetorical genre that has, in a sense, only come into its own in this century, is that in which the expression of the speaker assumes dominance in the text, oral or written, with the consequence that the persuasive appeal, or the literary art, or the scientific proof, or the explanation is reduced to a secondary or tertiary role. Cursing, some prayer, manifestos, gripe sessions, some contracts, or journals are forms that can take on this major role. Interest in this type of discourse is found usually among professionals concerned with psychological counseling, education, composition training, or philosophical wholeness of personality.

I will arbitrarily limit my coverage to the latter two categories. In the training for composition teaching, three names have come to the fore, insisting that one of the best ways to get a student to write in any genre is to let him express himself freely. Afterward, with some minimum scribal fluency, the student can move on to expository writing or literary creations with more ease. Ken Macrorie, *Uptaught* (1970), Peter Elbow, *Writing Without Teachers* (1973), and Lou Kelley, *From Dialogue to Discourse* (1972), have all presented this viewpoint convincingly.

But expressive discourse need not be pedagogical in order to justify its existence. It may be regarded as the most fundamental of all language experiences. This issue is addressed by a philosophical tradition, deriving originally from Hegel's *The Phenomenology of Mind* (1967) and transmitted through Martin Heidegger, *Being and Time* (1962), Jean-Paul Sartre, *Being and*

Nothingness (1953), Maurice Merleau-Ponty, *The Primacy of Perception* (1964) and *Phenomenology of Perception* (1962), and Georges Gusdorf, *Speaking (La Parole)* (1965). The last mentioned is the most explicit statement of the position insofar as discourse explicitly is concerned. The tradition of Sartre, Merleau-Ponty, and Gusdorf has been put to rhetorical use by James L. Kinneavy in *A Theory of Discourse* (1980).

Mass Media and Small Group Media

With the advent of contemporary mass media, the channel of communication has become virtually as central as the message; indeed in the phrase of Marshall McLuhan, the medium is the message. McLuhan's most extensive analysis of this phenomenon is his *Understanding Media: The Extensions of Man* (1964). Earlier Walter J. Ong, in *Ramus, Method, and the Decay of Dialogue* (1958), had chronicled the move from an oral to a visual universe in media.

Today, no one interested in rhetoric can ignore the importance, even for the written word, of film, television, radio, and even the modern magazine itself. And the computer as a medium is already affecting secretarial practice and methods of teaching composition. Probably the two dominating influences at present in media theory are structuralism and Marxism, though there are some thinkers not affiliated with either school who have done excellent work. The members of the Frankfurt school, mentioned above under political and commercial rhetoric, must also be mentioned in this connection. A somewhat similar approach to the problem of the influence of mass media on the populace is the study of Michael Real, *Mass-Mediated Culture* (1977). Herbert J. Gans, in *Popular Culture and High Culture* (1968), questions the legitimacy of looking upon certain types of cultural genres as superior to the mass media genres. John G. Cawelti, in *Adventure, Mystery, and Romance* (1976), examines such popular genres as the detective story, the western, and the social melodramatic novel.

In the field of television, Raymond Williams, *Television: Technology and Cultural Form* (1975), and John Fiske and John Hartley, *Reading Television* (1978), are excellent. The first is an intelligent Marxist reading, and the second is a semiotic study of television and society. Horace Newcomb's anthology, *Television: The Critical View* (1982), offers various perspectives on the medium. For the cinema, Thomas Schatz's *Hollywood Film Gen-*

res (1981) uses Continental and structuralist techniques to investigate the cinema.

Both film and television pose the question of the rhetoric of the visual image. Some excellent work has been done in this area. Roland Barthes in *Mythologies* (1972) and in *Image—Music—Text* (1978) pioneered in this area. Bill Nichols's *Ideology and the Image* (1981) is also excellent.

Mass media are not the only media that have been subjected to careful analysis in this century. In the field of small group media at least a few of the important studies ought to be mentioned, particularly as they relate to family relationships. Some of these are: Harold H. Kelley, *Personal Relationships: Their Structures and Processes* (1979), Harold H. Kelley and John N. Thibaut, *Interpersonal Relations: A Theory of Interdependence* (1978), Murray S. Davis, *Intimate Relations* (1973), and Mark Knapp, *Social Intercourse: From Greeting to Goodbye* (1978).

Semiotics and Semiology

It could be argued, with some plausibility, that the most pervasive structure of American and European discourse analysis has been provided by the semiotic framework of "syntactics, semantics, pragmatics," which has also provided the structure of this essay, and has been adopted by logicians, by linguists (structural or transformational), by discourse analysts, by rhetoricians, by literary theorists, by information theorists, and by semioticians themselves. I have referred above to the semiotic influence, precisely because of its pervasiveness. When the triad is translated into discourse terms as *subject matter* (referent, semantic), *text* (referend, syntactic), and *sender* and *receiver* (pragmatic), it becomes the familiar communication triangle at the base of much contemporary rhetorical thinking.

Although semiotics, in a formal sense, is almost totally a twentieth-century discipline, its early history, especially the work of Charles Sanders Peirce, reaches back into the nineteenth century and earlier. Roman Jakobson in *Coup d'oeil sur le développement de la sémiotique* (1976) traces the early history of the discipline up to and including Ferdinand de Saussure. For a more contemporary look, Thomas A. Sebeok's anthology, *The Tell-Tale Sign: A Survey of Semiotics* (1975), provides, if not a history, at least a geography.

Any work on semiotics must begin with and continue to consult *The Collected Papers of Charles Sanders Peirce* (1960, latest volume). The long section in volume 1, paragraphs 219–307, is almost the beginning of the discipline; and in volume 1, paragraphs 300–417 he applies his triad to phenomenology and metaphysics, in volume 2, paragraphs 100–104 to logic, paragraphs 105–10 to "speculative rhetoric," and so on. These should be supplemented with *Semiotics and Significs: The Correspondence Between Charles S. Peirce and Lady Victoria Welby,* edited by C. S. Hardwick and J. Cook (1973). The most useful secondary work on Peirce, for me is that of Murray G. Murphey, *The Development of Peirce's Philosophy* (1961).

Much of the terminology and many of the concepts of modern semiotics derive from Charles William Morris's *Signs, Language, and Behavior* (1946). He systematically applied Peirce and others to discourse theory. His earlier *Foundations of the Theory of Signs* (1938) was part of a concerted attempt by a number of major modern philosophers and scientists to make semiotics the foundation of an international view of sciences and philosophy.

In France, undoubtedly the most significant figure in semiology, an attempt to apply semiotics to entire cultural systems of meanings, has been Roland Barthes. In his *Mythologies* (1972) he analyzes many modern cultural forms (sports, striptease, and so forth) and then in the last chapter erects a theory of these cultural systems of "myth." A more theoretical treatment is to be found in his *Elements of Semiology* (1968). Also on the French scene is Julia Kristeva, two of whose books are *Desire in Language: A Semiotic Approach to Literature and Art* (1980) and *Semeiotike: Recherches pour une sémanalyse* (1969).

Possibly the most extensive treatment of semiotics has been by Umberto Eco in *A Theory of Semiotics* (1976) and *The Role of the Reader* (1979). In the first Eco erects a major alternative to the system of Morris; in the second he applies his system to particular texts and takes cognizance of the reader, a component of meaning he had largely ignored in his first book.

Rhetoric as Metaphor

As was pointed out in the first section of this chapter, rhetoric in Europe in the nineteenth and twentieth centuries has often been simply equated to figures of speech. And this notion persists in some areas, but with a particular twist deriving mainly from Nietzsche. With the publication of some of Nietzsche's lectures on rhetoric in the Musarion edition, *Gesammelte Werke.*

Fünfter Band: Vorlesungen 1872–1876 (1922), scholars have seen the importance of his treatment of metaphor from an epistemological standpoint. If all our language is metaphorical, and, consequently, only a partial and inaccurate rendition of reality, even science and philosophy are condemned to metaphor and rhetoric in their reports of the world, according to Nietzsche. Jacques Derrida takes up this theme, using Nietzsche, and applies this theory to all discourse, including science and literary criticism. His treatment, "White Mythology," first appeared in French in *Poétique* (1971), in an edition that also included a translation into French of much of the Nietzsche material from the Musarion edition, as well as several articles on Nietzsche's views of rhetoric.

Derrida in his article reviewed the work of Gaston Bachelard, *La Formation de l'esprit scientifique* (1938) and G. Canguilhem, *Etudes d'histoire et de philosophie des sciences* (1973), both of whom had studied the use of metaphor by scientists in great detail. Derrida finally rejected Bachelard's thesis that it is possible to erect science and a literary criticism, even though language has metaphor as its base. This position was also defended in a lengthy reply to Derrida by Paul Ricoeur, in *The Rule of Metaphor* (1977). Derrida responded with "The Retreat of Metaphor."

Both Genette and Barthes regret the narrowing of rhetoric to this figural view. However, a Belgian group of rhetoricians, the Groupe Mu, has made this concept the basis for its *Rhétorique générale* (1971), edited by Jacques Dubois and others. It is probably significant that the work has also been translated into Spanish.

Possibly the most influential work in English in the Nietzsche-Derrida tradition is that of Paul de Man, *Allegories of Reading: Figural Language in Rousseau, Nietzsche, Rilke, and Proust* (1979). De Man does consider "persuasion" as an alternative to a figural notion of rhetoric, but he questions whether they may not be the same in the long run.

Rhetoric and the Teaching of Composition

Most of the interest in the contemporary study of rhetoric in departments of English has come about because of the "literacy crisis," as it is called, in our schools and universities. There is much evidence that, for a number of reasons, students cannot write as well as they used to some thirty or forty years ago. Yet high school and college graduates still must write in their sub-sequent careers—more, in fact, than most of them imagine. The business of teaching students to write in a culture that is, on the surface at least, more dominated by the television and radio than by the written media has become a major preoccupation of English and other departments. Indeed, it is this aspect of rhet-oric that, probably more than any other, has inspired this book and that is the major professional commitment of most of the authors of the chapters.

Consequently, it is fitting that the volume should close with some of the exciting work underway in this area. Most of it, it must be admitted, is of fairly recent date; there has probably been more written in this area in the past thirty years than in the previous three centuries. It is difficult, therefore, to limit the coverage of this area, just as it has been difficult to limit the coverage of all of the concerns of this chapter. I will try to follow the general schema followed in the chapter as a whole. Conse-quently, I will first give some bibliographic material, then some general theories of composition, then some theories on in-vention and process, then some approaches to arrangement, a few modern views of revision, some concerns with student di-alects, some pedagogical approaches, and finally a word about the subject matter of the students' writings.

The most thorough bibliographic coverage of this field is by Gary Tate, editor of *Teaching Composition: 10 Bibliographical Es-says* (1976). This volume includes some excellent essays, though most of them are outdated after only six years. The topics cov-ered are invention, organization, style, modes of discourse, basic writing, media, linguistics, rhetorical analysis, related fields, and dialects.

"Heuristic Procedures and the Composing Process: A Se-lected Bibliography" (1982), by Richard Leo Enos, Barry M. Jereb, Paul L. Kravits, and Honora Mary Rockar, is almost as extensive in coverage as the Tate volume and is considerably more up-to-date. In addition it is more useful since the entries in each of the fifteen sections are alphabetized. Two other useful supplements to Tate are the annual composition bibliography in *College Composition and Communication* by Richard Larson and the quarterly supplements of *Rhetoric Society Quarterly*.

Several useful anthologies can serve as an introduction to the teaching of composition. Donald Graves, in *Rhetoric and Com-position: A Sourcebook for Teachers of English* (1976), and E. P. J.

Corbett and Gary Tate, in *The Writing Teacher's Sourcebook* (1981), have assembled articles or chapters of books on most of the issues treated in this section and have additional bibliographic recommendations. In addition, Donald McQuade has edited a fine collection of more scholarly work in *Linguistics, Stylistics, and the Teaching of Composition* (1979). Somewhat more limited in scope, but exhaustive for its field, is *Sentence Combining and the Teaching of Writing* (1979) by Donald A. Daiker, Andrew Kerek, and Max Morenberg.

The periodical most dedicated to the teaching of composition is *College Composition and Communication*. Also treating such issues quite frequently are the three periodicals of the National Council of Teachers of English: *College English, English Journal*, and *Language Arts*. *Research in the Teaching of English* publishes empirically based scholarship on composition.

The dominant theoretical views of the field of composition are the following. James Moffett, *Teaching the Universe of Discourse* (1968), has a theory with roots in Piaget and general semantics. James N. Britton's *The Development of Writing Abilities (11-18)* (1975) centers on the functions of language and is also Piaget-based. Frank J. D'Angelo, *A Conceptual Theory of Rhetoric* (1975), draws heavily from the historical topics combined with psycholinguistics for a different theoretical base. Richard E. Young, Alton L. Becker, and Kenneth L. Pike, in *Rhetoric: Discovery and Change* (1970), use a tagmemic heuristic approach to composition. James L. Kinneavy, in *A Theory of Discourse* (1980), uses a semiotic base combined with the historical liberal arts as a foundation for his aims and modes of discourse.

The last fifteen years have seen the rise of an emphasis on process in composition teaching, with the consequent deemphasis of the approach of being simply satisfied with the end product. The results have been pedagogical, psychological, and rhetorical. One of the early voices in this area was Gordon R. Rohman, "Pre-Writing: The Stage of Discovery in the Writing Process" (1966). Young, Becker, and Pike's book mentioned above was also quite influential, as was Janice Lauer's "Heuristics and Composition" (1970). The psychological aspect of the movement can be seen particularly in Linda S. Flower and John R. Hayes, "The Cognition of Discovery: Defining a Rhetorical Problem" (1980); the same authors also have written "The Dynamics of Composing: Making Plans and Juggling Constraints" (1980). Janet Emig, in *The Composing Processes of*

Twelfth Graders (1971), also represents a psychological study of the writing process.

The study of the organization of the parts of a discourse insofar as it relates to the teaching of composition has not been nearly as interesting a field as either general composition theory or invention and process. However, a few studies ought to be mentioned. Richard L. Larson's bibliographical essay in the Tate volume, mentioned earlier, is a good survey of the material available. Herbert A. Simon, in *The Sciences of the Artificial* (1969), addresses the problem of creating the structures of the artificial but does not go into rhetorical concerns in any depth. At the level of the sentence, Ross Winterowd's "The Grammar of Coherence" (1970) attempts to isolate the possible ways of combining sentence concepts. Another approach to combining parts of a discourse has been the recent work of some scholars in what has come to be called coherence and cohesion. One of the better studies in this area is Stephen P. Witte and Lester Faigley, "Coherence, Cohesion, and Writing Quality" (1981).

At the sentence and the paragraph level, the twentieth century has seen some interesting developments. Francis Christensen, in *Notes Toward a New Rhetoric* (1967), elaborated a new theory of paragraph development, largely based upon his research in Hemingway. Kenneth L. Pike, in "A Linguistic Contribution to Composition" (1964), applied tagmemic theory to composition, as did Alton L. Becker, in "A Tagmemic Approach to Paragraph Analysis" (1965). Paul Rodgers, Jr., in "A Discourse-Centered Rhetoric of the Paragraph" (1966), argued for a more holistic view of the relation of the paragraph to the entire theme.

Certainly the most spectacular and interesting work on the sentence in teaching composition has been the work of the sentence combiners, some following the work of Christensen and some following the lead of Kellog Hunt, who has shown that the sentence complexity of the student developed systematically from the lower grammar grades through college. His most influential report was *Grammatical Structures Written at Three Grade Levels* (1965). John C. Mellon (1969), Frank O'Hare (1973), and Donald Daiker et al. (1979) made experimental studies using the sentence combining techniques in high school and freshman college composition classes, in all three cases with significant results compared to traditional techniques.

Joseph M. Williams, in *Style: Ten Lessons in Clarity & Grace* (1981), has made an excellent combination of linguistics and rhetoric in studying problems of sentence structure and punctuation. He is not a sentence combiner, but he has learned from the movement.

Syntax and vocabulary were both an issue in a heated controversy in the sixties (somewhat abated, but not solved today) about the use of nonstandard and minority dialects in the teaching of composition. Certainly the most stimulating articles on this subject came from the pen of James H. Sledd. "Bi-Dialectalism: The Linguistics of White Supremacy" (1969) and "Doublespeak: Dialectology in the Service of Big Brother" (1972) both aroused considerable controversy. Geneva Smitherman's "English Teacher, Why You Be Doing the Thangs You Don't Do?" (1972) focused the issue in an article written in black dialect. In 1974, the National Council of Teachers of English and the Conference on College Composition and Communication both approved a statement on "Students' Rights to Their Own Language."

Possibly the most telling finding of this century relating to grammar has been the accumulated evidence from empirical research that the isolated teaching of formal grammar (traditional, structural, or transformational) cannot be shown to have any significant effect on improved writing, reading, or speaking skills. Ingrid Strom's "Research in Grammar and Usage and Its Implications for Teaching Writing" (1960) summarizes sixty years of research on the topic.

Some worthwhile work in revision as a process in teaching composition has also challenged traditional notions. Richard Braddock and his associates summarized early work on the subject in *Research in Written Composition* (1963). Nancy I. Sommers in "Revision Strategies of Student Writers and Experienced Adult Writers" (1980) has emphasized the danger of letting revision degenerate into a concern for mechanics. Ellen W. Nold, in *Revising: Toward a Theory* (1979), attempts to put what we currently know into a manageable synthesis that the teacher can use in teaching revising.

Two or three isolated works that have been influential in different areas must still be mentioned. E. D. Hirsch, Jr., in *The Philosophy of Composition* (1977), posed a theory of composition almost solely concerned with style—readability, as he called it.

He has since come to give more importance to concerns of subject matter and "cultural literacy," as he calls it—see his article "Culture and Literacy" (1980), in which he faces one of the most divisive issues in English departments today, the split between teachers of literature and teachers of composition. He favors teaching composition while teaching literature. Others today, on the contrary, would divorce the teaching of composition from any systematic reading activity—it is this tendency Hirsch is attacking. Still others, however, are insisting that composition be taught in other departments, with students writing on materials in their own fields of study. A recent book by scholars in different disciplines exemplifies this approach to writing across the curriculum, as the movement has come to be called. Elaine P. Maimon et al., *Writing in the Arts and Sciences* (1981), address writing in the humanities, the social sciences, and the natural sciences.

Conceivably the most creative work in scholarship in composition in this century has been the masterpiece of Mina P. Shaughnessy, *Errors and Expectations* (1977). By analyzing thousands of essays by entering freshmen into the CUNY schools in New York, she arrived at a systematization of their errors into intelligible and finite patterns. Her work, more than any other single piece of research, has influenced the teaching of basic writing in hundreds of institutions in this country. It is a remarkable synthesis of theory and practice, written in a lucid and sympathetic prose. It is a fitting work with which to bring this essay to a close.

Bibliography

The sections in the bibliography correspond to the sections in the text of the chapter. Readers are advised to check all sections related to their interests for works that overlap.

I. Introduction, Definition, and Boundaries

Applebee, Arthur N. *Tradition and Reform in the Teaching of English.* Urbana, Ill.: National Council of Teachers of English, 1974.

Berlin, James A., and Robert P. Inkster. "Current-Traditional Rhetoric: Paradigm and Practice." *Freshman English News* 8 (Winter 1980): 1–4, 13–14.

Bitzer, Lloyd F., and Edwin Black, eds. *The Prospect of Rhetoric. Report of the National Developmental Project.* Sponsored by Speech Communication Association. Englewood Cliffs, N.J.: Prentice-Hall, 1971.

Booth, Wayne C. *The Rhetoric of Fiction.* Chicago: University of Chicago Press, 1961.

Corbett, Edward P. J. *Classical Rhetoric for the Modern Student.* 2d ed. New York: Oxford University Press, 1971.

Genette, Gérard. "La Rhétorique restreinte." *Figures III.* Paris: Editions du Seuil, 1972.

Goth, Joachim. *Nietzsche und die Rhetorik: Untersuchungen zur deutschen Literaturgeschichte.* Tübingen: Max Niemeyer Verlag, 1970.

Hairston, Maxine. "The Winds of Change: Thomas Kuhn and the Revolution in the Teaching of Writing." *CCC* 33, no. 1 (February 1982): 76–82.

Hart, James Morgan, J.U.D. "The College Course in English Literature, How It May Be Improved." *PMLA* 1 (1886): 84–94.

Horner, Winifred Bryan. *Historical Rhetoric: An Annotated Bibliography of Selected Sources in English.* Boston: G. K. Hall, 1980.

Kinneavy, James L. *A Theory of Discourse.* New York: W. W. Norton & Co., 1980.

Murphy, James J., ed. *The Rhetorical Tradition and Modern Writing.* New York: The Modern Language Association of America, 1982.

Perelman, Chaim. *The Realm of Rhetoric.* Translated by William Kluback. Notre Dame: University of Notre Dame Press, 1982.

Rhetorica: A Journal of the History of Rhetoric (forthcoming, 1983). Davis: University of California Press for the International Society for the History of Rhetoric.

Richards, I. A. *The Philosophy of Rhetoric.* New York: Oxford University Press, 1936.

Richards, I. A., and C. K. Ogden. *The Meaning of Meaning.* New York: Harcourt, Brace, and World, 1923.

Ricoeur, Paul. *The Rule of Metaphor: Multidisciplinary Studies of the Creation of Meaning in Language.* Translated by Robert Czerny. Toronto: University of Toronto Press, 1977.

Weaver, Richard M. *Language Is Sermonic: Richard M. Weaver on the Nature of Rhetoric.* Edited by Richard L. Johannesen, Bernard Strickland, and Ralph T. Eubanks. Baton Rouge: Louisiana State University Press, 1970.

Young, Richard E. "Paradigms and Problems: Needed Research in Rhetorical Invention." In *Research in Composing,* edited by Charles Cooper and Lee Odell, pp. 29–47. Urbana, Ill.: National Council of Teachers of English, 1978.

II. Reference Works

Arts and Humanities Citation Index (1976–). Philadelphia: Institute for Scientific Information.

Barthes, Roland. "L'Ancienne rhétorique—aide-mémoire." *Communications* 16 (1970): 172–229.

Current Index to Journals in Education (1969–). Phoenix: Oryx Press.

Dyck, Joachim. "Rhetorical Studies in West Germany 1971–1973: A Bibliography." *RSQ* 8 (Spring 1978): 77–81.

———. With addenda by Peter Jehn. "Rhetorical Studies in West Germany 1974–1976: A Bibliography." *RSQ* 7 (Winter 1977): 1–19.

Gunther, Franz. "La Recherche rhétorique aux Etats-Unis." *Communications* 16 (1970): 235–37.

Lanham, Richard A. *A Handlist of Rhetorical Terms: A Guide for Students of English Literature.* Berkeley: University of California Press, 1969.

Lacoste, Michèle. "Choix bibliographique." *Communications* 16 (1970): 230–35.

Lausberg, Heinrich. *Handbuch der literarischen Rhetorik: Eine Grundlegung der Literaturwissenschaft.* 2 vols. Munich: Max Heuber Verlag, 1960.

Matlon, Ronald J. *Index to Journals in Communication Studies Through 1979.* Falls Church, Va.: Speech Communication Association, 1980.

Morier, Henri. *Dictionnaire de poétique et de rhétorique.* Paris: Presses Universitaires de France, 1961.

Pike, Kenneth L. *Language in Relation to a Unified Theory of the Structure of Human Behavior.* 3 vols. Glendale, Calif.: Summer Institute of Linguistics, 1960.

Resources in Education (1974–). Washington, D.C.: U.S. Government Printing Office..

Rhetoric Society Quarterly (1969–). St. Cloud, Minn.: Rhetoric Society of America.

Rhetorik: Ein internationales Jahrbuch (1980–). Stuttgart: Fromman-Holzboog.

Social Sciences Citation Index (1969–). Philadelphia: Institute for Scientific Information.

Woodson, Linda. *A Handbook of Modern Rhetorical Terms.* Urbana, Ill.: National Council of Teachers of English, 1979.

III. Situational Context

Bitzer, Lloyd F. "The Rhetorical Situation." *PR* 1 (1968): 1–14.

Burke, Kenneth. *A Grammar of Motives.* Berkeley: University of California Press, 1969.

Derrida, Jacques. *Dissemination.* Translated by Barbara Johnson. Chicago: University of Chicago Press, 1981.

Fish, Stanley. *Is There a Text in This Class? The Authority of Interpretive Communities.* Cambridge: Harvard University Press, 1980.

Harari, Josué, ed. *Text Strategies: Perspectives in Post-Structuralist Criticism.* Ithaca, N.Y.: Cornell University Press, 1979.

Kinneavy, James L. "The Relation of the Whole to the Part in Composition and in Interpretation Theory." In *Linguistics, Stylistics, and the Teaching of Composition,* edited by Donald McQuade, pp. 1–23. Akron, Ohio: Language and Style Books, 1979.

Pratt, Mary Louise. *Toward a Speech Act Theory of Literary Discourse.* Bloomington: Indiana University Press, 1977.

Rostagni, Augusto. "Un Nuovo capitolo nella storia della retorica e della sofistica." *Studi italiani de filologia classica,* n.s. 2 (1922): 148–201.

Said, Edward W. *Beginnings: Intention and Method.* Baltimore: Johns Hopkins University Press, 1975.

Turner, Roy, ed. *Ethnomethodology: Selected Readings.* Baltimore: Penguin Books, 1974.

Untersteiner, Mario. *The Sophists.* Translated by Kathleen Freeman. Oxford: Basil Blackwell, 1954.

Vatz, Richard. "The Myth of the Rhetorical Situation." *PR* 6 (Summer 1972): 154–61.

Wood, Houston, and Hugh Mehan. *The Reality of Ethnomethodology.* New York: John Wiley & Sons, 1975.

IV. Communication Theory, Hermeneutics, and Pragmatics

Bobrow, Daniel, and Donald Norman. "Some Principles of Memory Schemata." In *Representation and Understanding: Studies in Cognitive Science,* edited by Daniel Bobrow and Allen M. Collins, pp. 131–50. New York: Academic Press, 1975.

Bultmann, Rudolf. "New Testament and Mythology." In *Kerygma and Myth: A Theological Debate,* edited by Hans Werner Bartsch, translated by Reginald H. Fuller, pp. 1–45. London: S. P. C. K., 1953.

Cherry, Colin, ed. *Pragmatic Aspects of Human Communication*. Theory and Decision Library, no. 4. Hingham, Mass.: Kluwer Boston, 1974.

Daneŝ, Frantisek. "One Instance of Prague School Methodology: Functional Analysis of Utterance of Text." *Methods and Theory in Linguistics*, edited by Paul Garvin, pp. 132–46. The Hague: Mouton, 1970.

Gadamer, Hans-Georg. *Truth and Method*. Translated by G. Barden and J. Cumming. New York: The Seabury Press, 1975.

Heidegger, Martin. *Being and Time*. Translated by John Macquarrie and Edward Robinson. New York: Harper & Row, 1962.

Journal of Communication (1951–). Philadelphia: Annenberg School of Communication, University of Pennsylvania.

Journal of Pragmatics (1977–). Amsterdam: North-Holland.

Kintsch, Walter. *The Representation of Meaning in Memory*. Hillsdale, N.J.: Erlbaum, 1974.

Mathesius, Vilém. "On Linguistic Characterology with Illustrations from Modern English." In *A Prague School of Linguistics*, edited by Josef Vachek, pp. 59–67. Bloomington: Indiana University Press, 1964.

Miller, George A. *Communication, Language, and Meaning: Psychological Perspectives*. New York: Basic Books, 1973.

Minsky, Marvin. "A Framework for Representing Knowledge." In *The Psychology of Computer Vision*, edited by Patrick H. Winston, pp. 211–75. New York: McGraw-Hill, 1975.

Morris, Charles W. *Signs, Language, and Behavior*. Englewood Cliffs, N.J.: Prentice-Hall, 1946.

Schank, Roger, and Robert Abelson. "Scripts, Plans, and Knowledge." In *Thinking: Readings in Cognitive Science*, edited by Philip N. Johnson-Laird and Peter C. Wason, pp. 421—32. New York: Cambridge University Press, 1977.

Schramm, Wilbur. *Men, Messages, and Media: A Look at Human Communication*. New York: Harper and Row, 1973.

Shannon, Claude E., and Warren Weaver. *The Mathematical Theory of Communication*. Urbana: University of Illinois Press, 1964.

Van Dijk, Teun, and Walter Kintsch. "Toward a Model of Text Comprehension and Production." *Psychological Review* 85 (September 1978): 363–94.

V. Informal Logic

Adorno, Theodor W. "Sociology and Empirical Research." In *Critical Sociology*, edited by Paul Connerton, pp. 237–57. New York: Penguin Books, 1976.

Baier, Kurt. *The Moral Point of View: A Rational Basis of Ethics*. Ithaca, N.Y.: Cornell University Press, 1958.

Bernstein, Richard J. *Praxis and Action: Contemporary Philosophies of Human Activity*. Philadelphia: University of Pennsylvania Press, 1971.

Connerton, Paul, ed. *Critical Sociology*. New York: Penguin Books, 1976.

Ehninger, Douglas. *Influence, Belief, and Argument: An Introduction to Responsible Persuasion*. Glenview, Ill.: Scott, Foresman and Co., 1974.

Habermas, Jürgen. *Theory and Practice*. Translated by John Virtel. Boston: Beacon Press, 1973.

Horkheimer, Max. "Traditional and Critical Theory." Translated by J. O. O'Connell and others. In *Critical Sociology*, edited by Paul Connerton, pp. 206–24. New York: Penguin Books, 1976.

Nisbett, Richard, and Lee Ross. *Human Inference: Strategies and Short-comings of Social Judgment*. Century Psychology Series. Englewood Cliffs, N.J.: Prentice-Hall, 1980.

Perelman, Chaim, and L. Olbrechts-Tyteca. *The New Rhetoric: A Treatise on Argumentation*. Translated by John Wilkinson and Purcell Weaver. Notre Dame: University of Notre Dame Press, 1969.

Pollock, Friedrich. "Empirical Research into Public Opinion." Translated by Thomas Hall. In *Critical Sociology*, edited by Paul Connerton, pp. 225–36. New York: Penguin Books, 1976.

Toulmin, Stephen E. *The Uses of Argument*. Cambridge: Cambridge University Press, 1958.

Turner, Roy (see III, *supra*).

VI. Dialectic, Exploration, and Epistemology

Adorno, Theodor W. "Subject and Object." In *The Essential Frankfurt School Reader*, edited by Andrew Arato and Eike Gebhardt, pp. 497–511. New York: Urizen Books, 1978.

Burke, Kenneth (see III, *supra*).

Cherwitz, Richard A. "Rhetoric as 'A Way of Knowing': An Attentuation of the Epistemological Claims of the 'New Rhetoric.'" *SSJ* 42 (Spring 1977): 207–19.

———. "Toward a Rhetorical Epistemology." *SSJ* 47 (1982): in press.

Dialectica (1947–). Neuchâtel, Switzerland: Société Dialectica.

Feyerabend, Paul K. *Against Method: Outline of an Anarchistic Theory of Knowledge*. London: Verso, 1978.

Gonseth, Frédéric. "L'Idée de dialectique aux entretiens de Zurich." *Dialectica* 1 (1947): 21–37.

Grassi, Ernesto. *Rhetoric as Philosophy: The Humanist Tradition*. Translated by John Michael Krois and Azizeh Azodi. University Park: Pennsylvania State University Press, 1980.

Heidegger, Martin (see IV, *supra*).

Ijselling, Samuel. *Rhetoric and Philosophy in Conflict: An Historic Survey*. Translated by Paul Dunphy. The Hague: M. Nijhoff, 1976.

Johnstone, Henry W. "Truth Communication and Rhetoric in Philosophy." *Revue Internationale de Philosophie* 23 (1969): 405–6.

———. *Validity and Rhetoric in Philosophical Argument: An Outlook in Transition.* University Park, Pa.: Dialogue Press of Man and World, 1978.

Kinneavy, James L. (see I, *supra*).

Kuhn, Thomas S. *The Structure of Scientific Revolutions.* 2d ed. Chicago: University of Chicago Press, 1970.

Lukacs, Georg. *History and Class Consciousness: Studies in Marxist Dialectics.* Translated by Rodney Livingstone. London: Merlin Press, 1974.

Pre/Text (1980–). Charleston, Ill.: Eastern Illinois University.

Popper, Karl, *The Logic of Scientific Discovery.* Translated by Julius and Lan V. Fried. London: Hutchinson & Co., 1959.

Ruszkiewicz, John J. *Well-Bound Words: A Rhetoric.* Glenview, Ill.: Scott, Foresman and Co., 1981.

Scott, Robert L. "On Viewing Rhetoric as Epistemic: Ten Years Later." *CSSJ* 27 (Winter 1976): 258–66.

Young, Richard E., Alton L. Becker, and Kenneth L. Pike. *Rhetoric: Discovery and Change.* New York: Harcourt, Brace and World, 1970.

VII. Information Theory, Journalism, and Technical Writing

Alred, Gerald J., Diana C. Reep, Mohan R. Limaye, with the assistance of Michael A. Mikolajczak. *Business and Technical Writing: An Annotated Bibliography of Books, 1880–1980.* Metuchen, N.J.: Scarecrow Press, 1981.

Balachandran, Sarojini, ed. *Technical Writing: A Bibliography.* Urbana, Ill., and Washington, D.C.: American Business Communication Association and Society for Technical Communication, 1977.

Bar-Hillel, Yehoshua. *Language and Information: Selected Essays on Their Theory and Application.* Reading, Mass.: Addison-Wesley, 1964.

Charnley, Mitchell V., and Blair Charnley. *Reporting.* New York: Holt, Rinehart and Winston, 1979.

Charrow, Veda R. *Linguistic Theory and the Study of Legal and Bureaucratic Language.* Washington, D.C.: Document Design Project, 1981.

Information Sciences (1968–). New York: Elsevier North-Holland.

Journalism Quarterly (1924–). Lawrence, Kans.: Association for Education in Journalism.

Kinneavy, James L. (see I, *supra*).

MacDougall, Curtis. *Interpretive Reporting.* New York: Macmillan, 1977.

Meyer, Philip. *Precision Journalism: A Reporter's Introduction to Social Science Methods.* Bloomington: Indiana University Press, 1979.

Mills, Gordon H., and John A. Walter. *Technical Writing.* 4th ed. New York: Holt, Rinehart and Winston, 1978.

Racker, Joseph. *Technical Writing: Techniques for Engineers.* Englewood Cliffs, N.J.: Prentice-Hall, 1960.

Redish, Janice C. *The Language of the Bureaucracy.* Washington, D.C.: Document Design Project, 1981.

Schiller, Herbert I. *Communication and Cultural Domination.* White Plains, N.Y.: International Arts and Sciences Press, 1976.

Shannon, Claude E., and Warren Weaver (see IV, *supra*).

Siebert, Frederick S., Wilbur Schramm, et al. *Four Theories of the Press: The Authoritarian, Libertarian, Social Responsibility, and Soviet Communist Concepts of What the Press Should Be and Do.* Urbana: University of Illinois Press, 1956.

Wells, Rulon S. "A Measure of Subjective Information." In *Twelfth Symposium in Applied Mathematics,* edited by Roman Jakobson, pp. 237–44. Providence, R.I.: American Mathematical Society, 1961.

VIII. Propaganda, Political Rhetoric, and Commercial Advertising

Adorno, Theodor W. *Introduction to the Sociology of Music.* Translated by E. B. Ashton. New York: Continuum Publishing Co., 1976.

Advertising Age (1930–). Chicago: Crain Communications.

Barghoorn, Frederick C. *Soviet Union Propaganda.* Princeton: Princeton University Press, 1964.

Doob, Leonard. *Public Opinion and Propaganda.* 2d ed. Hamden, Conn.: Shoe String Press, 1966.

Fisher, Walter R. "Genre: Concepts and Applications in Rhetorical Criticism." *WS* 44 (1980): 288–99.

———. "Reaffirmation and Subversion of the American Dream." *QJS* 59 (1973): 160–67.

Goffman, Erving. *Gender Advertisements.* New York: Harper & Row, 1979.

Gronbeck, Bruce E. "Rhetorical History and Rhetorical Criticism: A Distinction." *ST* 24 (November 1975): 309–20.

———."The Rhetoric of Political Corruption: Sociolinguistic, Dialectical, and Ceremonial Processes." *QJS* 64 (1978): 145–72.

Habermas, Jürgen. *Communication and the Evolution of Society.* Translated by Thomas McCarthy. Boston: Beacon Press, 1979.

———. "On Systematically Distorted Communication." *Inquiry* 13 (1970): 205–18.

Hadsmovsky, Eugen. *Propaganda and National Power: The Organization of Public Opinion for National Politics.* Translated by Alice Mavrogordato and De Witt Mavrogordato. New York: Arno Press, 1972.

Journal of Advertising (1972–). Lawrence, Kans.: School of Journalism.

Journal of Advertising Research (1960–). New York: Advertising Research Foundation.

Kleppner, Otto, and Norman Govoni. *Advertising Procedures*. 7th ed. Englewood Cliffs, N.J.: Prentice-Hall, 1979.

Lasswell, Harold D., Nathan Leites, and Associates. *Language of Politics: Studies in Quantitative Semantics*. New York: G. W. Stewart, 1949.

Lasswell, Harold D., et al. *Propaganda and Promotional Activities: An Annotated Bibliography*. Chicago: University of Chicago Press, 1969.

McLuhan, Marshall. *The Gutenberg Galaxy: The Makings of Typographical Man*. Toronto: University of Toronto Press, 1962.

Marcuse, Herbert. *One-Dimensional Man: Studies in the Ideology of Advanced Industrial Society*. Boston: Beacon Press, 1964.

Ogilvie, David. *Confessions of an Advertising Man*. New York: Atheneum, 1980.

Public Opinion Quarterly (1937–). New York: Elsevier North-Holland.

Quarterly Journal of Speech (1915–). Annandale, Va.: Speech Communication Association.

Rosenfield, L. W. "A Case Study in Speech Criticism: The Nixon-Truman Analog." *CM* 35 (1968): 435–50.

———. "August 9, 1974: The Victimage of Richard Nixon." *Communication Quarterly* 24 (1976): 19–23.

Sandage, Charles, et al. *Advertising: Theory and Practice*. 10th ed. Homewood, Ill.: Irwin, Richard D., 1979.

Swanson, David L. "The Requirements of Critical Justifications." *CM* 44 (1977): 306–20.

Swanson, David L., and Linda L. Swanson. "The Agenda-Setting Function of the Ford-Carter Debate." *CM* 45 (1978): 347–58.

IX. Religious Oratory

Brilioth, Yngve. *A Brief History of Preaching*. Translated by Karl E. Mattson. Philadelphia: Fortress Press, 1965.

Broadus, John A. *On the Preparation and Delivery of Sermons*. Rev. ed., edited by Jesse Burton Weatherspoon. New York: Harper & Brothers, 1944.

Caplan, Harry, and Henry H. King. "Italian Treatises on Preaching: A Book-List." *SM* 16 (September 1949): 243–252. Others in the series in the same periodical are the following: for Spanish, 17 (June 1950): 161–70; for Scandinavian, 21 (March 1954): 1–9; for Dutch, 21 (November 1954): 235–47; for studies in English, 22 (1955): 1–159, special issue; for German, 23 (1956): 5–106; the second in the series, for French, appeared in *QJS* 36 (October 1950): 296–325.

Crocker, Lionel, ed. *Harry Emerson Fosdick's Art of Preaching: An Anthology*. Springfield, Ill.: Charles C. Thomas, 1971.

Fosdick, Harry Emerson. "What Is the Matter with Preaching?" In *Harry Emerson Fosdick's Art of Preaching: An Anthology*, edited by Lionel Crocker, pp. 27–41. Springfield, Ill.: Charles C. Thomas, 1971.

Preaching Today (1966–). St. Louis: The Christian Preaching Conference (originally *Preaching*, from 1966 to 1970).

Rahner, Karl, S.J., ed. *The Renewal of Preaching: Theory and Practice*. Concilium, Theology in the Age of Renewal, vol. 33. New York: Paulist Press, 1968.

Ritschl, Dietrich. *A Theology of Proclamation*. Richmond, Va.: John Knox Press, 1960.

Rosenberg, Bruce A. *The Art of the American Folk Preacher*. New York: Oxford University Press, 1970.

Semmelroth, Otto. *The Preaching Word: On the Theology of Proclamation*. New York: Herder and Herder, 1965.

Thompson, William, and William Toohey, eds. *Recent Homiletical Thought: A Bibliography, 1935–65*. Nashville: Abingdon Press, 1967.

X. Rhetorical Criticism

Baird, A. Craig. *Rhetoric: A Philosophical Inquiry*. New York: The Ronald Press Co., 1965.

Bitzer, Lloyd F. (see III, *Supra*).

Bitzer, Lloyd F., and Black, Edwin (see I, *Supra*).

Black, Edwin. *Rhetorical Criticism: A Study in Method*. New York: The Macmillan Co., 1965.

Bryant, Donald. "Rhetoric: Its Function and Its Scope." *QJS* 39 (December 1953): 401–4.

Communication Monographs (1934–). Annandale, Va.: Speech Communication Association (originally *Speech Monographs*).

Simons, Herbert W. *Persuasion: Understanding, Practice and Analysis*. Reading, Mass.: Addison-Wesley Publishing Co., 1976.

XI. Women's Voices

Bell, Roseann P., Bettye J. Parker, and Beverly Guy-Sheftall, eds. *Sturdy Black Bridges: Visions of Black Women in Literature*. Garden City, N.Y.: Anchor Press, 1979.

Eisenstein, Hester, and Alice Jardine, eds. *The Future of Difference*. Boston: G. K. Hall, 1980.

Feminist Studies (1972–). College Park, Md.: Feminist Studies.

Fisher, Dexter, ed. *The Third Woman: Minority Women Writers of the United States*. New York: Houghton Mifflin Co., 1980.

Gaudin, Colette, et al. "French Readings: French Texts/American Contexts." *Yale French Studies* 62 (1981): 2–236. Special issue.

Gilbert, Sandra M., and Susan Gubar. *The Madwoman in the Attic: The Woman Writer and the Nineteenth-Century Literary Imagination*. New Haven: Yale University Press, 1979.

Gilbert, Sandra M., and Susan Gubar, eds. *Shakespeare's Sisters: Feminist Essays on Women Poets*. Bloomington: Indiana University Press, 1979.

Hedges, Elaine, ed. "Women Writing and Teaching." *CE* 34 (October 1972): 1–106. Special issue.

Hull, Gloria T., Patricia Bell Scott, and Barbara Smith. *But Some of Us Are Brave: Black Women's Studies*. Old Westbury, N.Y.: The Feminist Press, 1982.

Kolodny, Annette. "Dancing Through the Minefield: Some Observations on the Theory, Practice, and Politics of a Feminist Literary Criticism." *Feminist Studies* 6 (Spring 1980): 1–25.

———. "The Feminist as Literary Critic." *Critical Inquiry* 2 (September 1976): 821–32.

———. "A Map for Rereading: Or, Gender and the Interpretation of Literary Texts." *New Literary History* 11 (Spring 1980): 451–67.

———. "Some Notes on Defining a 'Feminist Criticism.'" *Critical Inquiry* 2 (Autumn 1975): 75–92.

McAllester, Susan, ed. *A Case for Equity*. Urbana, Ill.: The National Council of Teachers of English, 1971.

McConnell-Ginet, Sally, Ruth Borker, and Nelly Furman, eds. *Women and Language in Literature and Society*. New York: Praeger Publishers, 1980.

Marks, Elaine, and Isabelle de Courtivron, eds. *New French Feminisms*. Amherst: University of Massachusetts Press, 1980.

Olsen, Tillie. *Silences*. New York: Delacorte Press/Seymour Lawrence, 1978.

Rich, Adrienne. *On Lies, Secrets, and Silence*. New York: W. W. Norton & Co., 1979.

Showalter, Elaine. "Feminist Criticism in the Wilderness." *Critical Inquiry* 8 (Winter 1981): 179–205.

Signs: Journal of Women in Culture and Society (1975‑). Chicago: University of Chicago Press.

XII. Self-Expression

Elbow, Peter. *Writing Without Teachers*. New York: Oxford University Press, 1973.

Gusdorf, Georges. *Speaking (La Parole)*. Translated by Paul T. Brockelman. Evanston: Northwestern University Press, 1965.

Hegel, G. W. F. *The Phenomenology of Mind*. Translated by J. B. Baillie. New York: Harper & Row, 1967.

Heidegger, Martin. (See IV, *supra*).

Kelley, Lou. *From Dialogue to Discourse: An Open Approach to Competence and Creativity*. Glenview, Ill.: Scott, Foresman and Co., 1972.

Kinneavy, James L. (see I, *supra*).

Macrorie, Ken. *Uptaught*. Rochelle Park, N.J.: Hayden Book Co., 1970.

Merleau-Ponty, Maurice. *Phenomenology of Perception*. Translated by Colin Smith. New York: Humanities Press, 1962.

———. *The Primacy of Perception*. Translated by James Edel. Evanston: Northwestern University Press, 1964.

Sartre, Jean-Paul. *Being and Nothingness: An Essay on Phenomenological Ontology*. Translated by Hazel Barnes. New York: Washington Square Press, 1953.

XIII. Mass Media and Small Group Media

Barthes, Roland. *Image–Music–Text*. Translated by Stephen Heath. New York: Hill and Wang, 1978.

———. *Mythologies*. Translated by Annette Lavers. New York: Hill and Wang, 1972.

Cawelti, John G. *Adventure, Mystery, and Romance: Formula Stories as Art and Popular Culture*. Chicago: University of Chicago Press, 1976.

Davis, Murray S. *Intimate Relations*. New York: Free Press, 1973.

Fiske, John, and John Hartley. *Reading Television*. New York: Methuen, 1978.

Gans, Herbert J. *Popular Culture and High Culture: An Analysis and Evaluation of Taste*. New York: Basic Books, 1968.

Human Communication Research (1974–). New Brunswick, N.J.: International Communication Association.

Journal of Broadcasting (1956–). Athens, Ga.: Broadcast Education Association.

Journal of Popular Culture (1967–). Bowling Green, Ohio: Popular Culture Association.

Journal of Popular Film and Television (1972–). Bowling Green, Ohio: Bowling Green State University.

Kelley, Harold H. *Personal Relationships: Their Structures and Processes*. New York: Halsted Press, John Wiley & Sons, 1979.

Kelley, Harold H., and John N. Thibaut. *Interpersonal Relations: A Theory of Interdependence*. New York: John Wiley & Sons, 1978.

Knapp, Mark. *Social Intercourse: From Greeting to Goodbye*. Boston: Allyn & Bacon, 1978.

McLuhan, Marshall. *Understanding Media: The Extensions of Man*. New York: McGraw-Hill, 1964.

Newcomb, Horace, ed. *Television: The Critical View*. 3d ed. New York: Oxford University Press, 1982.

Nichols, Bill. *Ideology and the Image: Social Representation in the Cinema and Other Media*. Bloomington: Indiana University Press, 1981.

Ong, Walter, J., S.J. *The Presence of the Word: Some Prolegomena for Cultural and Religious History*. New York: Simon and Schuster, 1970.

————. *Ramus, Method, and the Decay of Dialogue*. Cambridge: Harvard University Press, 1958.

Real, Michael. *Mass-Mediated Culture*. Englewood Cliffs, N.J.: Prentice-Hall, 1977.

Schatz, Thomas. *Hollywood Film Genres*. New York: Random House, 1981.

Social Text (1979–). Madison, Wis.: Coda Press.

Williams, Raymond. *Television: Technology and Cultural Form*. New York: Schocken Books, 1975.

XIV. Semiotics and Semiology

Barthes, Roland (see XIII, *supra*).

————. *Elements of Semiology*. Translated by Annette Lavers and Colin Smith. New York: Hill and Wang, 1968.

Eco, Umberto. *The Role of the Reader: Explorations in the Semiotics of Texts*. Bloomington: Indiana University Press, 1979.

————. *A Theory of Semiotics*. Bloomington: Indiana University Press, 1976.

Jakobson, Roman. *Coup d'oeil sur le développement de la sémiotique*. Studies in Semiotics, 3. Bloomington: Indiana University Press, 1975.

Kristeva, Julia. *Desire in Language: A Semiotic Approach to Literature and Art*. Edited by L. S. Roudiez. Translated by T. Gora, A. Jardine, and L. S. Roudiez. New York: Columbia University Press, 1980.

————. *Semeiotike. Recherches pour une sémanalyse*. Paris: Editions du Seuil, 1969.

Morris, Charles William. *Foundations of the Theory of Signs*. Chicago: University of Chicago Press, 1938.

————. *Signs, Language, and Behavior*. New York: George Braziller, 1955.

Murphey, Murray G. *The Development of Peirce's Philosophy*. Cambridge: Harvard University Press, 1961.

Peirce, Charles Sanders. *The Collected Papers of Charles Sanders Peirce*. Volumes 1–6 edited by Charles Hartshorne and Paul Weiss; volumes 7–8 edited by Arthur Burks. Cambridge: Harvard University Press, 1960.

————. *Semiotics and Significs: The Correspondence Between Charles S. Peirce and Lady Victoria Welby*. Edited by C. S. Hardwick and J. Cook. Bloomington: Indiana University Press, 1973.

Sebeok, Thomas A., ed. *The Tell-Tale Sign: A Survey of Semiotics*. Lisse: De Ridder, 1975.

Semiotica (1969–). The Hague: Mouton.

XV. Rhetoric As Metaphor

Bachelard, Gaston. *La Formation de l'esprit scientifique*. 9th ed. Paris: Vrin, 1975.

Barthes, Roland (see II, *supra*).

Canguilhem, G. *Etudes d'histoire et de la philosophie des sciences*. 3d ed. Paris: J. Vrin, 1973.

De Man, Paul. *Allegories of Reading: Figural Language in Rousseau, Nietzsche, Rilke, and Proust*. New Haven: Yale University Press, 1979.

Derrida, Jacques. "The Retrait of Metaphor." *Enclitic* 2 (Fall 1978): 5–33.

————."White Mythology: Metaphor in the Text of Philosophy." Translated by F. C. T. Moore. *New Literary History* 6 (Autumn 1974): 5–74.

Dubois, Jacques, et al. *Rhétorique générale*. Paris: Librarie Larousse, 1971.

Genette, Gérard (see I, *supra*).

Nietzsche, Friedrich. *Gesammelte Werke. Fünfter Band: Vorlesungen 1872–1876*. Munich: Musarion Verlag, 1922. Pp. 287–319.

————. "[Rhétorique et langage: Textes traduits, présentés et annotés par Philippe Lacoue-Labarthe et Jean-Luc Nancy]." *Poétique* 5 (1971): 99–143.

Ricoeur, Paul. *The Rule of Metaphor: Multidisciplinary Studies of the Creation of Meaning in Language*. Translated by Robert Czerny. Toronto: University of Toronto Press, 1977.

XVI. Rhetoric and Composition

Becker, A. L. "A Tagmemic Approach to Paragraph Analysis." *CCC* 16 (December 1965): 237–41.

Braddock, Richard, Richard Lloyd-Jones, and Lowell Schoer. *Research in Written Composition*. Urbana, Ill.: The National Council of Teachers of English, 1963.

Britton, James N., et al. *The Development of Writing Abilities (11–18)*. London: Macmillan Education, 1975.

Burke, Kenneth (see III, *supra*).

Christensen, Francis, and Bonnijean Christensen. *Notes Toward a New Rhetoric: 9 Essays for Teachers*. 2d ed. New York: Harper & Row, 1978.

College English (1939–). Chicago: National Council of Teachers of English (formerly *English Journal, College Edition*).

Daiker, Donald A., Andrew Kerek, and Max Morenberg. *Sentence Combining and the Teaching of Writing*. Conway, Ark.: Language and Style Books, 1979.

D'Angelo, Frank J. *A Conceptual Theory of Rhetoric*. Cambridge, Mass.: Winthrop Publishers, 1975.

————. *Process and Thought in Composition*. 2d ed. Cambridge, Mass.: Winthrop Publishers, 1980.

Emig, Janet. *The Composing Processes of Twelfth Graders*. Research Report no. 13. Urbana, Ill.: National Council of Teachers of English, 1971.

Enos, Richard Leo, et al. "Heuristic Procedures and the Composing Process: A Selected Bibliography." *RSQ* Special Issue no. 1 (1982).

English Journal (1912–). Chicago: National Council of Teachers of English.

Flower, Linda S., and John R. Hayes. "The Cognition of Discovery: Defining a Rhetorical Problem." *CCC* 31 (February 1980): 21–32.

———. "The Dynamics of Composing: Making Plans and Juggling Constraints." In *Cognitive Processes in Writing*, edited by Lee Gregg and Erwin Steinberg, pp. 3–30. Hillsdale, N.J.: Lawrence Erlbaum, 1980.

Graves, Donald. *Rhetoric and Composition: A Sourcebook for Teachers of English*. New York: Hayden Book Co., 1976.

Halliday, M.A., and Ruqaiya Hasan. *Cohesion in English*. New York: Longman's, 1976.

Hirsch, E. D., Jr. "Culture and Literacy." *Journal of Basic Writing* 3 (Fall/ Winter 1980): 27–47.

———.*The Philosophy of Composition*. Chicago: University of Chicago Press, 1977.

Hunt, Kellogg W. *Grammatical Structures Written at Three Grade Levels*. Research Report no. 3. Urbana, Ill.: National Council of Teachers of English, 1965.

Kinneavy, James L. (see I, *supra*).

Larson, Richard L. "Structure and Form in Non-Fiction Prose." In *Teaching Composition: 10 Bibliographical Essays*, edited by Gary Tate, pp. 45–72. Fort Worth: Texas Christian University Press, 1976.

Lauer, Janice. "Heuristics and Composition." *CCC* 21 (December 1970): 396–404.

McQuade, Donald, ed. *Linguistics, Stylistics, and the Teaching of Composition*. Akron, Ohio: Language and Style Books, 1979.

Maimon, Elaine P., et al. *Writing in the Arts and Sciences*. Cambridge, Mass.: Winthrop Publishers, 1981.

Mellon, John C. *Transformational Sentence-Combining: A Method for Enhancing the Development of Syntactic Fluency in English Composition*. Research Report No. 10. Urbana, Ill.: National Council of Teachers of English, 1969.

Moffett, James. *Teaching the Universe of Discourse*. Boston: Houghton Mifflin Co., 1968.

Nold, Ellen W. *Revising: Toward a Theory*. ERIC Report ED 172 212. Bethesda, Md.: Educational Resources Information Center, 1979.

O'Hare, Frank. *Sentence Combining: Improving Student Writing without Formal Grammar Instruction*. Research Report no. 15. Urbana, Ill.: National Council of Teachers of English, 1973.

Pike, Kenneth L. "A Linguistic Contribution to Composition." *CCC* 15 (May 1964): 82–89.

Research in the Teaching of English (1967–). Urbana, Ill.: National Council of Teachers of English.

Rodgers, Paul, Jr. "A Discourse-Centered Rhetoric of the Paragraph." *CCC* 17 (February 1966): 2–11.

Rohman, Gordon R. "Pre-Writing: The Stage of Discovery in the Writing Process." *CCC* 16 (May 1966): 106–12.

Shaughnessy, Mina P. *Errors and Expectations*. New York: Oxford University Press, 1977.

Simon, Herbert A. *The Sciences of the Artificial*. 2d ed. Cambridge: MIT Press, 1969.

Sledd, James H. "Bi-Dialectalism: The Linguistics of White Supremacy." *EJ* 58 (December 1969): 1307–15.

———. "Doublespeak: Dialectology in the Service of Big Brother." *CE* 33 (January 1972): 439–57.

Smitherman, Geneva. "English Teacher, Why You Be Doing the Thangs You Don't Do?" *EJ* 61 (January 1972): 59–65.

Sommers, Nancy I. "Revision Strategies of Student Writers and Experienced Adult Writers." *CCC* 31 (December 1980): 378–88.

Strom, Ingrid. "Research in Grammar and Usage and Its Implications for Teaching Writing." *Bulletin of the School of Education, Indiana University* (1960).

"Students' Rights to Their Own Language." *CCC* Special Issue (October 1974).

Tate, Gary, ed. *Teaching Composition: 10 Bibliographical Essays*. Fort Worth: Texas Christian University Press, 1976.

Tate, Gary, and E. P. J. Corbett, eds. *The Writing Teacher's Sourcebook*. New York: Oxford University Press, 1981.

Williams, Joseph M. *Style: Ten Lessons in Clarity & Grace*. Glenview, Ill.: Scott, Foresman and Co., 1981.

Winterowd, W. Ross. "The Grammar of Coherence." *CE* 31 (May 1970): 828–35.

———. "Topics and Levels in the Composition Process." *CE* 34 (February 1973): 701–9.

Witte, Stephen P., and Lester Faigley. "Coherence, Cohesion, and Writing Quality." *CCC* 32 (May 1981): 189–204.

Young, Richard E., Alton L. Becker, and Kenneth L. Pike (see VI, *supra*).

INDEX

This index includes primary authors for the first five sections, their works, and the secondary authors. For the last section it includes all authors, their books, and the important journals in the fields that Professor Kinneavy covers in his contemporary survey. There is an additional listing of journals and their abbreviations on pp. ix–x.